Jean Cocte__

Titles in the series Critical Lives present the work of leading cultural figures of the modern period. Each book explores the life of the artist, writer, philosopher or architect in question and relates it to their major works.

In the same series

Jean Genet
Stephen Barber

Michel Foucault
David Macey

Pablo Picasso
Mary Ann Caws

Franz Kafka
Sander L. Gilman

Guy Debord
Andy Merrifield

Marcel Duchamp
Caroline Cros

James Joyce
Andrew Gibson

Frank Lloyd Wright
Robert McCarter

Jean-Paul Sartre
Andrew Leak

Noam Chomsky
Wolfgang B. Sperlich

Jorge Luis Borges
Jason Wilson

Erik Satie
Mary E. Davis

Georges Bataille
Stuart Kendall

Ludwig Wittgenstein
Edward Kanterian

Octavio Paz
Nick Caistor

Walter Benjamin
Esther Leslie

Charles Baudelaire
Rosemary Lloyd

Jean Cocteau

James S. Williams

REAKTION BOOKS

For J.

Published by Reaktion Books Ltd
33 Great Sutton Street
London EC1V ODX, UK

www.reaktionbooks.co.uk

First published 2008

Copyright © James S. Williams 2008

All rights reserved
No part of this publication may be reproduced, stored in a retrieval system,
or transmitted, in any form or by any means, electronic, mechanical,
photocopying, recording or otherwise, without the prior permission
of the publishers.

Printed and bound in Great Britain by
Cromwell Press, Trowbridge, Wiltshire

British Library Cataloguing in Publication Data

Williams, James S,. 1963–
    Jean Cocteau. – (Critical lives)
    1. Cocteau, Jean, 1889–1963   2. Authors, French – Biography
    I. Title
    848.9'12

ISBN-13: 978 1 86189 354 3

Contents

Introduction: The Living Artist and the Posthumous Work   7

1   Paradise Lived and Lost   18
2   Natural-born Legend   25
3   Prince in Exile   34
4   Russian Lessons   45
5   Cocteau's First War   55
6   The Greatest Battle   67
7   Happy Families   75
8   Genius of France   85
9   A Child Carrying a Cane   94
10   *Annus Mirabilis /Annus Miserabilis*   104
11   Lost in the Wilderness   114
12   An Ass Bearing the Lord   123
13   Miracle or Simulacrum?   131
14   Body and Blood of a Poet   142
15   Tripping Across the World   153
16   Enter Apollo   165
17   World War Redux   176
18   No Man's Land   187
19   Club Santo-Sospir   201
20   The Long Haul   214
21   Jean Cocteau is Dead, Long Live Cocteau!   225

References   239
Select Bibliography   245
Acknowledgements   251
Photo Acknowledgements   253

Cocteau with an empty picture frame. Photo by Man Ray, 1922.

Introduction:
The Living Artist and the
Posthumous Work

When I write I disturb. When I make a film I disturb. When I paint I
disturb. When I exhibit my paintings I disturb, and I disturb if I don't.
I have a knack for disturbing . . . I will be disturbing after my death.
My work will have to wait for that other death, the slow death of my
knack for disturbing. Perhaps it will emerge victorious, unencumbered
by me, liberated, youthful, and shouting: phew!

Cocteau, *Diary of an Unknown*

In a short colour film made in 1958 by Jacques Demy and Jean
Masson entitled *Le Musée Grévin*, Jean Cocteau staged a remarkable
encounter with his own wax image. The wax figure of a mature
Cocteau sitting across the table sporting a bow tie is presented by
the real Cocteau as his Parisian alter ego, who receives the public
honours but also takes the blows. If this fabricated double is false
and hateful, it is because, as Cocteau puts it, 'the Parisians have
turned me into a character I should not like to meet'. Yet as always
with Cocteau this is only half the story, for he claims also to be very
grateful for this noisome false self who takes the heat in his place.
He instructs the wax impostor to return to Paris on the evening
train so that he can return in peace to his work. This is crucial to
Cocteau's general concept of artistic invisibility, one that becomes a
veritable obsession in his later work, according to which the Poet's
true self, that is, the autonomous writing self or 'Night', strikes a
form of compromise with the public – the fabrication of a false self
– in order to remain in safe obscurity and thus free from the

trappings of celebrity. The message could not be more clear: the more visible the man, the greater the invisibility of the artist and the more authentic the work.

Putting aside for a moment the question of whether the solution proposed here can ever be that simple, the waxwork scene exemplifies Cocteau's supreme talents as a performer and his compulsive desire to stage aesthetically the drama of his own life. It also invites the question: who was the 'real' Jean Cocteau? The Protean dancer on the artistic high wire, as he liked to see himself, inspired by the gravity- (and gender-) defying American trapeze artist Barbette, or an all-too-human contortionist desperately seeking to justify himself to others and to himself? Which is to say, the public extrovert or the private loner? For of all the many contradictions and paradoxes that define Cocteau, none is perhaps more striking than the fact that his prodigious output in virtually every artistic field and medium betrayed a fragile and lonely man wracked by self-doubt and feelings of alienation. Within the space of a sentence he could swing perilously from self-promotion to self-pity, from self-denigration to self-defence, from self-expansion to self-annihilation. What was rich duality one moment could be internal division the next, and the reader is made either complicit or reversed into the enemy accuser 'vous', subjecting him to yet further trial and humiliation. As the wax scene suggests, there is with Cocteau a very thin line between self-castigation and public accusation that was all too real. For having appeared during the late 1910s and early 1920s the very incarnation of the *moderne* and the quintessence of French wit and elegance (Edith Wharton once memorably described Cocteau as a man 'to whom every great line of poetry was a sunrise, every sunset the foundation of the Heavenly City'), he experienced a rapid fall from grace, dismissed as a social chameleon, plagiarist and crude effect-seeker, a producer of mere 'cocktails'. For many he was an all-performing dandy of unbearable lightness, a *touche-à-tout sublime* or 'sublime Jack of all trades', an uncommitted aesthete blessed with 'the talents of a polymath and the instincts of a dilettante'.[1] In particular, he was deemed frivolous for diversifying in too many different art forms (the French adjective *versatile*, applied to Cocteau, carried a particularly negative charge). For those left struggling to keep up with Cocteau artistically, he was simply the joker in the modernist pack, more sham than shaman. André Breton regarded him with particular homophobic virulence as an affront to artistic manhood, and with his Surrealist troops attempted to sabotage every project in which Cocteau was involved. The situation was not helped by his highly public personal life: what passed as alternative and glamorously bohemian in his own immediate circle began to seem to outsiders merely decadent, and the whiff of scandal – in particular drug-taking and the charge of corrupting young men – never left him. With some justification and just a hint of paranoid megalomania, Cocteau considered himself the most hated and persecuted man in all France. Despite the astonishing range and scale of his artistic achievement, the result of almost 60 years of uninterrupted creative activity at the intersection of the major artistic and intellectual currents in Europe (at least up until the 1940s), he lived to see himself become one of the most underrated and outmoded figures in twentieth-century French literature.

Certainly there is always some collateral damage when an artist invests so much of himself in his work, yet to be 'Jean Cocteau' Cocteau paid an unusually heavy price. It was not just his persistent poor health, exacerbated by long years of opium use, which necessitated seven separate treatments for detoxification. Cocteau put himself continually on the line, at once consumed by the world and consuming others in order to gain greater self-consistency and 'weight'. He lived a perpetual identity crisis and by his own admission experienced continual anguish and turmoil, from the moment of his father's suicide when he was just nine to the tragic early deaths of his closest male friends and lovers. He experienced a profound need to identify and fuse with others simply to exist: 'I love others and exist only through them', he explained. A chosen or conscripted other positioned as either Master or Muse or Mentor offered the possibility of restoring a sense of identity, which he felt to be lacking due to an insurmountable 'difficulty of being', the title of his crucial collection of biographical essays of 1947. So completely did Cocteau define himself through others that he would absorb them even to the point of mimeticism, giving rise to an awesome ability to imitate others' mannerisms. The success of such performances was inevitably short-lived and provoked an unsatisfiable desire for plenitude. At times he felt himself to be literally *écorché vif* like his young literary aliases – Jacques in *The Miscreant*, Guillaume in *Thomas the Impostor* – who are all assailed by the dilemma of how to live, constantly projecting themselves on to others and transferring their desires. It resulted in a life punctuated by repeated moultings, metamorphoses and reincarnations.

It is all too easy now to look back on Cocteau as a rather sad and pathetic figure buzzing around in feverish circulation, an *arriviste* perpetually not arriving where he wanted to be, hiding his personal malaise and self-doubt behind his frenetic activity and always ready at a moment's notice to roll up his sleeves and attempt once again to win over the public. Propelling his long arms and graceful hands in arabesques above his head, he literally charmed his audience into submission with the metallic ring of his sonorous nasal voice, his theatrical delivery and his cascading chatter (he was dubbed by friend and foe alike 'the greatest talker in France'). A mood of fatalism has taken its toll on critics who often start with the premise that the one undisputed proof of Cocteau's greatness – his mercurial presence and magnetic conversation that turned his life into a work of art itself – simply dried up the day he died, to be lost forever.

And yet:

The idea that Cocteau's public performance was his one true novel or poem, a fateful logic applied to another 'doomed' gay artist, Oscar Wilde, betrays ultimately an indifference both to his life and his work. Indeed, too often an over-obsession with the fanfare of Cocteau's public persona – the scandal and parade, the glossy surfaces and masks, the who's who of his address book, his apparent flirting with movements such as Dada and Surrealism – has obscured the unwavering intelligence and seriousness of a man whose fundamental asceticism produced one of the most coherent and original artistic statements of the twentieth century. A man who never saw himself as of this world was also one of its most perceptive observers, continually probing the modern condition and asking what it is to be human. His life's work, sliding back and forth as it does between optimism and pessimism (and all combinations of the two), constitutes a virtual manual on how – and how not – to live and to be. Cocteau's artistic strength was precisely to chronicle his own existential crisis by becoming his own subject of experimentation and recording the vicissitudes of his being with implacable honesty and courage. His restless self-construction through the Other revealed itself finally to be an existential 'work in progress', that is, a continuous putting into question of the Self. His mental agility, insatiable curiosity and demand for new stimuli, thoughts and sensations, together with his potent imagination and inventiveness, meant that he took nothing for granted and was always changing gear en route to new and altered states of artistic being, whether the waking dream, *le merveilleux*, the hypnotic trance of opium or the sensory zones of cinema. Moreover, his audacious montages of images, sounds, ideas and forms are what enabled him to gain new insights about himself in his quest for greater equilibrium and self-acceptance. By always embracing change and pursuing new directions he became one of the most vital and dynamic of contemporary artists, all the more so when the great mutations in his life and career matched those taking place in French society as a whole. This accounts for his unique status within French culture: having moved brilliantly from the exclusive world of the Salons to the new media in the 1910s and '20s, he became a cross-pollinator of art and culture, a go-between and *passeur* of the Right and Left Banks, of Montmartre and

Montparnasse, and more generally of high and popular culture and the marginal and aristocratic fringes of society. He was in the finest sense an operator and fixer, a man of a thousand connections and resources who made things happen, in the process opening up new portals within French society and culture. To take just one example: working as so often in parallel with and against the mainstream – Cocteau was in theory an elitist but in practice and at heart a populist – he co-founded the first Festival du Film Maudit at Biarritz in August 1949.

Cocteau's ever-evolving artistic project, sustained by his unwavering belief in the absolute value of art and his own poetic vocation, gave him an indispensable sense of personal consistency and futurity, and it is perhaps only the work – or rather the continual return to his work as in the waxwork scene described above – that provided a centre to his life. He measured his personal health by the success of his experimentation with form, however oblique and unpredictable, as well as his capacity for artistic self-transformation and renewal. This did not guarantee a happy ending, of course. After all, if poetry was the only religion for Cocteau, it was also one without hope or cure. The stakes of his high-octane project remained invariably high, for so implicated was he in his work that if it generated no tangible sense of progress or discovery then his tormented self was at risk of sinking irrevocably into the void. His best works are those that bear the visible traces of their journey from the brink, both in their formal undecidability and hybrid composition through the confounding of genres, irrational plots, shocks and surprises, forms of syncretism, etc., and in their author's strange unwillingness ever to let go (the staggering number of prefaces, forewords, postfaces and 'prospectuses' that buttressed his œuvre). Produced during intense creative bursts, his work often appears as a collection of rapid-fire images, disconnected statements, aphorisms and bullet points. Freshly minted aphorisms, witty one-liners and improvised speculations are left intact or simply juxtaposed rather than honed into arguments of logical progression. The key was to shoot straight and hit the target, which he invariably did again and again (one of the most accurate portraits produced of Cocteau was a photograph taken by Berenice Abbott in 1927, in which he appears to fire a gun directly into the lens of the camera).

The drama of Cocteau's search for being and identity is what lay at the root of his daily project to reveal the Invisible, or rather to wait for the Invisible to reveal itself suddenly to him, if only for a fleeting second. It is why he was particularly attracted to cinema, which he regarded, to put it at its most simple, as making the subjective objective and the invisible visible. Presenting himself as both a medium and a humble artisan, Cocteau wished for his viewers to share in his endless delight and fascination with the serendipity of the cinematic machine, its *trouvailles* and epiphanies. There is a genuine pathos here, for despite appearances to the contrary – his idealism and cult of youth, his need of fantasy and fabulation, his apparent aloofness and detachment – Cocteau was a profoundly materialist artist who sought always to remain on this side of the Real with death-bound humankind. He always thought with and through his hands in order to cut through physically to the most basic of our emotions (desire, anguish, terror, ecstasy, loss, etc.). This runs exactly counter to what so many critics have perceived as either cultivated technique or melodramatic ruse (the Cocteau of the famous quip: 'I am a lie that always tells the truth').

To sum up, the febrility of Cocteau's fractured being is what actually provided for the extraordinary synergy and exhilaration of his work. The organic link between a creator and his creation was his abiding concern, and it made him suspect that whatever he painted was essentially a self-portrait with its own separate identity. The artist was always his own true model, and since creative work in Cocteau's view was born of an exhalation *from within* (i.e., of the self) rather than inspired *from without*, it was necessarily biographical. This is to say, the individual work cannot help but betray the influence of its creator, even if, in the Oedipal terms preferred by Cocteau, the work also seeks to destroy its maker. There was therefore no real need for him to attempt a 'straight' autobiography or lubricious *journal intime*. His most overtly autobiographical moments, such as his volume of memoirs *Diary of an Unknown* (1952), constitute merely the extreme of a corpus always grounded in the biographical real and are exceptional only in that they establish a very different tone, usually resigned, often depressive, at times merciless. By the same token, the avowed fictions are always biographically suggestive precisely because they experiment with narrative form in order to investigate further the mysteries of the self. What is crucial here is that Cocteau, who fully assumed the obligations and responsibilities of his artistic practice, treated all his creative acts and public gestures, however successful, as part of a continuous process of exploration of artistic and personal fields, rather than as the preamble to a *magnum opus* in the manner, say, of Proust. As he put it at one point, an individual work (*une œuvre*) is only of value if conceived as part of a larger whole (*un œuvre*).[2] It is never a matter of this one individual poem or that particular play or film. We identify with the author and *all* his work, which is to say, with the creative gesture itself.

It is Cocteau's no-nonsense approach to art along with his urgent primary themes that provided his project with an overall unity and clarity of purpose, beyond the obvious fact that he labelled all his work *poésie* because part of the same basic act of producing (Greek *poein*, 'to make'). As the fellow recipient of an honorary doctorate from Oxford in 1956, W. H. Auden, expressed it, Cocteau's 'attitude is always professional, that is, his first concern is for the nature of the medium and its hidden possibilities'.[3] Even in the one major visual art form he never really practised, photography, Cocteau broke new ground, for by posing for some of the world's greatest photographers (Henri Cartier-Bresson, Jacques-Henri Lartigue, Man Ray, Irving Penn, etc.) and exploiting a range of stage accessories such as mirrors and screens, he produced a series of highly stylized self-images running from dark narcissism to

Philippe Halsman, *Dream of a Poet*, a 'living painting' with Cocteau, 1949.

self-fragmentation and self-parody. Each constructed image, more a micro art-installation, enabled him to explore alternative identities and personae, and in so doing to document his personal progress. These seductive images of vulnerability also offered, of course, a means for Cocteau to market his own public image and celebrity, just as his hand-drawn five-pointed star sealed his work like a personal logo or trademark. This tireless self-promoter was one of the first media self-publicists of the twentieth century, and rare to non-existent are the photographs where he was caught unawares (one notable exception was taken outside the Palais de Justice in Paris after a narcotics raid in January 1947).

How then, finally, are we to bring together Cocteau's multi-life, multi-work and multi-performance when he so cleverly and persistently blurred the usual boundaries, making his life the stuff of myth and generating in the process no end of public misunderstanding and confusion? So essential was affective experience for Cocteau that his achievement of loyal friendship and deep commitment to a chosen other was arguably where his life and work came together most powerfully. Pathologically incapable of hurting or hating anyone, Cocteau had an instinctive gift for f riendship and was unstinting in his concern for others. If he viewed the search for personal self-identity as a precarious and almost impossible task, he never once doubted the worth and durability of friendship, which he considered a calm and continuous 'spasm' freed from the dangers of infatuation and temporary passion.[4] Cocteau enjoyed significant relationships with a number of strong women, beginning with his mother, whose bond was absolute, yet it was with his younger male lovers and companions who were also his artistic collaborators in varying degrees that Cocteau pursued most extensively his ideal of true friendship. It is not simply that friendship was often the inspiration and decisive catalyst for the work (Cocteau's formative relationships are all closely tied up with the major turning points in his career), but that it lay at the very heart of his aesthetic project, which could best be defined as an ethico-erotic engagement with questions of the Self and Other. In order for art to be beautiful, it must, according to Cocteau, 'project' a moral force. He talked in terms familiar from the French *moraliste* tradition of the 'moral progress' and 'line' of his work, which he associated with 'the style of the soul'. The style of the man and the method of his practice were inextricably linked and together they formed the basis for an art of friendship and collaboration that encouraged new ways of artistic and communal being.

Cocteau was a totally new breed of modern artist, and because his art is intrinsically biographical for the reasons given it is best approached as part of a continuous 'life project' defined by tension and contradiction, for example, between a wish to be 'beyond' history (which he regarded as the process whereby truths become lies) and a simultaneous need to participate in historic events. A similar discrepancy exists between the warm intelligence of his heart and his dry, sometimes brittle, clipped style that could cut clean like a blade through sentiment. To take Cocteau in this parallel fashion, in process and performance, is to respect the open, generous spirit of his life and the sheer energy and all-embracing sweep of his artistic concerns. Already in his essay *Cock and Harlequin* of 1918, anticipating that his work would be truly understood and celebrated only when he himself had passed away and was thus no longer a disturbance, Cocteau concluded emphatically: 'ONE MUST BE A LIVING MAN AND A POSTHUMOUS ARTIST'. So much in advance of his times, his unique and complex œuvre has perhaps now found, nearly half a century after his death, an audience more willing and better prepared to appreciate its unerring capacity to disturb, astound and inspire.

1

Paradise Lived and Lost

Jean-Maurice Cocteau was born early in the morning of 5 July 1889
in the wealthy Parisian suburb of Maisons-Laffitte, twelve miles
north-west of Paris near the forest of Saint-Germain.[1] He weighed
six and a half pounds and was, by all accounts, a hale and hearty
good-looking baby with bushy black hair. He was baptized
two weeks later. His father, Georges, aged 47, was the gentle,
withdrawn son of a public notary from Le Havre and had worked
in his father-in-law's law firm before becoming a *rentier* of
independent means. Cocteau's mother, Eugénie (née Lecomte), was
descended from a Parisian family of stockbrokers with connections
in the diplomatic corps, finance and the navy. Place Sully in
Maisons-Laffitte was where Jean spent his vacations from 1891 to
1894, along with his older siblings, Paul and Marthe. The rest of
the time the family lived in Paris in the mezzanine of a mansion
owned by Cocteau's maternal grandparents at 45, rue La Bruyère
in the then elegant Pigalle area of the ninth *arrondissement*.

For Cocteau, early childhood was a magical time in a safe, high-
bourgeois Catholic world, and he would always hark back to it
nostalgically as a time of beautiful smells, in particular the lime and
lilac trees and heliotrope set amongst the villas and manicured lawns
of Maisons-Laffitte. The town, named after the banker Jacques
Laffitte, was an oasis of leisure complete with a fashionable horse-
racing track and stables, a seventeenth-century château, village fairs
and occasional social happenings. The young Jean proudly rode

Entrance to the park, Maisons-Laffitte, in the 1890s.

around it on his newly invented bicycle imported from England. With his keen eyes and pointed face he was the cynosure of every eye, fussed over and mollycoddled by both parents, above all his mother, who fostered in him a sensibility for all that was marvellous and extraordinary. Yet he was also a rather small, delicate, and at times nervous and unstable child. His favourite cousin, Marianne Lecomte (the future Mme Singer), two years his senior and closest companion, would later talk of Jean as a charming 'droll little boy, very frail'. A scoliotic backbone forced him to make odd lateral movements as he walked, including a slight listing of one shoulder compensated for by the other (this did not stop him, however, from being immediately enrolled into dancing lessons). He was entrusted to a German governess, Joséphine Ebel (or Jéphine as he called her), with whom he enjoyed physical warmth, lying in her lap at dinner table and listening enraptured while she read him fairy tales. Intoxicated by literature, he created a bedroom wonderland whenever he was able to bunk off school. Meanwhile, his otherwise silent father, a not untalented amateur painter, initiated him into drawing, and he quickly learned to mimic the style of the two most famous illustrators and caricaturists of the day, Sem and Leonetto Cappiello, demonstrating a remarkable gift for likeness. Like his mother, Cocteau also excelled at the piano, playing on a Rossini bequeathed to the family. His maternal grandfather, Eugène, an amateur chamber musician as well as a collector of *objets d'art*, organized regular musical quartets, for Paris was then a city of *mélomanes* and many *soirées musicales* took place in the private homes of French high society. Being forced to sit listening to Wagner, Cocteau developed a counter-knowledge of the earlier musical repertory and he could soon identify most arias.

All was possible in this most perfect of respectable bourgeois worlds where art was essentially a cultivated hobby and a means of pleasure. It stirred no feelings of revolt in Cocteau, precisely because his family was exactly what he wished, that is, an ever-ready and attentive audience. He would later explain his hybrid taste for music, art and the theatre by the fact that his family was a touch unconventional and eclectic in its tastes. In 1895–6, the year he entered primary school, he was taken to Le Nouveau-Cirque, frequented then by all social classes from *le gratin* to *le crottin*, and became fascinated by famous clowns like Foottit and his black partner Chocolat. He also went to the Palais de Glace in the Champs-Elysées, a skating rink where he first caught sight of Colette and her famous bulldog, as well as the slightly louche idols of the *Belle époque*, such as the music-hall performer Polaire and Liane de Pougy. He was in the audience for the first films screened by the Lumière brothers in their cellars near the Old England department store in the Boulevard des Capucines. Later he would attend the Théâtre du Châtelet to watch popular boulevard shows such as *La Biche au bois* and *Le Tour du monde en 80 jours*, as well as theatres like the Vaudeville and the Renaissance, La Scala and the Eldorado on the Boulevard de Strasbourg, where the great actors and tragedians like Sarah Bernhardt, Coquelin *aîné*, Réjane and Lucien Guitry reigned like gods.

Cocteau's first major acts of creativity were inevitably inspired by the theatre, and this included the ritual spectacle of his mother getting ready for an evening at the Comédie-Française. With the rich smell of her perfume, her beauty and jewels, she embodied the ceremony and glamour of the theatre, and he watched in awe and fascination at the painstaking care with which she prepared her costume. On Sundays, when all was quiet, the young wunderkind would stage his own dramatic shows and dress up to become whoever he wished to be, male or female. With his friend René Rocher (future director of the Vieux-Colombier theatre in Paris), he built in the courtyard of the Paris home a small model stage, experimenting with ingenious machines and fantastic settings along with exotic costumes sewn by Jéphine. A born *bricoleur*, Cocteau could make a project suddenly materialize in his hands and he revealed an outstanding graphic precision and acuity of gaze. By the age of five the precocious Jean had already established his own repertoire of boulevard plays and tragedies, including one he wrote in verse about Nero. There was a sense here of grand self-creation, of a self-Pygmalion dreaming of a 'total art'. When a little later he wrote his first verse he immediately declaimed it in front of a chosen audience and acted out all the roles. Indeed, he had a narcissistic wish to be everyone and everywhere and so monopolize the scene, for aesthetic beauty seemed to confer on him a sense of being. Yet this desire to be the most sensitive soul in the world went hand in hand with a terrible feeling of solitude as soon as the scenes came to an end and the spell was broken. A single unconquered look could open up doubts and anxieties and require that he re-examine and justify himself. Similarly, if he was unable to convince anyone of his worthy sincerity, he suddenly felt anxious and even afraid ('I'm naïve, not immodest, I only want to love', would become a constant refrain).

The joy of these early halcyon times for Cocteau came crashing down on 5 April 1898, when his increasingly isolated and depressive father placed a gun to his head and shot himself dead in his bed in the Paris home. Why suicide? Georges' apparent fears of the value of certain shares and possible financial ruin would later prove unfounded. There was the vague suspicion that his beautiful wife may have been having an affair, and indeed there had always been a lingering rumour that Cocteau himself was illegitimate. He had, after all, arrived eight years after his older – and, by comparison, supremely well-balanced – brother, Paul, with whom he had little in common, and twelve years after his ultra-serious sister, Marthe. He looked physically different from both, and some even claimed to recognize in his face Indian or Arab features. In fact, Jean always privately suspected and hoped that he was the forgotten child of a diplomat or Persian prince. How, after all, could one so preternaturally gifted as himself be the natural product of such a bourgeois family and milieu? Suspicion fell on the celebrated society painter Joseph Wencker, a family friend who had produced several dashing portraits of Cocteau's elegant and socially attractive mother in 1888. Another possibility was Marcel Dieulafoy, a noted archaeologist who had excavated in Persia, yet this likewise remained at the level of idle rumour and speculation. Whatever the precise truth, it helped to foster in Cocteau an ineradicable sense of being not only different but alien.

Publicly, Cocteau remained silent on the matter of his father's death right up until the year of his own, when, during a long interview for French television entitled *Portrait-souvenir*, he stated that his father had killed himself 'for reasons that are no longer relevant', a tacit acknowledgement perhaps that he may have been a closet gay and, because unable to accept the fact, repressed it to breaking point. Cocteau never went further than this, however, which has caused less favourable critics to accuse him of not having the emotional guts or psychological wherewithal to deal directly with his trauma. The result, they claim, was both an immature life and a fundamentally inauthentic body of work. Cocteau admitted that whenever he passed by rue La Bruyère he would run hell for leather so as not to see or hear anything. He also suffered for a long time a recurring nightmare in which his dead father turned into an anonymous parrot or cockatoo that his mother was unable to distinguish from all the others perched nearby. The sudden, violent death of his father at such a young age would resound in Cocteau's work in its continual leanings towards death, morbidity and violence, and it engendered many paternal phantoms and countless images of suicide. Whenever any paternal figures appear, which is in itself extremely rare, they are either totally weak (viz. the failed inventor Georges in *Les Parents terribles*) or else on the path to virtual extinction, like Jacques' father in *The Miscreant* who simply 'effaced himself'.

The period immediately following his father's death was especially difficult for Cocteau. His maternal grandmother died a year later, followed soon after by the death of a close school-friend. The shock of a golden age now forever lost and the fear of a proliferation of death would never leave him, and it gave rise to bouts of depression and feelings of emptiness, afflicting him even on summer vacations in the Swiss lakes with his family or at Vierzy in northern France, where he stayed with his paternal grandfather. On a visit to Venice in 1908 he experienced, as he later put it, the

> [b]itterness of being alone amongst the crowds, the melancholy of never feeling that one belongs in the places one loves the most, the revulsion of not being many-in-one and of living a captive in our narrow measure of space, the lassitude of passing through the normal phases of a tenderness for which we desire immediate reciprocity.[2]

We observe here both Cocteau's cruel realization that he could not be everyone in the scene he beheld and his soon-to-be familiar frustration that total control eluded him. Back in Paris, his maternal grandfather took him to the Conservatoire, and in April 1900 he attended the Exposition Universelle, where the flamboyant American dancer Loïe Fuller, dancing with expressive swirls under multi-coloured projector lights, imprinted on him an entirely new set of impressions and sensations. Otherwise, Cocteau was now brought up exclusively by women and above all by his all-consuming mother, who resolved to remain a widow. Buying sailor outfits for her *petit prince*, she attempted to perpetuate his earlier blessed childhood. Yet it seems that in his pre-teen years Cocteau also became openly antagonistic towards her. During one particularly unpleasant and dangerous episode on a train when returning from Switzerland, he effectively betrayed his mother to French customs. He had asked her to hide a case for him and then promptly denounced her, as a result of which she was forced humiliatingly to undress in public and be subjected to a body search.[3] Perhaps Cocteau felt responsible for his father's disappearance, which enabled him to become the sole intimate of his mother, sparking off an Oedipal crisis that became a veritable obsession in his work. In fact, Madame Cocteau was a rather difficult and demanding person, by turns authoritarian and pious, coquettish and *mondaine*, and her traits of anxiety, possessiveness and melancholy would serve later also to define her son. A fusion had formed between them, and from now on until her death they would write at least one letter to each other every day, in which they told each other everything (or almost everything). Indeed, they would live together virtually like a married couple until Cocteau was well over 40. The die had already been cast. Requiring love from all sides and unable to separate himself from others, Cocteau now found himself doomed to float in an indiscernible space between everywhere and nowhere.

2
Natural-born Legend

In 1900 Cocteau entered sixth grade at Le Petit Condorcet, a school located just a few minutes away in the rue d'Amsterdam. He later claimed he was a terrible pupil with a short attention span, a virtual dunce who gained prizes only for less prestigious subjects such as drawing and gymnastics as well as German because he was aided by Jéphine. In fact, reports described him as an intelligent student with a lively and subtle mind although weak-willed, 'irregular' and easily distracted. The public side of Jean's naughty, controlling genius was beginning to form. With insolent charm he obliged both fellow pupils and teachers to read aloud his verse. He could produce classical Alexandrine rhymes at the slightest whim and exhibited any little sketch or caricature to hold and bewitch his audience. The misery and tedium as well as daily tortures and detentions of school life were alleviated by the often brazen autoerotic antics of the boys (the classroom reeked of gas, chalk and sperm, he later observed) and the events of the Cité Monthiers just off the rue de Clichy. This was the school playground, which became during winter the scene of snowball fights. One in particular would haunt him forever. It starred an older, ruggedly handsome thirteen-year-old co-pupil called Dargelos, who was already a grown man with jet-black hair and fleshy lips while his peers were still boys. Cocteau wrote later that Dargelos was a supremely arrogant duffer who always went unpunished, but again this was far from the actual truth. He was, however, cock of the

Cocteau at school (front row, second from left), *c.* 1901.

walk and, for the young Jean who followed him around blindly,
a 'vamp' who embodied the 'supernatural' sexuality of virile beauty
and initiated the younger boys into the pleasures of sex. The fight
in question resulted in a crime: a snowball thrown by Dargelos
containing a stone struck the chest of another schoolboy and
immediately killed him. This would become in Cocteau's work
a virtual primal scene of fatal male beauty starring a shameless,
untutored faun, symbol of a superior, amoral force. The combined
angelic and Orphic figure of Dargelos was so intensely imprinted
in Cocteau's retina that he would project it in different ways on
to all the young men with whom he subsequently fell in love, and
it lies at the root of all his drawings of idealized male figures. A
decade later he would write: 'At an age when gender does not yet
influence decisions of the flesh, my desire was not to reach, not to
touch, nor to embrace the elected person, but *to be* him . . . What
loneliness!'[1] Cocteau was fated to crave love in order simply to
be, igniting a compulsive desire for identification with a hyper-
masculine ideal – his perfect complement – that could, of course,
never be truly satisfied.

Cocteau's academic progress degenerated when he entered
Le Grand Condorcet and he was eventually expelled from the *lycée*
in 1904 for 'disciplinary reasons'. He was then sent to the Fénelon
school, where he continued to draw, moving on to caricatures
of his cosy bourgeois world with its sports and entertainments.
Consumed by new alternative pursuits including palmistry, he duly
failed the *baccalauréat* in 1906 and underwent a succession of
idiosyncratic private tutors, notably Monsieur Dietz, a professor
at the Lycée Buffon who had also been a tutor for André Gide.
Cocteau first went to stay with Dietz at his home in the Val André
in Brittany to cram for the *baccalauréat*, but after another dismal
failure returned to Paris to attend the boarding school that Dietz
ran on the rue Claude Bernard. On 30 December 1906 Cocteau's
first fully fledged show, entitled *Sisowath en ballade*, was staged
by Dietz's pupils. A farce about the king of Cambodia, this mini-
spectacle of tableaux revealed already Cocteau's taste for cliché
and burlesque metamorphosis (he appeared on stage himself as a
'man-object'). Although he suffered yet another stinging failure at
the *baccalauréat* in 1907, in every other respect Cocteau's life was
now starting to become more worldly and cosmopolitan. He was
fifteen, good-looking and utterly charming. Every Thursday and
Sunday he would combine allowances with his schoolboy friend
Carlito Bouland to rent a stage-box at the Eldorado theatre, where
famous singers such as Dranem and Mistinguett performed.
Another vaudeville actress and singer there called Jeanne Reynette
signed personal photographs for Cocteau with theatrically
extravagant messages (these were probably written by Cocteau
himself, who took care to preserve them for posterity). It was
Mistinguett, however, who most captivated the young boys. Like
a child-vamp she was selling a lyric and crude gutter-life with her
famous onomatopoeic refrains that require no translation. One
such went: 'Je suis Mam'zelle, sans façon,/ Je rigole, je batifole,/ Et
j'adore le rigodon'. Cocteau became infatuated with 'la Miss', who

was equally beguiled by this intelligent and always animated *petit monsieur* with his fox-like nose, thick eyebrows, delicate lips and hair combed in the style of the young Victor Hugo. She would later confide coyly to friends that she had slept with Cocteau, although she 'had never been to bed with him'. She had rather 'imparted' some worldly wisdom by performing on him an intimate form of *déniaisement*.

Cocteau was on an amorous roll. He had another brief 'affair', this time with a music student called Christiane Mancini, who was both his age and his equal and who donned a long, black velvet robe. The intensity of her declaration of love clearly frightened him and he rebuffed his new 'companion' in a particularly cold, almost ruthless way, his cruelty a premonition of some of the verses of Baudelairean sadism he would later dedicate to her in his first collection of poetry. Then, at seventeen, he fell passionately in love with the actress and cabaret singer Madeleine Carlier, a genuine Parisian *cocotte* from Montmartre who had survived the boulevard. Here again the facts remain sketchy. Cocteau described 'la môme Carlier', seven years his senior, as a 'very simple but very fashionable girl', and she was by all accounts the first person he actually wanted to possess rather than simply identify with. He was besotted by her and after her performances they spent long evenings together, during which he drew her in erotic poses. Unfortunately, she was maintained by a mysterious Greek gentleman and then fell instead for Cocteau's friend Carlito. This devastated him and, in what would quickly establish itself as his reflex response to emotional crisis, he experienced a total void. His fiercely jealous mother forbade him ever to see again this 'slut' of the *demi-monde*. Did Cocteau talk of an engagement with Carlier in order to defend himself from his mother's over-protective attitude? Or was this more a wish on his part to invent and magnify heterosexual relationships and so counter any suggestion of innate homosexuality (Cocteau was never bisexual as such)? Either way, the collapse of the affair left him feeling mortally wounded. If the young Cocteau could break young girls' hearts, his own, too, could just as easily be crushed.

Cocteau's romances with different women, however real or imagined, were not the only formative experiences of this period. Around the age of fifteen, after failing the *baccalauréat* and just before entering the Val André, he did a runner to Marseilles. The full facts of this escapade, which lasted no more than a couple of months, will never be fully known, but it appeared that he lived incognito in the highly dangerous Vieux Port, and specifically the Chinese-Annamite quarter around the notorious rue de la Rose. He later called this 'year' in Marseilles one of the best periods of his life, yet took care never to speak about it in any detail. Whatever the precise circumstances of this flight, Cocteau certainly experienced for the first time personal liberation and a sense of experimentation that stretched from taking drugs to exploring his sexuality, following his liaison with his putative first gay lover, a famous jockey at Maisons-Laffitte called Albert Botten. Eventually, Cocteau's maternal uncle Raymond, a high-ranking officer in the diplomatic service, was informed of the matter and arranged for the police to rescue him from his job as a dishwasher or 'servant' and have him sent back to Paris. (This was the same dashing gay uncle who, in 1906, as first secretary to the French Embassy in Berlin, was himself implicated in a scandalous affair involving Prince Eulenberg, a favourite of Kaiser Wilhelm II, centred around a group of sodomitic spiritualists called The Round Table.) Cocteau, it seems, had actually made it possible for his family to find him by sending a postcard from Marseilles, a fact that for some critics nullifies his experience. Yet this was a vitally formative period for Cocteau, a necessary rite of passage, and it conferred on him the special aura that he craved. It also traumatized his mother, and it is perhaps because of this fact, rather than out of any sense of personal shame, that he chose to remain somewhat opaque on the subject of his homosexuality (and indeed that of his father and uncle). Cocteau, it needs to be said, never suffered from any disabling complexes or inhibitions when it came to expressing his sexuality either in his life or his art.

Towards the end of 1907, just as his older siblings were conforming to social expectations (his brother became a stockbroker, his sister married to become the Comtesse Henri de la Chapelle), Cocteau moved with his mother and her valet Cyprien to an apartment in the rue Malakoff (now the rue Raymond-Poincaré) near the Arc de Triomphe. With all hopes of a regular schooling well and truly over, he decided he was going to be a poet. Through his mother he made contact with the Salon poet Lucien Daudet, son of the novelist Alphonse Daudet and an intimate of Marcel Proust. Eleven years his senior, the good-looking, highly precious and cultivated gay Lucien acted as a kind of double and model for Cocteau. Unambitious for himself, he was the first to recognize objectively Cocteau's talent, regarding him even as the natural inheritor of Proust. By offering him entry to the major Paris Salons, Lucien instilled in Cocteau a new self-confidence. Indeed, Cocteau suddenly found himself in his element, for this was an exclusive world of chamber concerts, games, charades and disguises totally insulated from the other emerging strand of the French *bourgeoisie* defined by positivism and scientism. When not performing as a kind of servant-*cavalier* to the elderly ex-Empress Eugénie, widow of Napoleon III, he also met the musician and poet Reynaldo Hahn (another of Proust's lovers), with whom he would soon collaborate on a one-act *pochade* called *La Patience de Pénélope*. Finally, through his friend René Rocher he made the acquaintance of one of the most popular tragedians of his day, the Romanian actor Edouard de Max.

Flirtatious, outrageously camp and helplessly addicted to both opium and ephebes, de Max paraded around Paris and the Bois de Boulogne in a flamboyant velvet suit when not staging his own private sybaritic delights at home. At one masquerade ball that took place at the Théâtre des Arts he arranged for Cocteau to arrive as Heliogabalus with red curls, a tiara, pearl-embroidered cloak, painted nails, de Max's own rings and a Napoleonic eagle perched on his head. De Max soon realized the error of this folly and with much embarrassment relieved Cocteau of his wig and sent him home (Cocteau would later describe de Max as 'the most naïve man in the world'). With his mother's full consent, however, Cocteau visited de Max alone in his flat in the rue Camartin and read to him in bed. In return, the actor gave him a personal photograph inscribed: 'To your sixteen years in bloom, from my forty years in tears'. De Max sought to be a kind of spiritual father to this delicate young creature, whom he considered a potential new Edmond Rostand, the poet and dramatist best known for *Cyrano de Bergerac*. Having reared himself on the poetry of Baudelaire, Verlaine and Jean Lorrain, Cocteau was now beginning to write a blend of Parnassian and Symbolist verse that bore all the hallmarks of poets like Rostand, Gabriele d'Annunzio and Gustave Kahn. His jottings seeped – and oh, how they seeped! – with the trials and tribulations of anxious love. Yet this poetry was also stunningly devoid of any reference to the Marseilles escapade, for at this stage the young Cocteau was consumed only by his natural desire to please.

On the morning of Saturday, 4 April 1908 de Max organized at his own expense a poetry recital largely in Cocteau's honour at the Théâtre Femina where he happened to be playing that year. His prestige attracted a starry and dressy audience that included the Minister of Public Education, the idiosyncratic translator and satirical poet Laurent Tailhade, and Catulle Mendès, the now ageing head of the Parnassian school of poets and survivor of the era of Hugo, Baudelaire and Théophile Gautier. This rumpled, larger-than-life Falstaff figure and literary broker would exert an early fascination on Cocteau and become his virtual impresario until his death in February 1909. It was Tailhade, however, who presented Cocteau in a short introductory lecture, proposing him as a new Rimbaud and praising him for his exquisite anguish and adolescent negativity, the standard tropes of Symbolist and post-Symbolist poetry. An assortment of invited actors and artists then participated in the readings, after which songs based on Cocteau's poems were performed by Jacques Renaud and Tiarko Richepin. Cocteau himself recited a selection of his poems, dazzling his audience with his natural presence and charisma, his verbal facility and *esprit*. By the end of the performance, gushing wildly with tears due to the huge applause, he found himself a star, effortlessly wafted, as he put it, on the wings of fame. It was now official: he was the new prince of French poetry. He had arrived! And crucially it had happened on the Paris stage. He would henceforth be in artistic and emotional thrall to what he called theatre's 'crimson and gold disease' and always define himself as a Parisian artist performing for an audience (real or imagined).

Over time Cocteau typically misremembered the *matinée poétique* that launched him, even claiming he was just seventeen and that the great stage actress Sarah Bernhardt had engineered the event. What was indisputable, however, was that the doors of the capital were now flung open. He was invited to participate in the Salon des Poètes, and his first published poem, 'Les Façades', appeared a few months later in July in the smart review *Je sais tout* accompanied by his photograph, a visual accessory that set a precedent in his work. The crucial figures of Paris's artistic elite, including Proust, Rostand and his son Maurice, the writer and playwright Roger Martin du Gard, and the theatre critic, playwright and Academician Jules Lemaître, all queued up to hear the young prodigy. Success would never again come so easily or taste so sweet. Cocteau had moved as if by magic from the maternal bosom of childhood to public glory without even having to evolve, adored by his audience just as he had been by his family.

But precisely because of this he demanded yet more unconditional praise and approbation in order to have a sense of selfhood and well-being. And the more he lived to please, the more he needed to please to exist. His fate was now effectively sealed. Only the adoring look of others could provide him with any real solidity.

The trip to Italy that Cocteau took shortly after with his mother to celebrate his overnight success introduced a further ingredient into this dangerous psychological mix. A young and romantic 23-year-old French writer, Raymond Laurent, shot himself on the steps of the church of the Salute in Venice on 24 September 1908, after apparently forcing himself amorously on to Cocteau. After his doomed attachments with mainly older women, so now began Cocteau's fatal attraction for younger men, although the actual cause of death here was not Cocteau himself but Laurent's American lover, Langhorn Whistler. The same wounds of loneliness and emptiness opened up within Cocteau as before, yet significantly, although clearly fearful of the possible public repercussions of the incident, he promptly wrote a sonnet ('by way of an epitaph') devoted to Laurent's memory, as well as a ballad ('Souvenir d'un soir d'automne au jardin Eaden'). With its oblique and mysterious allusions to the real incident, the ballad reveals Cocteau's compulsive need both to invoke the real and to reinscribe it as legend, thus displacing and ultimately dispersing his trauma as little more than a passing trifle. Such impressive detachment and powers of mental reversal would provide Cocteau with vital psychological armour. And despite a now growing awareness of death within his circle of family and friends, he remained focused, like Rastignac at the end of Balzac's *Old Goriot*, on pumping Paris for its glittering possibilities of success and acclaim – not glory for glory's sake so much as the chance to have an identity *tout court* and become, somehow, himself.

3

Prince in Exile

Between 1909 and 1910 Cocteau moved of his own accord out of his mother's apartment and rented a wing of the decaying Hôtel Biron (now the Musée Rodin) in the rue de Varenne, a secret bohemian space that housed at one time or another Auguste Rodin, Matisse, Rilke and Isadora Duncan. He eventually settled down with his mother in a large apartment at 10, rue d'Anjou, an altogether respectable address just off the rue du Faubourg Saint-Honoré. Now began his first full flush of youth and genius. With his Brillo-pad hair and elongated spaghetti fingers, nonchalant verbal brilliance, exquisite grace and charm rounded off by perfect manners, he cut an irresistible dash. Exempted from two years of military service on health grounds (either strings were pulled or else a doctor's certificate was produced to certify that he was a frail aesthete), he became a man about town, a Parisian dandy who had his portrait taken by the leading painters of the day. In Romaine Brooks's portrait of Cocteau from 1912 at the time of the Big Wheel, he is standing on a balcony with the Eiffel Tower in the back-ground, dressed in a suit and bow tie while holding a red rose and gloves like a pale Byron. The well-known society portrait painter and writer Jacques-Emile Blanche also produced a series of portraits of Cocteau around this time. Blanche recognized in Cocteau a throwback to Aubrey Beardsley, Proust and Wilde (the same *préciosité*, the same rhetorical poses, etc.), and although he admired Cocteau's evident artistic qualities, in particular his

Romaine Brooks, *Jean Cocteau at the Time of the Big Wheel* (1912), oil on canvas.

remarkable powers of observation, he also intuited with some disquiet that behind the razzle-dazzle and splendid mimicry lay a fragile, depressive adolescent. One full-length oil painting based on a photograph and executed in 1912 presented Cocteau, now 23, already like an old man with a walking stick in a garden, his angular features and slender silhouette captured in profile (see over). The painting's rather rough-hewn quality and lack of distinguishing features reveals a confused, complicated face, suggesting a young man slightly at odds with himself, lost in his own boredom and unsure what to do next.

What disturbed Blanche fascinated others such as Jules Lemaître, whom Cocteau now courted as a potential new sponsor and who named him Ariel. For Cocteau seemed to be a creature of pure gas without flesh, alighting on new experiences, stimulations, ideas and influences as he raced with gay abandon around

Jacques-Emile Blanche, *Jean Cocteau in Offranville* (1912), oil on canvas.

the capital in the company of young pals like Lucien Daudet, Maurice Rostand and a tall, elegant, rich and art-loving aristocrat, Comte Etienne de Beaumont. Together they believed they were the new *jeunesse dorée* and direct heirs to Byron and Shelley. Rostand, an extremely flamboyant dandy whose main inspiration was Aubrey Beardsley and who displayed an interest in transvestism (he was, for example, obsessed with Sarah Bernhardt), was totally enchanted by Cocteau. Together with the printer-cum-publisher François Bernouard they founded in 1910 an elegant and glossy poetry review on fine paper entitled *Schéhérazade*, certainly not the first de-luxe magazine devoted to poets, as Cocteau liked to profess, but one of the most handsome. It catered perfectly to the current vogue for all things Persian, its cover by the fashion illustrator and designer Paul Iribe featuring an ink drawing of a naked Sultana as a Beardsley vamp reclining on her chaise longue. The five issues that appeared were permeated by the late *Belle époque* / Art Nouveau style of the grand couturier Paul Poiret and included drawings by Pierre Bonnard and André Mare, poems by Nathalie Barney, Maurice and Edmond Rostand, fourteen previously unpublished pieces by Mallarmé, and Cocteau's own first fiction, a period Venetian trifle entitled 'Comment mourut Monsieur de Trèves'.

Cocteau's approach to his sexuality at this time was principally aesthetic, perhaps because he was still too affected by the deaths he had witnessed while growing up and because any intimate friendships he developed soon become tortuous. He toured Algeria with Daudet in 1910 precisely because he had fallen in love with a morose young male poet (name unknown) but had ended up waiting in vain. In what would become a characteristic guise, he felt like St Sebastian facing his archer and executioner. Immediately upon his return to Paris he met the upcoming and slightly older Catholic writer François Mauriac, who was currently receiving rave reviews for his poetry. Typically, it was Cocteau who made the first move by formally inviting Mauriac to the rue d'Anjou, but it was Mauriac who then wished to take things further, not only by meeting and exchanging letters with Cocteau but also by sending him poems. Wary no doubt of any kind of relationship while still on the rebound, Cocteau did not respond in kind, thus provoking a tension between the two that only festered over time. Cocteau continued to work through some of his thoughts about homosexuality in odd articles and writings for the literary journal *Comoedia*. In one entitled 'De Biais' (Slantwise) in the November–December 1910 issue he evoked a fictional Jahel in order to suggest that homosexuality was purer and nobler than heterosexuality, which was fatally linked to the original sin of Adam and Eve. Wilde was becoming a crucial influence, and themes of the mirror and double masks revealing the truth were starting to take shape in his work (he even attempted with his friend Jacques Renaud a stage adaptation of Wilde's *The Picture of Dorian Gray* entitled *Le Portrait surnaturel de Dorian Gray*, a 'pièce fantastique' in four acts and five tableaux). Of course, this was a period when many negative clinical and psychoanalytical theories of homosexuality abounded, by Charcot and Krafft-Ebing among others, all premised on the idea that homosexuality was a cause of instability as well as an unnatural and asthmatic nervousness associated with the 'female' sickness of hysteria. For some, this helped to explain why Cocteau had the look of a nervous insect or young 'male girl' and often felt physically weak and ill, experiencing recurring problems with hay fever, allergies, abscesses, skin problems, viruses and shingles, conditions he would often exaggerate for effect. At times he could even seem slightly hysterical, especially in the way he imitated and appropriated others due to his incapacity to inhibit his own skin. Moreover, at around the age of 22 he started to resemble further his mother (the same pointed nose, oblong eyes, black hair and slightly yellowish-brown complexion). Homosexuality was not publicly outlawed in France at this time, but it was nevertheless regarded as a matter of private shame and even contagious. For Cocteau, however, it was also firmly enmeshed in the rarefied and hermetic world of the Salons with their secret codes. Only very rarely would he branch out to sample the exotic tastes displayed by Daudet for rough trade and the world of low *queers*.

In addition to his regular company at the Salons, three crucial literary figures began to impose themselves on Cocteau and serve as guides for his artistic career. The first was André Gide, twenty years his senior and already a major writer with whom he would share for more than forty years an ambivalent, love–hate relationship born of both mutual respect and intense rivalry. Gide had co-founded in 1908 the *Nouvelle Revue française*, now established as one of the literary and critical powerhouses in France, and Cocteau craved Gide's cultural weight and intellectual prestige. In the first letter he sent to Gide in 1912 requesting a meeting, Cocteau claimed to have read nearly all his works and proposed that he (Gide) would find in him a Nathanael and 'prodigal son' (a reference to Gide's *Fruits of the Earth*). With customary reserve, Gide chose to remain aloof and even frosty towards the young man's advances, although in the course of time they would produce together more than 100 known items of correspondence, from personal letters to telegrams, in which they passed judgement on each other and developed their individual doctrines. The second major figure for Cocteau at this time was Proust, who, in the dark, cork-lined sanctuary of his apartment, was already dissecting the vanity and void of the very world that Cocteau was on a direct mission to conquer. The two were on the same aesthetic and personal wavelength thanks to their similar social origins and attitudes, and Proust became entranced by this young genius, whom he once addressed in a letter thus: 'You who enjoy representing the highest truths by a dazzling symbol that contains them all'. Proust understood exactly what made Cocteau tick, namely that he was always searching for new remarkable people to amaze and be amazed by precisely because he desperately needed to consolidate his existence with some external structure and meaning. Their personal dealings were heavily ritualized according to Proust's tastes, including dinners at the Ritz, nocturnal trysts and letters composed in rhyme. They also both shared a mischievous sense of humour and a desire to ridicule those whom they admired, to the point that Cocteau naturally began to imitate Proust in public.

By far the most significant of Cocteau's new acquaintances at this time, however, was the poet Anna de Noailles. De Noailles is much less well known now but at the time was considered by many as the greatest living poet of the post-Symbolist age. Thirteen years Cocteau's senior, this oriental-looking daughter of a Romanian prince and a Greek mother was his first great 'sister' in arms, and despite odd periods of silence and rivalry she would remain an abiding influence on him until her death (the last major text Cocteau completed before his own death would be a final assessment of her literary worth entitled *La Comtesse de Noailles, oui et non*). An undisputed queen of the Salons, de Noailles held forth in her bed at home on the rue Scheffer, preaching glory and immortality, recognition and love with an insistence that Cocteau could entirely relate to. They became like Siamese twins, enjoying a symbiotic, asexual friendship based on mutual adoration. Indeed, Cocteau copied her literary style and handwriting so well he earned the nickname of l'Anna-*mâle*. If she talked obsessively of fatigue, suffering, death and the uncomprehending world in hyper-precious vocabulary (*volupté, azur, éther, langueur, sublime*, etc.), then so did he. Moreover, he began to replicate her favourite form of conversation, the cascading monologue, firing off rhetorical questions and then instantly supplying the answer so that his audience could never catch its breath to interrupt him. He even started to receive guests while in bed and affected the same hanging head and hand gestures. De Noailles' fundamental lesson for Cocteau was that there could be no separation between public and private life. The literary was also the personal and sentimental, and everything had to be experienced directly through one's work.

What, then, of Cocteau's own artistic development? The first collection, *La Lampe d'Aladin*, published in 1909 at his own expense, featured dedications to many of the famous figures, artists and tragedians who had attended the momentous *matinée poétique*. A hypersensitive preface set the tone:

> Young like Aladdin, walking with fearful step, I have seen fruits, jewels, gleams and shadows. And, my heart filled with illusions, I have wept at the difficulty of giving them to the unbelieving world.

Cocteau's poetry was at one with his Parisian image of a Salon prince, and his cultivated pastel verses evoked Versailles, Watteau and Whistler as well as Beardsley and Wilde (an entire sequence was devoted to *Salomé*). All was enshrouded necessarily within the mortal ether of German Lieder and Nordic mists. Cocteau's second volume, *Le Prince frivole*, displayed on its cover the snatch of a Mozart score and was crammed with even more references, nods and winks to de Noailles, dedications to Mendès, Molière and Gautier, as well as larded with epigraphs from Voltaire and Byron. The poems featured the odd, knowingly risqué gay detail, such as allusions to Wilde's 'naked god that doesn't speak its name', yet other references to the *ancien régime* felt distinctly old-fashioned. Though clearly derivative in the vein of de Noailles, Henri de Régnier and Mendès, the collection was noted for being less of a pastiche than *La Lampe d'Aladin* and was praised by Proust for containing 'potential' greatness. Yet for most readers Cocteau's Poet spent more time reflecting on his aesthetic position and status than actually delivering the goods, resorting instead to the standard tricks of fashionable name-dropping and invocations of the Parisian *gratin*. The closing 'Sonnets de l'Hôtel Biron' refer explicitly to the ageing aristocrat dandy, the Comte Robert de Montesquiou, a model for both Huysmans' Des Esseintes and Proust's Baron de Charlus and on whom Cocteau was now partly modelling himself (he even began to sport a cane and turned-up satin cuffs while aping extravagant little 'agonies'). Cocteau forever tried to obtain an audience with this poison-tongued snob, yet Montesquiou regarded him as little more than a pretentious young upstart on the make and consistently snubbed him, which, of course, only made Cocteau more keen to prize and imitate him.

Cocteau's third collection, *La Danse de Sophocle*, published not over-enthusiastically by Mercure de France, received only a lukewarm response heaped with much faint praise of the kind 'how can one criticize the dance when the dancer is so charming?' (a reference to the young Sophocles in the quotation from *Athenaeus* used as an epigraph). It also bore too evidently the sublime mark of de Noailles, some poem titles matching word for word her brand of personal and romantic lyricism (de Noailles herself stated rather ambivalently of the volume: 'I like it more with each new page'). There were many obligatory poems on insomnia and death, including one that proclaimed itself a little ominously 'The last song of the frivolous prince', where Cocteau seemed to be turning away from the influence of Rostand. Initially, Cocteau could not understand the unfavourable critical reaction, which he attributed to pure jealousy and public incomprehension in the face of genius, although he certainly had not helped things by comparing himself in the collection to a white butterfly rubbed in pollen. Serious questions were now being asked about the real nature of his talents, and even the sympathetic Proust, who had a lucid sense of Cocteau's marvellous gifts, warned him of dissipating his natural abilities. It was, however, a highly patronizing review in the September 1912 issue of the *Nouvelle revue française* by Henri Ghéon that stung Cocteau the most, for it suggested that although he showed excellent promise and was outstandingly equipped for producing 'frivolous' Parisianism (in other words, poetry *lite*), he had a long way to go before becoming a proper artist. Since Ghéon was Gide's lover at the time, Cocteau suspected that Gide was behind the piece, the first major salvo in their long and often bitter struggle for personal and literary influence. If Gide admired his junior's consummate social ease, wit and imagination, he nevertheless believed that Cocteau was in danger of misusing his prodigious talents because of his Parnassian mannerisms and over-cultivated elegance.

The truth was that Cocteau himself knew that he had not really progressed as a poet. Poetry was really just a clever parlour game, rather than, as he would later describe it, a priestly vocation and struggle conceived in great solitude, where the Muses are like praying mantises ready to swallow up and devour their young male poets. He was merely the latest and most proficient exponent of the Salon school, whose rules and themes were thoroughly pre-determined. By conforming to existing models, there was nothing particularly original about his approach or style, and certainly nothing that we now recognize as 'Cocteau'. Reproducing generic and highly affected, often mawkish verse, 'Sophocteau' (as Montesquiou unkindly dubbed him) could see himself becoming less a *prince frivole* than a *prince du ridicule*. He had waltzed through his youth like a precocious, pampered social butterfly, acclaimed by snobs and aesthetes who were more seduced by his poetic image than his actual poetry. His premature success now looked an altogether false start, and he knew he would have to turn his back on the world of the Salons in order to be truly himself. He immediately forbade the republication of his first three volumes and later excised them completely from his bibliography. Eventually, too, he would renounce any lingering Wildean traces and tendencies. He would henceforth always be suspicious of fame and crave recognition only from those he genuinely respected. But what new school of art would he have to enter to acquire the right kind of training? As ever with Cocteau the result would be a combination of a chance encounter, excellent timing and the arrival of one or more Great Men.

4

Russian Lessons

On 19 May 1909 Cocteau attended the Paris premiere of the Ballets
Russes at the Théâtre du Châtelet. The mixed programme included
Le Pavillon d'Armide with a score by Tcherepnin, Borodin's *Danses
polovstiennes* from his opera *Prince Igor*, and *Le Festin*, a suite of
dances set to the music of various Russian composers. Cocteau
was enchanted by the spectacle and above all by the performance
of the company's star dancer, Vaslav Nijinsky, as Armide in a costume
of white, silver and yellow. He was subsequently introduced to
the company's director Serge Diaghilev and dutifully followed
the entire six-week season, making notes, drawings and caricatures
of what he saw both front- and back-stage and developing his
own witty graphic style in the process. The experience would
yield for Cocteau vital insights into the connections between
lived experience and artistic practice.

Diaghilev's principal aim in forming the Ballets Russes in 1908–9
had been to revolutionize both the form and the status of ballet in
Western Europe. For this he had commissioned music by Debussy,
Ravel and Stravinsky, costumes and décor by Léon Bakst and
Alexandre Benois, and choreography by Michel Fokine that
expressed sound as movement. Dance seemed for the first time to
provide a synthesis of all the other arts, and the Ballets Russes had
an immediate influence on contemporary dress style and interior
decoration in France, notably Bakst's pistachio greens and Benois'
variations on white and black. Diaghilev was really the purveyor

of a kind of luxury avant-garde, eager to court controversy in the wealthy elite on whom the ballet depended for its core audience. Nicknamed Chinchilla on account of a streak of white in his dark hair, he was a large man of enormous energy, artistic flair and drive (in Cocteau's drawings he appears a virtual hippopotamus). He also had a forceful personality and was by turns authoritarian, whimsical, sarcastic, inflexible and vindictive. Misia Edwards, his sole female intimate and confidante, served as the company's Polish 'queen' and capricious muse. As for Stravinsky, he had arrived in Paris in 1910 with *Firebird* and, true to form, it was Cocteau who sought him out and introduced himself rather than the other way round. Yet it was Nijinsky who fascinated Cocteau most on account of his potent mixture of animality and fragility, at once desirable and androgynous, half-angel and half-leopard. He presented for Cocteau a unique, hybrid spectacle of desire, pain and sacrifice. In a little-known volume, *Vaslav Nijinsky: six vers de Jean Cocteau, six dessins de Paul Iribe* (1910), which contains six one-line pieces of verse accompanied by Iribe's Beardsley-inspired woodcuts, Cocteau signed a veritable love-letter to Nijinsky, portraying him in his role as the Sultana's black slave in *Schéhérazade*, the most sumptuously oriental of all the company's ballets. Nijinsky represented for Cocteau a new type of artistic model and performer due to the absolute contrast he offered between performance and reality. If on stage he was god-like, a mixture of winged grace and slender power, once off he appeared strangely hunched, over-muscled and awkward. In fact, backstage between scenes he was often caught gasping and on the point of fainting. Throughout all his writings on Nijinsky, where he explains that the dancer possessed both superhuman vigour and feline grace, Cocteau celebrated a total devotion to art but also an aesthetics of clumsiness and weakness, an 'art of suffering' taken to the point of paroxysm. Indeed, with his fusion of body, ideal and will, this 'barbarian of genius' set a new aesthetic standard for Cocteau, for whom the Dionysian hopes and expectations of Nietzsche as expressed in *Le Gai Savoir* were, it seemed, at last being realized. Nijinsky could potentially do anything, and Cocteau fancied himself similarly as a superhuman entity charged with spreading the fire of the divine. In Cocteau's books, it took one to know one.

The Ballets Russes soon became a kind of family for Cocteau, and he in turn became their 'Jeanchick' and unofficial French mascot. He functioned really as a counterpoint to Diaghilev because he was unstintingly enthusiastic and hands-on in his approach, always larking about and creating mirth. For the first time Cocteau had entered an openly gay artistic milieu with its own extravagant and exotic aesthetic, and Diaghilev's pederastic court, described famously by Stravinsky as a homosexual Swiss Guard, was rife with desires, petty jealousies and favourites. Like an autocratic father Diaghilev was always suspicious of Cocteau whenever he got too close to his own private property – and one-time lover – Nijinsky, yet Cocteau had a purely platonic passion for the dancer and stood up to Diaghilev with cool resilience (he was also protected to some degree by Bakst). For the moment the two enjoyed a good working relationship, and off-duty with other members of the company they would visit the area around the Madeleine commonly known as 'Sodome et Gomorrhe'. They met regularly at Misia's flat on the Quai Voltaire, where Misia found the slightly frail and sharp-featured Cocteau 'irresistible' because of his conversational gifts and rare harmony of intellect, control and timing.

So confident and immersed did Cocteau become in the workings of the ballet company that with the hubris of youth he even believed he had surpassed his models in each domain (Sem in drawing, de Max in the theatre, etc.). In 1911 he designed a pink and mauve poster of Nijinsky in his rose-coloured tunic for *Le Spectre de la rose*, as well as one of the lead ballerina, Karsavina. The images were highly derivative of both Bakst and Toulouse-Lautrec and bore more resemblance to Cocteau himself than to the dancers. He also wrote a short promotional text advertising future ballets and their stars that appeared in the magazine *Comoedia Illustré*, where he waxed lyrical about Nijinsky who 'defie[d] heaven in a thousand different ways'. Cocteau was eventually commissioned by Diaghilev to write the script for one of the company's first French works, *Le Dieu bleu*, in collaboration with Frédéric de Madrazo and Reynaldo Hahn. The audience reception to the first performance in May 1912 was lukewarm. The major problem, surprisingly, was a lack of real sensuality, for if Cocteau had wished to raise Nijinsky to a new Nietzschean level he ended up merely feminizing him. There was also an embarrassing mismatch between the pleasant yet slender French melodies of Hahn, Fokine's choreography, the exorbitant sets of Bakst (temple, costumes, pearls, etc.), and the lashings of blue make-up. Despite the remarkable sight of Nijinsky as the Blue God rising up from an Indian blue pool, this over-baked effort marked the extreme of an aesthetic of exoticism and luxury that Diaghilev would very quickly abandon. It was unceremoniously dropped from the repertoire and would ultimately suffer the same fate as Cocteau's first collections of poetry on his list of collected works. The company's Paris season was saved two weeks later, however, by *L'Après-midi d'un faune*, the first modern 'anti-ballet' with choreography by Fokine and music by Debussy, where, in the first of his great scandals, Nijinksy performed as a faun in a skin-tight spotted leotard designed to make him seem more naked than naked, a bunch of grapes hanging loosely over his genitals. Nijinsky now revelled in his newly restored virile masculinity, as if fully vanquishing the feminine tendencies of *Le Dieu bleu*.

With his depersonalization of gesture and reduction of expression, Nijinsky had undergone a complete self-transformation, thereby offering Cocteau yet another kind of model, that of self-renewal. For Cocteau now realized that he would have to turn his back on what increasingly appeared an affected *style fleuri* (he was already beginning to express some major reserves about the all-too-precious poetry of Anna de Noailles). And then one night after a performance in 1912, while crossing the Place de la Concorde, Diaghilev bellowed out to Cocteau the following instruction: 'Astound me! I'll wait for you to astound me.' This was more than simply a challenge and artistic ultimatum on Diaghilev's part, since it was tinged with a measure of contempt for a man who had never charmed him (like some hysterical super-male Diaghilev had even taxed Cocteau for being too feminine). Yet Diaghilev's words touched Cocteau to the very core, and from that night on, as if replacing one kind of primal trauma (personal) with another (artistic), his recurring childhood dream of his father as an indiscriminate parrot finally abated. The imperative now was to provide a response to Diaghilev and somehow 'die' in order to be artistically reborn.

Shortly afterwards, on 29 May 1913, Cocteau attended the premiere of Stravinsky's *The Rite of Spring*. This momentous artistic event at the brash, new Théâtre des Champs-Elysées lasted just 35 minutes and was the first true scandal that Cocteau had witnessed. The audience's reaction was one of genuine shock and Diaghilev personally had to quell the massive booing and even riots in the aisles by flashing on the house lights before the police arrived. The evening had begun innocuously enough with a performance of *Les Sylphides*, but that was the essence of the shock: a comprehensive raid on prevailing aesthetics. Beyond the outrageous costumes and bizarre story of pagan sacrifice the show was an extraordinary synthesis of two different and bold modernist inventions: Nijinsky's physically unnatural dancing and difficult choreography, and the elemental savagery of Stravinsky's complex, dissonant multi-rhythms, with insistent stamping chords and throbbing vertical blocks of sound. It was a revelation. Cocteau now discovered that the real essence of creation was contradiction and controversy. Stravinsky epitomized the 'Astonish me!' of Diaghilev and immediately became the only valid artistic model for Cocteau, a symbol of rebellious youth, at once savage, volatile and destabilizing. Stravinsky was clearly an enchanter, a dynamo who could harness and transform raw power, and he compelled Cocteau to turn away utterly from what he now regarded as the soft cushion of Orientalism. Art could no longer be a simple matter of pleasing according to the bourgeois rules of supply and demand. It needed to be, like *The Rite of Spring*, a 'great insult to habit' and ignite a volcanic explosion. Cocteau was realizing rather belatedly that this was now the period of primitivism. There had, of course, been a *frisson nouveau* in the arts for a while, from Fauvism in painting (Matisse, Derain, Vlaminck) to Mallarmé's apocalyptic purism. The challenge for Cocteau was to fuse this new spirit with what he had learned from the Ballets Russes, namely discipline and artistry. A collaboration with Stravinsky was the obvious way forward.

David sprang superficially from the composer's earlier ballet score for *Petrushka* and was quite traditional in its heroic mythological vein, based around the theme of a travelling circus with acrobats performing outside a tent in which the real show 'David' unfolds. Cocteau appointed himself librettist, choreographer and set-designer, and the role of David was offered to Paulet Thévenaz, a young Swiss painter and dancer who earned his living by teaching at the recently founded Paris School of Dalcroze Eurythmics. Thévenaz taught Cocteau callisthenics and choreography, encouraging him to conceive of his body as an instrument in itself. He was also probably Cocteau's lover for a short while, although details again are lacking about the precise nature of their relationship. In March 1914 the two went off to Leysin to work with Stravinsky, who was then recovering from typhoid and was still a little suspicious of Cocteau, whom he viewed as largely a careerist and more interested in the provocation caused by *The Rite of Spring* than anything else. As for Cocteau, he claimed to have Stravinsky's best creative interests at heart, yet this was also his deliberate pitch for the avant-garde and he was already in discussions with the Théâtre du Vieux-Colombier and its director, Jacques Copeau, editor-in-chief of the *Nouvelle Revue française*. Stravinsky played his cards very close to his chest and strung Cocteau along with hopes and promises. The delicate period of negotiation between the two lasted several long months and included even a forlorn trip together to London. Stravinsky found Cocteau's endless flatteries and solicitations extremely vexing, but Cocteau, sensing mounting resistance, typically chose to delude himself that things were really moving forwards. Like a jilted lover he sent importunate and increasingly desperate letters to Stravinsky of the kind 'David is our moment', but the project was doomed and Stravinsky pulled out, claiming it was not as important artistically as his score for the opera *Le Rossignol*, which Diaghilev had just commissioned (extra money, among other incentives, was promised by the jealous Diaghilev). Stravinsky had effectively sacrificed *David*, and with it Cocteau. It was the first of Cocteau's many crises with the composer and the first of many such ruptures with his chosen collaborators.

Cocteau had lost out on a whole set of levels: not only on a spiritual marriage and collaboration with Stravinsky, but also on a union with the avant-garde and the Left Bank through a possible opening of the gates of the *Nouvelle Revue française*, and, in personal terms, on a relationship with Thévenaz, who suddenly abandoned him, taking off in 1914 with Copeau's dance trip to America, where he would remain until his early death in 1921. As was now the pattern, Cocteau was utterly devastated and inconsolable: 'It's all over', he declared. Cue the void. Yet Cocteau's overarching desire to generate the youthful, revolutionary and orgiastic effect of *The Rite of Spring* would now help him through. More than lovers and collaborators, what was at stake now was to re-conceive the very nature of his artistic practice. He would not publish another volume of poetry for seven years. Moreover, he would now cultivate a sobriety of order and silence by withdrawing temporarily from Paris (he went back to Leysin) and lay claim to an aesthetics of minimalism, writing properly for the first time in prose, a fact viewed by many in the avant-garde as a *volte-face* rather than an advance. And this meant himself sacrificing his other Chosen One, the noble Anna de Noailles who had done so much to raise his game and whom he was now starting publicly to mock. To be sure, Stravinsky would continue to serve as a proclaimed Master, yet Cocteau's new ambition was to be his own master and probe the secrets of his own bizarre self. He had understood immediately the importance of Freud's discovery of the unconscious and took it very seriously, even to the point of consuming large intakes of sugar, regarded then as the best nutrient for dreams and a fast track into the interior world. His method was summed up by the daring formula of his new novel: 'Whatever the public reproaches you for, cultivate it: it's you'.[1] From now on, Cocteau would be forever – partly out of necessity, partly out of wish-fulfilment, and in ways not always intended – his own *poète maudit*.

Dedicated to Stravinsky and invoking *The Rite of Spring* as a 'masterpiece' and 'ferocious eclogue' in its opening pages, *Le Potomak* is essentially a direct satirical attack on the bourgeoisie that pitches two clans against each other: the pompous, complacent and over-fed bourgeois Mortimers from the provinces, and the cruel and ravenous Eugènes with their companions, the Humeuses. The Eugènes are really Cocteau's family (Eugène, we recall, was one of his own baptismal names and Eugénie his mother's name). The text narrates visits by Cocteau and his friends to 'Le Potomak' (a troping on the American river), a formless aquatic monster hiding under the church of the Madeleine in a subterranean aquarium with a tubular protrusion. It is a 'megoptera coelenterous' that bears resemblance to a film projector, storing dreams and spewing them forth in reels. Accompanied by two moulting animal figures,

Persicaire and Argemonde (when Persicaire comes out of its skin, someone dies, another awakens – the novel rigorously upholds the rules of metamorphosis), the narrator goes down on three occasions to Le Potomak's lair as if in a dream or descent to hell. Cocteau said that before *Le Potomak* he had always been awake, hence this was the first outpouring of his sleep and he is clearly at grips with his own interior life and private demons. 'A drama is taking place in the work', the narrator states, adding: 'From a bourgeois family, I am a bourgeois monster'.[2] *Le Potomak* perhaps possesses his mind, or even *is* his mind, with an obsessive attraction for both the oral and anal that characterizes so much of Cocteau's work. He observes it, polyp-like and faecal, as it digests and expunges its multifarious contents formed of a diet of gloves, a music box playing Wagner, a programme of the Ballets Russes, etc. – all influences that Cocteau was now in a rush to jettison. Some of the more poignant expressions towards the end (e.g., 'Limp is now the hand that reached out only for mine') are derived directly from two letters he had written to Gide about how Thévenaz had dumped him.

Le Potomak revealed the measure of Cocteau's increasing personal investment in his work, yet the overall effect of this totally original autobiographical novel was of a strange hybrid: part *roman noir*, part philosophical dialogue, part lyrical confession, part stream of unconsciousness, and part abstract adventure featuring in very concrete terms savage rites and elemental forces. The seemingly plotless narrative is a complex collage of influences (Gide, Flaubert, Rimbaud, etc.) as well as literary forms, including aphorisms and bizarre *saynètes* (or playlets) that break away from an empty narrative shell shorn of all logical links. Straight dialogue segues abruptly into hermetic images, prose breaks out into riots of free verse, chunks of discourse alternate with macabre refrains and metaphysical lullabies, and words perform freewheeling puns. Included in this rich ferment are 64 drawings, formally simple geometrized forms with a comic-strip air and a hint of Breughel. This is what it was finally to be modern and experience the perceptual decentring of consciousness! Together with the 'Prospectus' that Cocteau added in 1916, where he acknowledged the influence of Gertrude Stein, the novel heralded a new *ars poetica* summed up in the simple statement: 'Ideas are born out of words'. Yet when *Le Potomak* was finally published in 1919 critics were left confused by its dizzying patchwork effect. Had Cocteau now joined the Left? No matter. He had at last come into his own, abandoned all signs of his comfortable *joliesse*, and his new preference for the shortcut would be put to the service of a twin literary and personal ideal: that of embracing every available art form in a continuous act of radical self-renewal. No sooner had Cocteau's self-transformation as a writer begun, however, than it was rudely interrupted by far more pressing concerns: the outbreak of war.

5

Cocteau's First War

When war broke out with Germany in August 1914 a major change
occurred in Cocteau. Seeing history enter his life for the first time,
he reverted to social type and became an ultra-patriotic Frenchman,
ready to defend the honour of the motherland: a 'Coq-ueteau', or
Gallic cock, no less. Initially, he approached the idea of war as pure
theatre with all the glamour and trappings of a grand spectacle.
Dining with friends at the fancy Larue restaurant, he happily mim-
icked the supposed sounds of war while donning a new blue officer
pilot's-style uniform designed by Paul Poiret (in rivalrous tribute
perhaps to his aviator brother Paul). In November he also met the
pioneer aviator Roland Garros, who initiated him into flying and
even took him on reconnaissance flights over the Alps. As a result
he adopted the star as his signature symbol and renamed himself
'Jean de l'Etoile'. Less than four months after the declaration of
war, in November 1914, he brought out the first issue of *Le Mot*,
a fortnightly review he founded with Paul Iribe, who served as
co-editor and co-illustrator. *Le Mot* was the wartime sequel to
Schéhérazade, but printed on much poorer paper. Gone was the
former's late Art Nouveau and late Symbolist aesthetic, replaced
now by often shrill, anti-German propaganda. While its chauvinism
was still relatively mild and light-hearted in comparison with some
of the other more jingoistic and intemperate magazines of the
period that rallied around General Poincaré's declaration of a *guerre
de droit*, it nonetheless marked an explicit move to the Right for

Cocteau and an entrenchment of his own fundamentally nationalist convictions.

Le Mot was a product of French popular culture, featuring hymns to French generals and military poems, patriotic *faits divers*, assorted images of Marshal Joffre, Joan of Arc, Reims Cathedral in flames and all manner of visual slurs against the enemy. Issue 7, for example, ran with the simple but nasty warning: 'the foreigner (*métèque*) cannot love our journal'. *Le Mot* also played on the primeval fear that German soldiers were amputating the hands of children. A series of harsh cartoons and sketches entitled 'Atrocités', comprising frightening figures of fat, stupid and sadistic Boches in the Eugène style of *Le Potomak*, all splattered together, directly echoed Goya's *Disasters of War*. Yet Cocteau also poked fun

LA CROIX DE FER.

Cocteau (pseudonymously signed 'Jim'), 'La Croix de Fer', from *Le Mot*, 20 (July 1915).

at French xenophobes, engaging in a long polemic with Saint-Saëns, who detested all foreigners. In addition to pouring obvious scorn on Wagner, the magazine resolutely abandoned the pre-war exotic aesthetic of the Ballets Russes, which was now considered unpatriotic, decadent and – sin of all sins – 'cosmopolitan'. Double-page spreads were signed variously Iribe, Cocteau (or 'Jim', in homage to Sim), Bakst and Raoul Dufy, yet invariably the drawings were of a high classical nature typified by clear lines that eschewed the play of shadow or volume. This style drew heavily on the innocence and naivety associated with the *images d'Epinal*, the folkloric and brightly coloured didactic broadsheets produced since the sixteenth century at Epinal in the Lorraine. Within the bold patriotic frame of *Le Mot* Cocteau penned one of his most celebrated phrases: 'Between TASTE and VULGARITY, both unpleasant, there remains an *élan* and a measure: THE TACT OF UNDERSTANDING JUST HOW FAR TO GO TOO FAR. *Le Mot* hopes you will follow it on this path of France' (emphases original). Problems arose only when Cocteau decided to feature the work of the emphatically Cubist painter Albert Gleizes, as well as Roger de la Fresnaye. Cubism, deemed 'Kubisme' through association with the soup 'Kub', was deemed now in polite circles a suspect German invention, although Cocteau successfully made it his own in works such as *Les Eugènes de la guerre* (around 1913–14), an intense collage coated with shards of English, French and German newspapers. The journal's explicit invocation of Cubism contributed to its early demise and it ceased publication on 1 July 1915 after nineteen issues.

What exactly was Cocteau's direct personal experience of the war? To his profound dismay he found himself repeatedly rejected by the army on medical grounds, so instead volunteered to become part of the auxiliary service and was posted with the Red Cross to distribute milk at railway stations. In September he joined the ambulance corps based around Reims, which formed part of an unofficial and improvised convoy organized by Misia Sert. He thus

experienced at first hand the bombing of Reims and witnessed the
battle of the Marne. He publicized the terrible fate of the wounded
and dying men he encountered in despatches for *Le Mot*, which
contained anecdotes about life with the ambulances. He sought
the support of the now staunchly right-wing writer and politician
Maurice Barrès, a leading contributor to France's war propaganda.
Twice Barrès refused to become involved in such practical human
issues, a stance Cocteau deplored and later mocked in *Visites à
Maurice Barrès* (1921) (Barrès' failure to act taught Cocteau always
to be suspicious of abstract theories and any self-proclaiming
ideologies). He was called back into action in March 1915, though
he did not end up joining the 13th artillery regiment to which he
had been originally posted but rather the 22nd section of the
military nurses and quartermaster corps. He left Paris in December
1915 as part of a now official ambulance convoy led by Etienne de
Beaumont that included other literati such as Bernard Faÿ.
Although now married, Beaumont still retained a queer persona,
obsessed as he was, like Cocteau, with youth, taste and flair. The
units included shower baths and Cocteau found himself with
Beaumont disciplined for 'offering' baths to soldiers. By Christmas
Cocteau was in Sector 131 near the mouth of the Yser that included
Nieuport-Ville, Nieuport-Bains, Coxyde-Ville and Coxyde-Bains, and
where the Red Cross served the 4th regiment of 'Zouave' (Algerian)
and Senegalese infantrymen, as well as the British division of
the Red Cross. Cocteau was drawn especially to the West African
sharpshooters, who approached war much in the same way as
he did, that is, as a kind of giant simulacrum. Under the influence
of the Senegalese, he started in his letters to family and friends to
cultivate a new syncopated form of speech marked by the elision
of articles, the reduction of verbs to infinitives and unanticipated
word-images. He also took photographs with his Kodak camera
provided by his mother, even though this was expressly forbidden
by the army. They include one of Cocteau smiling at the camera

Cocteau in the trenches near Nieuport, *c*. 1916.

beside a latrine bearing the slogan 'wc – Réservé au génie' (both
'corps of army engineers' and 'genius'), as well as photographs of
naked soldiers bathing.[1]

Around this time Cocteau was found guilty of 'profuse' (read:
sexual) 'kindness' with one of the Goumiers or Arab soldiers,
arousing the ire and jealousy of his commander. It is more than
probable that this event determined Cocteau's transfer in April
1916 to a new sector where there were no North Africans
whatsoever, only regular French *poilus*, although the precise facts
remain unclear. He was now part of a mobile unit containing a
library and x-ray apparatus and his morale slumped dramatically.
Cocteau could never really relate to either the officer corps or
the working-class soldiers, and the feeling was mutual. After all,
he sported a different uniform from theirs and was visibly bored
by their unintelligent prattle and dim laughter. For the first time
in his life he felt truly hated. He was obliged to go on perilous
missions to replace a soldier who had been forced to leave the
unit for 'card-sharping'. To everyone's surprise and disappointment,

he always managed to come back alive. Otherwise he was left totally on his own to guard the shower and latrines whenever the battalion marched off towards the Somme. It is at this point that the story of Cocteau's experience of war becomes rather blurred. In one version, a French marine captain discovered him by chance while guarding a shower bath. Commanded to follow, he found himself instantly adopted by the Marine Fusiliers stationed at Coxyde-Bains and was even allowed to wear their uniform. But Cocteau was soon exposed as a false Marine after being nominated for a Croix de Guerre and was frogmarched out of the camp by two policemen who had come to take him away for court-martialling. They effectively saved his life, however, for according to Cocteau Saint-Georges was bombed to shreds the next day and the entire unit killed, although no record of such a calamity exists. In a less dramatic version of the same event he was saved from a court martial by his friend, the diplomat Philippe Berthelot. He was then summoned to rejoin his own unit and left Nieuport-Coxyde before proceeding via Amiens to the Somme. By early July 1916 he was on hand to care for the first wounded, yet faced with the sheer scale and horror of the killing fields he began to suffer severe trauma. He quit the Somme abruptly in mid-battle in July and by the end of the month found himself back in Paris for good. In August he was officially released from his duties, classed physically unfit and transferred to a desk at military headquarters. Berthelot secured for him a post at the Maison de la Presse, the propaganda bureau of the Ministry of Foreign Affairs, whose members officially belonged to the 22nd division. Cocteau's first war was all but over.

Now began the myth. Early on in the conflict he had glimpsed a certain 'Raoul de Castelnau' who appeared out of the blue one day proclaiming that he was the nephew of the famous General de Castelnau. This casual association with a name of military glory, together with his adolescence and display of both medals and wounds, was enough for him to be believed and respected by men and women alike. It was eventually revealed that Castelnau was not his actual name but simply that of the town where the 'mythomaniac' had been born. The hoaxer subsequently vanished but cropped up elsewhere, still plying the same story and still eagerly believed. Cocteau wrote about this anecdote and the dissimulations of war in an article (published in the issue of *Le Mot* for 1 May 1915) that ends: 'The story will probably be continued.' And so it was, much later, with his novel of 1923, *Thomas the Impostor*, subtitled 'Histoire', which takes place against the backdrop of the Great War in the two sectors that he had known best, Flanders and Champagne, and which concerns a hoax 'visited upon' the protagonist, Guillaume Thomas. Asked if he is related to the general De Fontenoy because he is called Thomas de Fontenoy, Thomas replied yes and imme-diately became him. The book was inspired by other real events directly lived or witnessed by Cocteau, including the bombing of Reims, an episode in June 1916 when a group of artists visited the Front, the story of Misia Sert (Madame de Bormes in the novel) leading an unofficial ambulance convoy, and the battle of the Marne. Cocteau presented the fiction of *Thomas the Impostor* as a kind of 'fabulous reality', for when the anti-hero is finally shot at the Front he confronts personal exigency with the fatal rule of make-believe he had made his own: '"A bullet!", he told himself. "*I'm done for if I don't pretend to be dead*". But in him, fiction and reality were one and the same. Guillaume Thomas was dead' (emphasis original).[2]

So much is already fictional and mythical about Cocteau's war that it is not possible to say that Guillaume's story represents simply the fictional version. Indeed, *Thomas the Impostor* is autobiographical in other profound ways, being in part a celebration of one of Cocteau's brief early lovers, Jean Le Roy. Not too much is known about this aspiring poet, whom Cocteau had met in Paris in April 1917. Le Roy reportedly sent letters to Cocteau from the Front sealed with a kiss, as well as a series of youthful poems (published posthumously as *Le Cavalier de Frise* in 1924 with a moving preface by Cocteau). He was really the first of Cocteau's young heroic men and pupils, a soldier-poet, 'young, handsome, good, brave, full of genius, simple – everything that Death loves', as Cocteau put it. He was clearly the inspiration for Thomas, who, for all his games of deception, is a gallant young man who strays bravely from the norms of conventional society and dies in pursuit of his dream with his 'imposture' still intact, as a true poet always should for Cocteau. It was on the battlefield that Le Roy died in April 1918 aged 23, the same age as another character in *Thomas the Impostor*, a young Marine called Roy, killed just as he is about to go on leave. As he admitted to Gide in a letter a month later, Cocteau felt as if had been 'amputated'.

To try to recover, Cocteau withdrew for two months during the summer to the Atlantic coast, where he joined the painter André Lhote and his wife in a little hideaway called Le Piquey, a beautiful secluded beach in a corner of Arcachon bay near Bordeaux. Bathing naked in the sun, he recharged by re-reading Nietzsche, yet when he finally returned to Paris he fell poorly again and, in what would constitute a recurring motif in his life, received a misleading diagnosis (of rheumatism and depression of arteries) from his physician, a virtual charlatan called Dr Capmas. Physically weak, barely alive, he felt annihilated by his grief for Le Roy, which found its best expression in the prose poem 'Visite', part of the collection *Discours du grand sommeil* dedicated to Le Roy and composed of poems Cocteau had written from 1916 to 1918. Originally called 'Secteur 131', 'Visite' is in part a nostalgic account of his old sector, chiefly concerned with the Marines, the Senegalese and the Zouaves. The narrator-poet imagines a dead solider (Le Roy) addressing him like a 'spectre from beyond the grave' and leading him to the Underworld. A phantasmatic identification with Le Roy then gives rise to repeated inversions as the poem swings back and forth perilously from 'I' to 'you' to 'us' to 'One', variously friend and foe. Cocteau's style here is direct and unaffected and serves as a repository for his general thoughts on life, love, pain and death. As such, the poem is typical of the collection as a whole, a mixture of war diary and self-chronicle that veers continually towards despair and desolation in its graphic accounts of the trenches and the 'tortuous bazaar' of life. The poet may discover the profound song and angelic force of the nightingale in the horror of the battlefield, yet he is consigned to solitude in poems like 'Désespoir du Nord' and 'Malédiction au laurier', which attack the false idea of glory and the blindly heroic aspirations of war.

With poems such as 'Visite', Cocteau discovered comprehensively for the first time that poetry was an 'architectural nausea always skirting the void' and a 'religion without hope' to which everything must be sacrificed, even one's natural verbal facility. He had, in fact, made giant strides both artistically and emotionally since his other slightly earlier series of poems about the war collected as *Le Cap de Bonne-Espérance*. With its idiosyncratic style of pagination this volume had attempted to imitate the swooping flights of Roland Garros, who died in a plane crash in action in October 1918 (legend has it that proofs of Cocteau's poems were found in his cockpit). Chopped up like propellers producing torrents of pure energy with onomatopoeic words, images and sounds, the typography was marked by Cocteau's by turns excited and tragic loopings and their syncopated charge. The verse was sustained by rhythm and speed, each soaring cluster of images in free flight leading downwards to be reformed in the face of the Unknown, as if suspended between language and silence, gravity and weightlessness, dreams and hyper-lucidity. During repeated public readings of the volume in 1917, notably in June before an audience of hand-picked guests at the home of the diplomat and soon-to-be writer Paul Morand, Cocteau seemed to lift off the ground like a prophet with his metallic voice. Yet few could really make much head or tail of the loaded magazines of images he was firing off in all directions and which included allusions to Picasso, Stravinsky, Sodom and Gomorrah, Gabriel, Ganymede and cinema (to name but a few). Some dismissed this new fragmented style as pidgin French ('le petit nègre') or, even worse, Cubist prose. The truth was that no one was yet convinced by Cocteau's sudden transformation into an all-out modernist. In his 1922 preface to the collection he later acknowledged the relative failure of his experiment, saying that he would melt down all the poems and remould them as Alexandrines. He wished to be – and knew he could be – everyone and everything (the standard Cocteau mantra), but right now it simply was not happening.

The other side of Cocteau's war was, of course, his experiences of leave. One period was spent at Boulogne-sur-Mer in early June 1916 with his new friend Valentine Gross, whom he had met in May 1914 and who was then visiting her mother. Two years older, very serious, girlish and tall (Cocteau called her a swan due to her long, graceful neck), Valentine was a bona fide artist, designer and illustrator and linked to the *Nouvelle Revue française* circle. She already had her own Wednesday Salon and was soon to become the wife of the artist and designer Jean Hugo, great-grandson of Victor Hugo. Under Valentine's influence Cocteau became artistically freer, and they collaborated on a series of drawings 'half-Kodak half-fresco' for a project she was putting together on dance movement from antiquity to the present day. It was all very gay and fun with hybrid drawings-cum-photographs of Scotsmen dancing in kilts, playing tennis and merging transfigured into Greek legend and myth (Castor and Pollux, Satyricon, etc.).[3] Yet Cocteau still had a lot of catching up to do in matters of art. Cubism had been underway now for seven years and Montparnasse was now home to a whole new cosmopolitan avant-garde, a melting pot of central and eastern European, Jewish and Yiddish influences. Situated geographically at the halfway point of the

Nord–Sud metro line running from Montmartre to Montparnasse, Cocteau would make it his business to do the rounds of modernism and acquaint himself with all that was new in the art world. Through Valentine he met the crucial figures of what would eventually become known as the Paris School (Braque, Derain, Modigliani, Gris, Kisling), and as if making up for lost time he literally plunged himself into the smoke and stench of the Bar Tabarin, a skating rink where all kinds of bohemian low life would congregate. As if documenting his own progress, he took during the course of one day in August 1916 more than twenty snapshots of Picasso, the poet Max Jacob, Kisling et al. on the streets of Montparnasse, his one concerted experiment in photography.[4]

Cocteau would later talk romantically of the highly competitive and factionalized world of Montparnasse as a kind of paradise regained, a new Maisons-Laffitte. Yet this was a typical exercise in mythomania on Cocteau's part, since it is very doubtful that the hard-drinking young 'Montparnos' jockeying for position in the rough and tumble seedbed of modernism welcomed him with open arms, if at all. In fact, Montparnasse regarded him with deep suspicion, especially when he would turn up at their run-down studios with the likes of Poiret and Sert in their elegant costumes and furs. One exception was Modigliani, who in 1916–17 painted a portrait of Cocteau with pinched lips, long crooked nose and elongated neck, loftily seated in a high-backed chair and looking decidedly on edge (Cocteau considered it diabolical and proof that Modigliani actually hated him). Another was the poet Blaise Cendrars, with whom Cocteau founded a publishing house, Les Editions de la Sirène, to publish Apollinaire. For most in Montparnasse, however, Cocteau still remained more a commissioner of portraits and general *faiseur* than a personal friend. He knew he would have to try to blend in more and act the part (i.e., gaunt, brash, lazy), for this was certainly not a place to promote his natural brio, still less his homosexuality. In fact, if Cocteau seemed to be moving towards Left Bank bohemianism, privately he still indulged in his earlier interests and formative influences (de Noailles, Stravinsky, Bonnard, etc.). As for his own artistic projects, an ambitious plan to stage with Gleizes an ultra-modern version of *A Midsummer Night's Dream* at the Cirque Médrano, with sets by Lhote, came to nothing. Instead, a new project began to take shape in his mind that harked back to David and would soon consume him completely. It would all hinge on his collaboration with two very different artists, one of whom would serve as his artistic point of reference for his entire life.

6

The Greatest Battle

Before returning to the Front in May 1916, Cocteau had given the maverick composer Erik Satie a sheaf of notes containing some jumbled-up ideas for a provocative new spectacle called *Parade*. For Cocteau, who had met Satie through Valentine, the composer was not only a shy, complex genius but also a totally committed professional who trained – and even retrained – himself with the discipline of a schoolmaster.[1] Cocteau was drawn to Satie because his music, with its crisp, pure lines, appeared timeless, unlike that of Stravinsky, say, which was defiantly of the moment. Hence, a little later Cocteau followed up his notes with a libretto scored for two voices. This excited and inspired Satie, since his own style, combining music hall and counterpoint, seemed to complement Cocteau's perfectly with its alternating humour and pathos. Cocteau would have to wait a while for Satie's reaction and input, however, since the composer was notoriously slow to deliver.

The other great master of the time for Cocteau was Picasso. After initial scepticism towards him on account of his perceived high-society worldliness and theatricality, Picasso was suddenly very keen to make contact with Cocteau. They met in Paris in the autumn of 1915 between Cocteau's periods at the Front. The painter Edgar Varèse brought Picasso to 10, rue d'Anjou, where Cocteau lay in bed with a heavy cold. As so often, Cocteau would later reinvent the event, even claiming that Varèse had conducted him in the spring of 1916 to Picasso's studio on the Rue Schoelcher, where he had taken part in 'a meeting written in the stars', despite his fear of the 'black arrow' of Picasso's eye. This reads, of course, like a retroactive *coup de foudre* with an Oedipal twist, and indeed Cocteau courted Picasso as much as Picasso had himself courted Braque between 1908 and 1914, that is, like a virtual lover. Picasso was soon totally charmed by Cocteau, although the power relations were established from the beginning heavily in the painter's favour. Picasso was a man of few words who liked to dominate and impress, while Cocteau was a man of too many words who liked to admire. Hence, Cocteau's many meetings with the super-virile Picasso came to resemble so many glorious castrations, each commemorating afresh the original ('The way Picasso contemplates me with a moist eye', he rhapsodized). Cocteau described Picasso's movements as 'the twists of a matador', but in truth the artist often behaved more like an unpredictable bull.

So it was that Cocteau invited Picasso to collaborate with him and Satie on *Parade*, even though Picasso had not executed work for the stage before. During the course of 1916 the project began to take shape. The obvious producer was Diaghilev, who duly proposed that all involved, including the choreographer Léonide Massine, decamp to Rome, where his troupe was currently engaged. All the components for the ballet were thus first assembled in Paris then transported in February 1917 to Rome. Before Cocteau and Picasso left for Italy however (minus Satie, who never strayed far from his home of Arcueil-Cachan just south of Paris), there were scenes of rivalry, chicanery and general ego-bruising, the 'dog fights of great art' as Cocteau later called them. Indeed, the three-way process of collaboration was at times paranoia-inducing for Cocteau, for as the work progressed Picasso began inexorably to wrest the project out of his hands. Satie had initially been very happy to accept Cocteau's ideas for sound, because at that point he regarded Cocteau as 'the man of ideas' as well as an 'adorable maniac'. Yet Satie was equally intimidated by

Picasso, whom he recognized as his own new master. Under Picasso's command there was to be no dialogue or cinema-style captions, and the accumulated noises of trains, planes, gongs, sirens and futurist-style Morse-code signals (what Cocteau called his 'trompe l'oreille') were to be eliminated, although Cocteau managed at least to retain a trace of his *bruitages* with a typewriter clicking out imitations of a dynamo.

Once in Rome Cocteau proceeded to woo Picasso and, to employ again an ocular metaphor, admitted he saw nothing of the Eternal City because his eyes were only for his new artistic model. The two were almost like a newly married couple, staying in adjoining rooms at the Hôtel de Russie in the Spanish Piazza. Because the master had a liaison with the dancer Olga Koklova (whom he would later marry in July 1918), so Cocteau pretended in an elaborate charade to court the young Maria Chabelska, who was to play the role of the Little American Girl. During the daytime the choreography of *Parade* came alive in a basement studio in the

Cocteau with Sergei Diaghilev (right) and Léonide Massine at Pompeii, 1917.

Piazza Venezia, where Cocteau was utterly captivated by the machine-like application of Picasso, in particular the way in which he could fuse elements of Futurism with classical art. He admired above all Picasso's wish not always to complete a work and the fact that his art was always changing form. Indeed, faced with the fast and furious productivity of Picasso, Cocteau felt increasingly insecure about his own progress. He saw his original libretto literally frittered away and his very words elided in favour of a metronome ticking to and fro as the Managers shuffled about portentously. All he could do during a trip to Naples in the spring and summer of 1917 was to take photographs of Picasso in the company of Diaghilev and Massine, even producing a Cubist-style portrait of the master. Yet Cocteau, who lived collaboration at an intense and even erotic level of fusion, would invariably end up justifying and rationalizing the process, later declaring: 'Since these mysteries escape me, I shall pretend to be their organizer'.

Cocteau had deliberately called *Parade* 'realist' to distinguish it from Cubism and also to emphasize that his ballet referred to something quite ordinary rather than any arcane theory. He intended it to be a self-consciously 'minor' spectacle, like a street-fair theatre of discontinuous visual surprises. The major visual inspiration for the aesthetic was again the quintessentially French *images d'Epinal* that he had tapped into for *Le Mot*. Indeed, the spectacle would be a magically transformed page of the *Cris de Paris* (1858), wherein the Parisian vendors become artists, critics and dealers trying to catch the public's attention (the verb *crier* (to shout) recurs throughout *Parade*). It was also manifestly a dialogue between Cubism and Futurism: on the one hand Cocteau's scaled-down Futurist *bruitages*, on the other Picasso's somewhat fragmented cityscape and skewed proscenium arch for the setting, plus his two Cubist constructions for the gesticulating Managers. Yet ironically, while Cocteau sought to make exaggerated interpretations of everyday gestures, Picasso edged rather conservatively towards the abstract. In fact, his designs for the characters and the overture curtain resurrected the earlier themes and symbolism of his Pink Period. Cocteau had really wanted Picasso to produce a drop-curtain echoing the mechanical style of film captions. Instead, based on a nineteenth-century Neapolitan gouache, it looked already distinctly old-fashioned and even a touch sentimental with its *saltimbanques* and buffoons in blue, white, red and green.

Cocteau returned to Paris alone in April 1917 to resume his work at the Maison de la Presse. The final preparations for *Parade* became a frantic rush to meet the date of the premiere, yet in what would become a familiar move Cocteau was keen to present it ahead of time on his own terms in order to frame its reception and perhaps in the process reappropriate the work. On the day of the first performance he published a short but brilliant piece in the newspaper *L'Excelsior* to justify his production, where he analysed the nature of realism in the theatre and argued that real objects lose their reality the moment they are placed in unreal surroundings. *Parade*, he proposed, concealed poetry beneath its course *guignol* skin. Cocteau was soon bitterly disappointed to discover that the preface to the programme, which Cocteau had personally asked Apollinaire to write, barely mentioned him. Indeed, Cocteau's unique role as originator, inventor and *animateur* of *Parade* was completely ignored in favour of Picasso's contribution. Apollinaire's actions can be put down in large measure to artistic rivalry, for he did not wish to appear less 'modern' than Cocteau, especially with his own play *The Breasts of Tiresias* soon to be produced. His preface had the virtue at least of introducing an exciting new term, *sur-réalisme*, a troping on Cocteau's *réalisme*, by which Apollinaire sought to promote a 'more complex art' as the starting point for a new manifestation of the *esprit nouveau* incorporating painting, dance, plastic elements and mime.

When the premiere of *Parade* finally took place on the night of 18 May 1917 at the Théâtre du Châtelet it was far from being the great scandal Cocteau later claimed. True, well before the end of the twenty-minute performance many were already angrily yelling out 'Boche!'. The Front, after all, was just 90 miles away and modernism was still viewed as a foul German import. Moreover, the show had been advertised by the theatre as a benefit performance for charities to help ill and wounded soldiers. Apollinaire, his head bandaged up from recent combat and wearing military uniform, was obliged personally to calm outraged patrons. Yet the brouhaha was not at all on the scale of that which greeted *The Rite of Spring*, precisely because many in the sophisticated audience emanating from both banks of the Seine had been hand-picked by Cocteau and they half expected a showdown of some kind. There were scattered catcalls and jeers but no major confrontations or demonstrations, certainly no stampede of women armed with hatpins as Cocteau later wrote (Paul Morand catalogued it simply as: 'Much applause and a few boos'). If *Parade* caused any genuine confusion and incomprehension at all it was because of its competing aesthetic elements and styles. Was there in all this an oblique critique of the mess and barbarism of war, the more sympathetic members of the audience wondered. Most failed to appreciate the show's realism, however, because they were all but dazzled by Picasso's great burlesque Cubist sculptures, even if not all the stage effects came off successfully due to mechanical difficulties. As for the press reaction, it was mixed to poor to plain condescending. Critics dismissed Satie's score as at once naive and over-intricate (it included a one-step derived from music hall and a *Ragtime*) and denigrated his Senegalese *tams-tams*, a charge that particularly upset the composer since Cocteau had imposed this on him. In *Le Carnet de la semaine* Jean Poueigh slated Satie for his lack of wit, skill and inventiveness, a move that precipitated a real scandal when Satie wrote Poueigh a vitriolic and scatological postcard calling him 'an unmusical asshole', as a result of which Poueigh took him to court and sued him for libel (ever the scene-stealer Cocteau became involved himself when he raised his cane at Poueigh's lawyer and was ushered away by the police, roughed up and fined). The press lambasted above all the *sottises* of Cocteau, casting him as a 'hysterical' librettist. Diaghilev was forced to withdraw the ballet after less than two weeks.

Parade stands now, of course, as one of the most important and influential works of the early twentieth-century French avant-garde. It was the first truly modern ballet and spawned a whole new tradition of ballet on commonplace themes with contemporary music and sets. There were revivals, first in London in November 1919, then in Paris in December 1920, with Cocteau's original ideas, notably for sound, fully restored. Although Satie and Picasso both boycotted the show, Cocteau felt totally vindicated. In personal terms, and putting aside the fact that he never really forgave Diaghilev for aiding and abetting Picasso's amputation of his original score (relations between Cocteau and Diaghilev were forever strained thereafter), he had finally delivered on his personal promise to astonish Diaghilev. The dancer Serge Lifar later went even further, claiming that everything new and current in ballet was invented by Cocteau in *Parade*. He had finally crossed the Rubicon and entered the Paris avant-garde. Just a few weeks after opening night, at a concert in homage first to Apollinaire then to Picasso at one of the essential 'Lyre et Palette' evenings at the Salle Huyghens gallery in Montparnasse, Cocteau's poems were read out aloud with those of Apollinaire, Cendrars and Jacob. The proprietors of the *Nouvelle Revue française* even started to warm towards him and treat him as a bona fide artist to be reckoned with, as did the poet Paul Reverdy, who opened the doors of his journal *Nord–Sud*. In subsequent critical writings Cocteau would return again and again to *Parade* as the decisive step in his artistic development, for with its multiple self-reflexive elements, its focus on the male body in performance and its cross-fertilizing ambition to marshal different

Cocteau at the Villa Croisset in Grasse on the French Riviera, 1918.

artists and artistic forms, it served as a template for all his future work. Crucially, Cocteau had conceived and overseen every stage of the project, from scenario and score to decor and choreography. Yet the long and protracted episode of *Parade* also revealed other important aspects of Cocteau's personality: his need for complete control over the production and reception of his work, his wish to forge his own artistic self-image, and his unrelenting desire to see projects through on his own terms. Despite his new-found success, however, Cocteau still felt distinctly underrated and misunderstood. Fortunately, the war was almost over, and even before the last shot had officially been fired a new concatenation of circumstances ensured, if only temporarily, that time and history were on his side.

7

Happy Families

On 9 November 1918, just two days before the signing of the Armistice, Apollinaire died from a combination of influenza and the deleterious effects of his head wound (Cocteau's doctor Capmas was called in and once again proved himself inadequate to the task of both diagnosis and treatment). Cocteau observed Apollinaire's terrible eyes of agony and later wrote an obituary. In truth, the friendship between Cocteau and Apollinaire had never been a particularly deep one and was often strained, little more than a strategic bond forged through various projects, a few jealously guarded mutual friends (Le Roy, Picasso) and the shared indignity of a mock trial staged by the Cubists following the production of Apollinaire's *The Breasts of Tiresias* in June 1917 (Cocteau had to account for the poem 'Zèbre' he had written for the programme). Now, in a poem entitled 'La Mort de Guillaume Apollinaire', delivered on 8 June 1919 at a *matinée poétique* in his memory, Cocteau offered a slightly derisory summation of Apollinaire as an 'amateur of tulips'. This, along with a tribute that appeared with others in the February 1919 issue of the magazine *sic*, was rightly read as Cocteau's first aggressive step in his campaign to assume the mantle of modern poet now left vacant by Apollinaire, who had incarnated the *esprit nouveau*, the one movement universally recognized – even if not always admired – by all the competing factions of early French modernism. In the compressed fish tank of the Parisian avant-garde, the battle for succession would be long and bitter.

Cocteau at this point was essentially *persona non grata* in the artistic circles that clustered in the new nerve-centres of Paris such as Paul Guillaume's art gallery for recitals of poetry and music at the Salle Huyghens, Valentine Gross's apartment in the Palais-Royal and the bookshop Aux Amis des Livres in the rue de l'Odéon, and which also crystallized around magazines like *Littérature*, *Dada* and *391*. Indeed, although he entered into correspondence with Louis Aragon and enjoyed reasonable relations with Francis Picabia, with whom he attended some Dada happenings, Cocteau found himself formally banned by André Breton from the pages of *Littérature* and ejected by *391*. Moreover, in meetings of his group at the Café Certa near the Gare Saint-Lazare in late 1919, Breton engaged in fierce competition for the headship of the avant-garde and even forbade Aragon from seeing Cocteau in order to ensure the purity of the cause. He wrote to Tristan Tzara in December 1919: 'My opinion – completely disinterested, I swear – is that he [Cocteau] is the most hateful being of our time', adding not so disingenuously 'hatred is not my strong point'. Breton's personal antipathy towards Cocteau, verging on sadistic virulence, was born of a lethal combination of personal jealousy, ideological contempt and ugly homophobia. The provincial Breton hated Cocteau for his precociousness and wit as well as his social ease and effortless Parisianism, of which his sartorial elegance was but the most obscene sign (Cocteau was currently adopting an English gentleman style of dress, including satin bow neck-tie, inspired by one of his new British Embassy friends, Reginald Bridgeman, private secretary to the ambassador). Above all, Breton profoundly resented the fact that Cocteau, who in his eyes both diluted and polluted Dada, was identified by the general public as a crucial artistic figure of the avant-garde whilst others like himself remained largely off the radar. Although he had not yet published anything of major note, he regarded himself as Apollinaire's natural successor and the new *chef d'école* (it was he, after all, not

Cocteau entwined with Tristan Tzara. Photo by Man Ray, 1924.

Cocteau, whom Apollinaire had asked to provide a preface for his Collected Works). Until he achieved his own artistic ends and ambitions, Breton would never waver in his mission to track down his nemesis.

Whatever he thought of Dada's wild excesses, Cocteau entered into the spirit of the movement in good faith. He collaborated on the *Anthologie Dada* and participated in a Dada *matinée* in January 1920 where, along with Jacob, Reverdy, Cendrars, Breton, Picabia, Satie and Tzara, he danced like a Dada dervish. For some he even started to act like a Dada 'pervert', producing gross phallic images and cartoons for Picabia of philandering fireman brandishing a phallic hydrant. For this and other acts Cocteau would become known briefly as an 'anti-Tzara', yet in one delightful and slightly later photograph from 1922 by the American photographer Man Ray Cocteau appeared with Tzara in an image of harmless male fun, intertwined in a large swirl of fabric (Cocteau on top, Tzara below). Cocteau soon tired of all the forced hoopla of Dada, however, in particular the barbs and insults (at one Dada demonstration at the Salle Gaveau in May 1920 Philippe Soupault savagely knifed a balloon marked with his name). He wrote a letter to Picabia declaring his formal 'break' with the movement, declaring: 'I have a physical obligation to act against Dada (never against you, nor against Tzara, nor against any others – friendship or the memory of one being sacred in my eyes).' In this fractious and volatile world of intellectual rivalry and betrayal, it is an incontrovertible fact that Cocteau usually came out with his personal integrity intact, since he always sought to separate the principles of friendship from professional matters. Picabia, meanwhile, published Cocteau's letter not in *391* but in a new magazine *Cannibale*, accompanied with his own highly sarcastic comments (Cocteau would later write that it was Picabia who first used the term 'Le Parisien' to describe him, an intended insult that he immediately reversed to his advantage and indeed cultivated).

In the face of such raw hostility Cocteau knew that if he was to be the new cock of the avant-garde roost he would have to branch out into arts other than poetry, just as Apollinaire had done, of course, with Cubist painting. Since *Parade* he had been frequenting a number of young composers who had gathered like disciples around their master, or rather 'anti-master', Eric Satie. Two young musicians in particular, the child prodigy Georges Auric and Francis Poulenc, paid court to Cocteau as much as to Satie, and they asked permission to set some of his verse to music. At the same moment in Rio de Janeiro, the young Darius Milhaud, secretary to the French ambassador Paul Claudel, attended successful performances of *Parade* and was inspired. These three young musicians, together with Arthur Honegger, Louis Durey and Germaine Tailleferre, had already taken part in various mixed programmes in Paris at Jane Batori's Théâtre du Vieux-Colombier, and in January 1918 they appeared on stage together for the first time. They would eventually be named 'Les Six' by the musician and journalist Henry Collet. All six were very different from each other and proclaimed no common aesthetic policy other than utter devotion to Satie and a shared revulsion for Debussy. Theirs was an art of brevity and harmonic puns, with sudden switches of key but little difference in mood beyond their mocking variations on great themes. They were consciously limited in range, yet Cocteau loved what he heard precisely because it corresponded to his own developing notion that 'music heard with one's head in one's hands' was no longer appropriate. He offered to act as their spokesman and publicist, and nearly all the group would set his poems to music, Poulenc most strikingly with *Cocardes*, although Cocteau's collaborations with Milhaud and Auric would prove to be the most extensive.

Cocteau, in fact, worked directly with musicians more than any other contemporary French writer, although he left all questions of singability to the composer and did not attempt to provide

Cocteau at the piano with Les Six, 1921. Left to right: Darius Milhaud, Arthur Honegger, Germaine Tailleferre, Francis Poulenc and Louis Durey (Georges Auric appears only in Cocteau's drawing in the background).

'musical' words (he knew from his time with Diaghilev that in order to take shape, a work of mixed media must be formed of autonomous components). The fact that Les Six corresponded so well to his hopes for a new path to modernism in his own image, one that was inclusive and non-sectarian, might suggest that this was no more than a consolation prize he was offering himself after his recent literary setbacks. Cocteau, after all, had music all to himself, since Breton had banned it along with homosexuality, while Tzara was still in thrall to raw noise. Yet Cocteau, an able enough musician in his own right and possessing a good tenor's voice, had always taken music very seriously. In time Les Six came to represent an ideal: not just a fresh kind of modern music but a new ethos of collaboration born of genuine friendship. Evoking Les Six many years later (and Cocteau would continue to be photographed with the group well into the 1930s, even though

Durey had already left in 1921), he emphasized their mutual understanding and spirit of freedom: 'Friendship brought us together without constraint. Each member blossomed according to his own abilities.'[1]

Les Six had initially been called by Cendrars the 'Nouveaux Jeunes' with Cocteau, in the umpteenth troping on his name, serving as *le coq-tôt* (literally, 'the early cock'). Together they tapped into the cult of youth in the immediate post-war period when, with the old powers and established orders now in disarray, everything suddenly seemed ready for the taking. This gave Cocteau the idea for an essay on the new music and its significance for the emerging generation. *Cock and Harlequin* (*Le Coq et l'Arlequin*), published in the spring of 1918 by Cocteau's own Editions de la Sirène, was a dazzling 74-page manifesto on the musical Renouveau, bursting with ideas and aphorisms about music, writing and painting. Subtitled 'Notes around music', it was really a polemical tract in the spirit of Nietzsche's *The Case Against Wagner*. It was illustrated with two 'monograms' of a cock and a harlequin by Picasso, as well as Picasso's earlier portrait of Cocteau in uniform. Written with the active support of Auric, to whom it is dedicated and who is positioned explicitly as an 'escapee from Germany' (i.e., from prevailing German aesthetics), *Cock and Harlequin* began with a simple formula: 'Long live the cock! Down with Harlequin', and then called for a complete renunciation of the prevailing 'Germanico-Slavo musical labyrinth', that is to say, of the pre-war aesthetic of Romanticism and Impressionism (in particular Debussy), which, with their vagueness, unnecessary complication and exotic tastes, were little more than 'after-effects' of Wagner. Cocteau argued for a new type of modernism that would paradoxically be also extremely classical, and he conceived this in characteristically nationalistic terms as 'French music for France'. The musical model now was Satie, who, with limpid and meticulous notations, 'clears, simplifies and strikes rhythm naked'. What this really translated into was 'the music of everyday life', taking its inspiration from the most varied local and popular sources (the café, music hall, fairground, circus, village dances, etc.), and what mattered most was rapidity and humour, that is, the minor mode, rather than any notion of the grand Sublime. The manifesto proceeded with startling formulas, contradictions and exaggerations, its quicksilver style rolling in original formulations delivered with the verve and pungency that would soon become the hallmark of Cocteau's critical style. With its cascading staccato *pensées* the essay captures not only the modern music he was promoting, with its techniques of syncopation and reliance on simplicity and cliché, but also for the first time his own dynamic oral manner. For Cocteau was firing bullets straight at the reader in a series of riffs and licks, repetitions and improvised turns. Included are some of his most famous axioms and sayings such as: 'Art is science in the flesh', and: 'Tact in audacity consists in knowing how far one may go too far'. Yet *Cock and Harlequin* also unfolds as a classic Cocteau exercise in self-redefinition and self-reclamation. In an extensive appendix, he offered yet further post-mortems on *Parade* and a small study of *The Rite of Spring* as if he were repackaging it for artistic legend. Was Cocteau finally getting his own back now on Stravinsky when he talked of the easy charms and even 'theatrical mysticism' of *The Rite of Spring*? Certainly he was upbraiding Stravinsky for following too much in the line of Debussy and Schoenberg, although he chose immed-iately to revise this statement with a qualifying footnote, as if he could not quite damn Stravinsky outright precisely because he was a friend.

Cock and Harlequin proved immediately very popular and influential with all young musicians, not just Les Six. Whilst more conservative artists like Jacques-Emile Blanche suspected that Cocteau was being drawn to the left by Picasso, modernists like Proust savoured the concise and piercing *coups de bec* of this unique *Coq*. Gide's reaction was characteristically ambivalent, however. In an 'Open Letter' to Cocteau published in the June 1919 issue of *Nouvelle Revue française* he praised *Cock and Harlequin* rather patronizingly for the way that Cocteau 'let himself go', yet also bitterly attacked the latter part where Cocteau justified the 'unserious' art of *Parade* (which Gide had still probably never seen). Gide claimed that Cocteau was overstretching himself, and in a further letter highlighted his 'double personality': personally charming but artistically unoriginal and artificial. Cocteau had got wind of the 'Open Letter' before its publication and masochistically accepted Gide's invitation to visit him at his home in Auteuil to hear him read the final draft. Gide described Cocteau's reaction as hysterical, and when Cocteau asked him to modify it he refused. Acting typically on impulse, Cocteau printed a virulent reply in August in *Les Ecrits nouveaux*, although it was much toned down since it originally contained doses of pure venom against Gide of the kind 'There is about you both the pastor and the Bacchante'. The nasty dispute between the two must, of course, be read in terms of literary politics, for the *Nouvelle Revue française* was now taking up Breton and Dada (albeit briefly), and its editor-in-chief Jacques Rivière was very happy to stoke up trouble. Yet the degree of provocation can only be fully understood in the context of the young 'mythomaniacs' who circulated between Cocteau and Gide and who jumped ship whenever they perceived grievances or felt rebuffed. So it was that Gide suspected Cocteau of wanting to seduce his young *protégé*, the future documentary filmmaker Marc Allégret, following an incident of pure jealousy that occurred in early December 1917, when Allégret made the mistake of singing Cocteau's praises too highly. Gide later admitted this was the root cause of his long hostility to Cocteau and the two broke off contact for several years. A truce was declared in 1922, but Cocteau only fully reconciled himself to Gide in 1949. Gide's cruel portrait of Cocteau as the scheming and supremely 'counterfeit' Count Robert de Passavant in his 1926 novel *The Counterfeiters* is just one of the many instances of revenge and recrimination in their ongoing personal and artistic feud. On the cusp of the new decade, however, with Les Six overturning all hierarchies and enjoying ever greater success, it was Cocteau, not Gide, who was in the ascendant and who would encapsulate the spirit of the Roaring Twenties.

8

Genius of France

During the early days of the new decade, as American jazz, *surprise-parties* and *fêtes nègres* swept through Paris, Cocteau was most often to be found at a new bar called La Gaya, owned by Louis Moysès and located in the rue Duphot near the Madeleine. The musicians featured there included the Conservatoire-trained pianist Jean Wiéner and the African-American banjoist and saxophonist Vance Lowry, who together provided the soundtrack for Cocteau's emerging aesthetic of the everyday. The bar also hosted the *samedis* when Cocteau and his assorted anti-Dada clan – baptized by Paul Morand the Société d'Admiration Mutuelle (Mutual Admiration Society), or SAM for short – met to experiment with new American-style cocktails and have fun, lots of it. The SAM included (among others) Les Six, Lucien Daudet, Valentine and Jean Hugo, the actor Pierre Bertin, Marie Laurencin (former partner of Apollinaire), the pianist Marcelle Meyer and the amateur painter Irène Lagut. Their extravagant evenings were largely dictated by Cocteau's pace and rhythms, and after meeting first usually at his or Milhaud's apartment all options were open: a restaurant in Montmartre, the Cirque Médrano, the street fair of the Foire du Trône, the Folies-Bergère, the *grands boulevards* to watch an American film, an amusement park like Luna Park or Magic City . . . Having briefly become a jazz critic for *L'Intransigeant*, Cocteau personally helped to bring over from London the Billy Arnold jazz band, the first jazz ensemble ever to play in a concert hall in France. He even improvised jazz himself during the long evenings at La Gaya, which soon became so successful that it was rumoured he had become a nightclub manager. During one such happening in December 1920 organized by Picabia, which featured a concert by Auric-Poulenc, he stepped up to play trombone, big drum, castanets, reed-pipe and car horn. For Aragon, Cocteau had now become himself a *poète orchestre*.

Cocteau was at the top of his game and firing on all cylinders, initiating by example a major revolution in cultural taste and sensibility. He caught brilliantly the hothouse atmosphere of jazz and Right Bank intrigue in a series of short newspaper articles on art, music and poetry that he penned for *Paris-Midi* from March to August 1919 (later to be published under the title *Carte blanche*). Racing with insouciant ease from subject to subject, Cocteau revealed himself always one step ahead of his peers, whom he took impish delight in outdoing through his sheer range and force of personality. He explained his role as enlightening the reader about the world of the arts, which encompassed all forms of culture high or low (Charlie Chaplin, whom he eulogized as a universal artist addressing all ages and peoples, served as his new working model). He announced the rising stars to watch and reported on the latest shows, *vernissages* and other happenings, interweaving contemporary events such as the victory celebration on 14 July 1919, as well as more personal subjects like Jean Le Roy, *Parade* and Mistinguett. At the same time he offered speculations and judgements on France and the value of art and artists, and in particular the power and 'lightness' of American films such as *Carmen of the Klondike* (1918). It was a dizzying and ingenious performance, all the more so since Cocteau's main readership had no idea of the backstage bickerings between the various factions of the avant-garde he was depicting. In acknowledging his sources Cocteau was also suggesting that he was in direct contact with the very people who despised him and was speaking on their behalf as a fully accredited member of the avant-garde. The only aspect that marred this achievement was again Cocteau's lingering nationalism and Germanophobia, for he mounted tendentious comparisons between the daring *élan* and improvisation of France and the stodginess of Germany, sneering, for example, that modern Germany merely aped America by swallowing everything like the digestive tube of an inferior animal, yet possessing neither the innocence of America nor the 'fertile dung-hill' of France. Whatever doubts he harboured about his mother country with its cult of death, injustice and contempt for youth, these could always be redeemed since it was totally desirable that a true artist work *against* society in order to impose his individual genius.

Did Cocteau's own major artistic activity at this time match up to such grand ambitions? The year 1920 saw the publication of a collection of 63 poems entitled simply *Poésies, 1917–1920*, a frontier work that charted a new pictorial universe, specifically material and concrete forms found within nature (terrestrial, marine, solar, etc.), and which destroyed the standard configurations of time and place in order to achieve a Cubist-like simultaneity. The same year also saw the publication with André Lhote of *Escales* (Ports of Call), his first collaboration with a painter. Printed in a large luxury format, the poetic fragments and black-and-white as well as colour drawings in matte blue, white and grey depicted a *louche bas-monde* of naked women in bars and *tabacs*, sailors in ports, steam-boats, the music-hall, etc. The overall effect was spicy and hybrid with references to myth (the Sirens, Ulysses, Aphrodite, Narcissus), Nieuport stacked up with its marine fusiliers all now dead, negresses and assorted prostitutes daubed in scarlet red, and 'la belle saison' with its corresponding 'fatal beauty' and syphilis (a special edition of the book was originally planned to incorporate a 'secret museum' of poems and pictures of an even more erotic nature).

It was for the stage, however, that Cocteau again produced his most significant and ground-breaking work. *Le Boeuf sur le toit; ou,*

'*The Nothing Doing Bar*', first performed on 21 February 1920, was the second of his major transpositions of the everyday, that is, non-sublime, non-folkloristic and non-exotic spectacles. Set in an American speakeasy during Prohibition, this pantomime-style ballet developed Cocteau's notion of a simplified theatre of violence, chance and surprise. Wearing huge, dehumanizing papier mâché heads, the actors and professional clowns performed a series of stereotypes (the Woman in a Low-Cut Dress, the Red-Headed Woman, the Negro Boxer and so on). It was all of a piece with Milhaud's musical theme, circus-like and slapstick, which returned like a rondo between authentic samba tunes. The visual source for Cocteau was again the *images d'Epinal*, with costumes and masks by Raoul Dufy. The effect was of a modern 'realist dream', where everyone on stage moved slowly in contradiction of the frenetic score. On the opening night, as part of his new strategy to pre-empt unwelcome scandal, Cocteau stepped in front of the curtain to say a few words and bring the audience on board. Apart from the oversize masks ordered by Cocteau, which looked slightly awry, the show proved a resounding success in front of a packed house and was critically acclaimed. The production crossed the Channel to London in July and opened at the Coliseum with an English cast as *The Nothing-Doing Bar*. Cocteau was billed now as 'the Parisian' and was on hand to supervise his 'great Parisian success'.

Le Boeuf sur le toit was followed up by the 'tragi-comedy' *The Eiffel Tower Wedding Party* (*Les Mariés de la Tour Eiffel*), conceived by Cocteau as a kind of secret marriage between Greek tragedy and an end-of-the-year variety show incorporating music hall and vaudeville. Although lacking a central theme and constructed more as a series of satirical skits, it presented the misadventures of a *petit-bourgeois* wedding party one 14 July. As in *Le Boeuf sur le toit* it was to be pantomimed by the dancers and other participants, but here two recorded voices spoke like a chorus about the actors' movements and 'qualities' through two giant phonographs on

'The Married Couple' from *The Eiffel Tower Wedding Party*, staged in Paris in July 1921.

either side of the stage complete with horns for mouths (during some performances Cocteau assumed one of the roles). The actors did not speak themselves (the influence of silent cinema), but moved like puppets in grotesque masks as if satirizing themselves. By stripping away all traces of theatrical illusion as well as individualism (the main characters have names like 'the Bride sweet as a lamb', 'the Father in Law rich as Croesus' and 'the Mother in Law phoney as a slug'), Cocteau was attempting here to rekindle both a sense of the marvellous and an archetypal humanity (much of the action and irony pivots on a pun, the word *cliché* meaning in French both banality and snapshot). In his extensive preface-cum-manifesto to the later printed text, he proclaimed with some justification that with *The Eiffel Tower Wedding Party* a new theatrical genre was forming in France on the fringes of ballet, opera, *opéra-comique* and boulevard, one that expressed the modern poetic spirit and encouraged new combinations of *féerie*, dance, acrobatics, pantomime, drama, satire, orchestra and speech. This was 'the plastic expression of poetry', Cocteau argued, employing for the first time his crucial term 'poetry *of* the theatre' (as opposed to '*in* the theatre').[1] During the gala preview at the Théâtre des Champs-Elysées in June 1921, there was, as anticipated, an anti-Cocteau Dada demonstration led by Tzara that overwhelmed the phonograph voices of Pierre Bertin and Marcel Herrand on stage. It did not diminish the show's overall success, however, which was ensured by the degree of collaboration involved: dance by Rolf de Maré's Swedish Ballet, sets by Irène Lagut inspired by Le Douanier Rousseau, costumes and masks by Jean Hugo, above all the eclectic music to which all Les Six contributed (notably Milhaud's fugue pastiche *Massacre at the Wedding* and Honegger's *The Funeral March of the General*). Cocteau rightly regarded *The Eiffel Tower Wedding Party* as the first work in which he owed nothing to anyone and which resembled nothing else in existence.

So high was Cocteau's artistic and social star now rising that by January 1922 Le Gaya had become too small to cater for all the party-goers he attracted. Perhaps because he sensed that both he and the bar were becoming a social fixture and even institution he eventually decided to abandon the evenings. Moysès immediately opened up a new cabaret bar called Le Boeuf sur le Toit in the rue Boissy-d'Anglas, midway between the Madeleine and the rue d'Anjou, where Wiener again performed accompanied by the Belgian pianist Clément Doucet as well as Vance Lowry. Le Boeuf sur le Toit would in time become another mythical club and bar where the best, most famous and most fabulous all gathered,

Poster for the 'Le Boeuf sur le Toit' nightclub in Paris (with Cocteau in the eye of the bull).

including now the dancer Caryathis (the future Elise Jouhandeau), who served as unofficial dancer for Les Six. The club would even enter daily vocabulary with popular expressions like *faire un boeuf* (to make a great success) and *un effet boeuf* (a fantastic impression), and it ensured Cocteau's place at the very centre of Parisian social and cultural life. To be sure, Le Boeuf sur le Toit was a snob cabaret attracting a new kind of luxury boho mix more interested in celebrity than the arts. Beauty, talent and renown were what mattered most, along with opium and homosexuality, for this was also a far more explicitly gay haunt even than Le Gaya and it brought out the full ramifications of the term *les années folles*. In fact, it was a rather brash and wild hang-out that allowed for – and positively encouraged – the enjoyment of binge drinking and the playing out of personal fantasies. A fresh catchphrase was launched by a Belgian chronicler to describe Cocteau, 'un cocktail, des Cocteaux', rather ironic since Cocteau was never really a drinker. Yet Cocteau was now 'it', the toast of the capital and the *nec plus ultra* of artistic chic. Not only was he brilliantly in sync with the emerging new society but he also personally embodied the *esprit nouveau* and drew to Paris foreign writers and artists in search of the *moderne*. Among those attracted by this new 'delight of Europe' were Alejo Carpentier, Mayakovsky, Edmund Wilson, Clive Bell, and Ezra Pound, who, in the autumn of 1921, corrected the proofs of Jean Hugo's translation of *Le Cap de Bonne-Espérance* for the *Little Review*.

It looked as though things had finally come together for Cocteau, yet despite his staggering artistic and social success he was still wracked by grave doubts and uncertainties. On Picabia's famous canvas *L'Oeil Cacodylate* hanging above the bar at Le Boeuf sur le Toit and looking down on revellers like an octopus (the title was an allusion to a patent medicine claiming regenerative powers), he had inscribed around an inserted photograph of himself the words 'Couronne de mélancolie' ('crown of melancholy'). To most this gesture was nothing more than a public pose, but it indicated to his closest friends that Cocteau's personal life and happiness were still far from assured. Indeed, it was obvious that behind the constant whirr of his social performance there lingered feelings of genuine turmoil, if not dread. Even at home he would hide behind his constructed self-image as the Poet, seemingly intimate yet always on stage and performing different personae. When he gave tours of his bedroom to invited guests he would describe the provenance of each object in a long monologue that caricatured famous people and brooked no discussion. In fact, the material clutter and organized chaos of Cocteau's room, a warehouse of light accessories that corresponded to the fashion of the period (twinkling objects of fun and chance, poetic baubles, mysterious

Portrait of Cocteau by
Henri Martinie, 1926.

fetishes), betrayed a growing vacuum at the heart both of his life
and his art. For although his artistic identity had now expanded
into exciting new fields, his poetry, which had initially made his
name, was no longer finding the same audience and he feared he
was losing his literary touch. But throughout this whole period,
beginning with the poetry recital in 1919 to commemorate
Apollinaire, there had hovered around Cocteau a teenager referred
to in one chapter of *Carte blanche* as 'the youngest of our young
poets'. This prodigious new ephebe would very rapidly assume
the role of Cocteau's new master. Would he – could he – also
provide a new direction and centre to Cocteau's life?

9

A Child Carrying a Cane

When, at the instigation of Max Jacob, Raymond Radiguet first
rolled up at 10, rue d'Anjou in June 1919, pale, weak-voiced, stoop-
ing and myopic, the wife of Cyprien, the domestic valet, introduced
him simply as 'a child carrying a cane'. The arrival of Radiguet was
for Cocteau 'a wonderful accident'. Just listening to the shy sixteen-
year-old who was still attempting to publish his first collection of
poems entranced him. He saw Radiguet as a young prodigy, just
as he had been, yet also his virtual mirror opposite on account of
Radiguet's introverted nature and reticence to the point of tacitur-
nity. Radiguet loved the idea of looking and growing old, since he
detested youth and was suspicious of easy charm and brilliance (all
the things that Cocteau seemed to stand for), and Cocteau detected
the palpable scorn and arrogance lying in his near-sighted glance,
his badly cut hair and chapped lips. For Jean Hugo, Radiguet
was simply sulky and arrogant, however awesomely mature in
his judgements, while for the poet André Salmon, who briefly
employed him, he could be offhand and insensitive with a gift for
being callous and cruel like an innocent child. Cocteau would later
write that Radiguet was so emotionally tough that it would take a
diamond to scratch his heart, and his cool insolence was no more
evident than in the dismissive letter he wrote to Breton rebuffing
the older poet's offer to be his protector. The dandified Radiguet
was certainly an equivocal creature to behold, dressed in a resin-
coloured jacket so large he continually had to roll up its sleeves,

Portrait of Raymond Radiguet by Albert Herlingue (undated).

striped black trousers, down-at-heel shoes, a straw derby and a monocle. Cocteau was prepared to overlook all this, however, so seduced was he by Radiguet's hairy physique and dark angelic looks, his sculpted Greek face and owl-like eyes, and above all his uncompromising charisma and ruffian audacity. He also admired Radiguet's capacity for complete self-absorption and his desire to observe and analyse in minute detail. In short, Cocteau saw in Radiguet a perfect admixture of man and child, perversity and innocence, strength and fragility. The fact that he would probably never be able to penetrate Radiguet's opacity or fathom his instinctive intelligence and precocious wisdom made the young man only more alluring and fascinating. The immediate imperative for

Cocteau was to mould such raw genius so there was no repeat of his own mistakes.

Cocteau installed Radiguet in a hotel room in the nearby rue de Surène so that he could set to work on publicity articles for Satie, Les Six and the Paris revival of *Parade*. Radiguet's father quickly suspected that their friendship had gone further than it should have, and Cocteau's mother surmised that some kind of exchange of sex for money was in operation (she would always regard Radiguet as a damned soul). In November Cocteau was forced to write to Radiguet's father to assure him that nothing untoward was taking place between him and his son (the letter was probably co-written by Radiguet). Cocteau even advised paradoxically that the precious Radiguet should avoid Paris altogether and remain in his home town of Saint-Maur-des-Fossés, fourteen kilometres to the south-east. In fact, from the very beginning Cocteau acted like an interfering godfather and tutor. While away from Paris during the summer of 1919 he wrote increasingly warm and friendly, though always respectful, letters to Radiguet that generated a further exchange of poems and letters of the kind 'Cher Monsieur . . . ' (Cocteau and Radiguet would always adopt formal terms of address for each other and even employ the *vous* form). He obtained employment for Radiguet, pulling strings again with Philippe Berthelot by promoting him as 'the Poet'. Once exempted from military service, Radiguet became a fully fledged member of the SAM and virtual mascot of Les Six. In public at Le Boeuf sur le Toit he and Cocteau were the ultimate odd couple, and Radiguet was more than happy to let people imagine that they were having an affair. For while Radiguet was physically turned on by mature women, he was also highly conscious of his sexual force over other men and purposely exploited it.

In May 1920 the two co-founded a magazine called *Le Coq*, a response to all the magazines that had snubbed Cocteau. While appearing to imitate Picabia's *391* with its folded format, fragmented

text and variegated typography, *Le Coq* surpassed it completely
with its sparking cocktail of anti-Dada wit, *désinvolture*, high spirits
and gaiety that sought to celebrate the 'pure' French spirit. The
June–July issues were all produced in a simple stark format of
light colours, and the first, in pale pink, included a text on the
cover by Auric entitled 'Bonjour, Paris!'. This was followed inside
by a statement of faith from Satie (essentially a two-fingers up at
Ravel), a protest by Radiguet against a Frenchman's obligation
always to be an intellectual and a side-swipe at Stravinsky while
celebrating his rival Schoenberg. All the numbers of *Le Coq* took
as their principal theme variations of the slogan that appeared in
the first issue: 'Return to poetry. Disappearance of the skyscraper.
Reappearance of the rose'. The second issue, in pale yellow with
the drawing of a cock and the words 'Je réveille', featured a piece
by Auric stating that American jazz may have woken up France
but from now on 'we' must 'reinvent nationalism'. Cocteau himself
declared provocatively that he was of the 'extreme Right' and
presiding over 'an Anti-Modern League'. The fifth issue (July–
September 1920) was called *Le Coq parisien*. In the last issue in
November 1920 (the publisher, François Bernouard, had run out
of funds), Radiguet, as a self-styled militant of 'non–originality',
wrote his 'Advice to great poets' and his famous precept (a
quote within a quote): 'Strive to be banal', in obvious negation
of Diaghilev's command to Cocteau (the last issue included the
announcement that a 'third' Cocteau was hatching and there
would be several more to come).

In August 1920, following an initial trip together to Carqueiranne near Saint-Tropez, Cocteau took Radiguet to Le Piquey.
Here he sought to hold down Radiguet long enough to nurture
his talent. They stayed at the Hôtel Chantecler, which was really
no more than a shack of wooden planks in the middle of dunes
and sand, pine trees and huts. So began 'the Le Piquey years',
during which Cocteau and Radiguet worked together in splendid

isolation and enjoyed affective and intellectual proximity. Their relationship was a kind of 'Mutual Inspiration Society' in that they both saw themselves as the twin stars of a new movement, a 'return to order' devoted to old virtues such as poetic rhyme, figuration and simplicity. Radiguet's room (they would always take separate rooms in hotels) was littered with the French classics (La Fontaine, Ronsard, etc.), and together they wrote the score for an *opéra-comique* by Satie entitled *Paul et Virginie* adapted from Bernardin de Saint-Pierre, as well as a musical farce inspired by Mallarmé entitled *Le Gendarme incompris*. Radiguet's brooding calm and power of analysis had a major stabilizing effect on Cocteau, who now suddenly found himself reading French poetry that pre-dated Baudelaire and discovering new artistic capabilities. Yet for all their intense fertile dialogue there was a distinct lack of gentle caresses and sweet nothings between Cocteau (now aged 30) and the untidy, sometimes rebellious boy he chose to call 'Boby'. Indeed, their relationship seemed at times little more than politeness on Radiguet's part. Yet for lack of erotic intimacy their relationship became a pure collaboration of minds to the point that a form of fusion took over. In a kind of chaste compromise Boby was even starting to write like Cocteau in a more laconic style suffused with death, while Cocteau, no longer constrained by the need to please, became more 'indecent' in his approach and thematics.

Things continued in the same vein during their stay in Carqueiranne in early 1921. Growing a beard and breathing in the Mediterranean enabled Cocteau to develop his new 'timeless' style and aesthetic while Radiguet wrote regular, classical and mellifluous poems and odes about Venus and the sea. In this natural haven Radiguet was content to be drawn at length by Cocteau, who, just as he would never verbally imitate Radiguet as he did everyone else, always drew him clothed, as if to do otherwise might detract from his purity. Indeed, unlike his erotic drawings of

Sketch of Radiguet
by Cocteau, 1923.

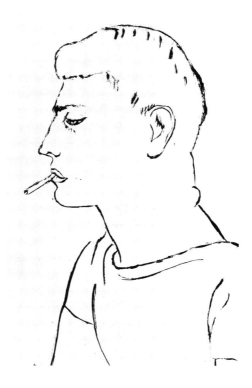

anonymous and super-endowed young men, Cocteau presented his
significant others in a gentle and flattering light, at once human
and beautiful and without any irony or caricature. He was one of
the finest celebrants of the male form in motion, and his devotion
to Eros of the male sex was achieved with a natural virtuosity and
spontaneity that brooked no second thoughts or compromise. No
two men are alike in his intimate drawings, and in the case of
Radiguet the range is even greater, for in certain images he appears
to flaunt egotistical virility like a *torero* with a contemptuous face
and obscene eyelashes. With his pencil Cocteau was thus inhabiting
Radiguet's naked sleeping body in the only way possible. The
pattern of Cocteau's love for another man had already been well

established, of course: he abdicated his very self, being and manhood in order to *be* (as opposed to *possess*) the other. On good days, when writing and collaboration were in full flow, this artistic solution paid off handsomely. Desire had been transported incandescently to a pure aesthetic level, and Cocteau was content to love from a discreet distance without being loved in return. This was a form of sublimation based on a passionate exchange of thoughts and ideas and beliefs. On bad days, however, when the ink dried up and Radiguet suddenly became incommunicado, Cocteau was reduced to making love for both of them. Even worse, he often had no choice but to wait and suffer all the anxieties and trepidations of a possessive and rejected lover. And if the strong and bold and exceptional Radiguet did not love him, then no one did, least of all himself.

In mid-April 1921 Cocteau and Radiguet returned to Paris, where Radiguet tried for the first time to engineer a space for himself away from Cocteau's now rather stifling attentions. He started to dissipate himself in drink and women, and when in the early summer of 1921 the pair went to the Auvergne to stay with Auric and Bertin he chose for the first time to behave badly. Cocteau was prepared to sweat it out, however, and promptly whisked Radiguet back to Le Piquey so that the young genius could resume work on *The Devil in the Flesh* (*Le Diable au corps*), a novel inspired by Radiguet's own illicit affair with the young wife of a soldier serving on the Front during World War One. Holding the manuscript of *The Devil in the Flesh* in his hands, Cocteau declared that originality consisted in trying to write like everyone else and precisely in not succeeding. During their stay Cocteau edited *Professional Secrets* (*Le Secret professionnel*), where he argued with real conviction that if poetry was rooted in the cliché and everyday reality, it was also a religious and ascetic mystery for a privileged elite. Yet with each passing day Radiguet became increasingly impatient with his guardian / mentor and his almost neurotic wish for control. On one occasion Cocteau even locked him up in his room until he had rewritten a part of the manuscript he had thrown into the fire. As Radiguet explained to his new confidant Auric, it was simply too much sometimes to be loved by an older man whom he could not desire. At one point he went AWOL and fled with Brancusi for twenty days, first to Marseilles, then Corsica, generating yet greater jealousy and distance between himself and his keeper.

The asymmetrical structure of desire between the two men nevertheless inspired from Cocteau *Plain-chant* (1923), perhaps the most personal and touching love poem he ever conceived (he acknowledged to Jacob that he had done no more than 'receive' these 40 pages of lyrical poetry in classical metre). Although in diverse types of rhyme and comprising over 33 discrete blocks of verse with references to Cocteau's own earlier work, as well as Picasso and Les Six, there is a coherent progression of themes here such as love, friendship, collaboration and poetic inspiration that all pay homage to the young 'angel' with whom the narrator is pressed against in his thoughts at night to the point that the two become 'a single machine'. The narrator is lucid and eternally vigilant, yet along with the slightly paranoid fears about the beloved escaping from him via sleep into another world ('I could kill you when I see you smiling in your sleep!', 'I will die, you will live, and that's what awakens me!', etc.), there is a strong yearning here for fusion: 'You hold my body tight with your little strength./ Why are we not a plant with the same bark,/ The same heat, the same colour,/ And whose single flower would be our kiss'.[1] *Plain-chant* is ultimately a *chant d'amour* matured during all those long nights Cocteau spent watching Radiguet asleep with his mouth open. There are many erotic allusions to a single bed, yet Cocteau provides no sense of sexual satisfaction. Like the striking series of drawings he executed of Radiguet in peaceful slumber during that summer, these verses of great erotic beauty feed directly into an aesthetics of the impossible (absence, the passage of time and the solitude this causes for the beholder).

Another remarkable volume of poetry produced by Cocteau during this period, and which also contains clear allusions to gay love, is *Vocabulaire*, the first evidence of his 'writing with four hands'. With the reference in the title to lexicon rather than syntax, the collection presents itself as another new *ars poetica* and a prelude to Cocteau's conversion to regular verse in a neo-classical vein with echoes of Ronsard and Apollinaire. Cocteau's conception of angelicism led him to strip bare and transcribe the invisible by willing himself as a Prometheus capable of illuminating the secrets of the world in flux and transformation. The most successful poem, 'L'Endroit et l'envers', is part of a series called 'Tombeaux', in which Sappho, Socrates and Narcissus express the joys of gay love. Here, homosexuality is linked to death and metamorphosis, and although death invades everything the poet finds relief from the labours of life and love through his unique sensitivity to the world's beauty. Another poem in the series, 'Les Oiseaux sont en neige', is a virtual ode to homosexuality and includes the arresting line: 'Rebuses of butterflies, you are transparent to me'. Here as elsewhere in the volume there is a fresh and elegant musicality to the language, yet to Cocteau's great disappointment *Vocabulaire* caught off-guard even those who were usually prepared to follow his artistic detours.

Feeling once again woefully misunderstood, Cocteau took Radiguet back to Le Lavandou, where the sun provided dependable consolation. There was nothing left to do but to change format once again, and so Cocteau embarked on his first proper novel, *The Miscreant,* one that by means of a fictional double would reveal his own fragility and disequilibrium. Radiguet, meanwhile, was already engaged on *Count Orgel's Ball* (*Le Bal du comte d'Orgel*), the story – no surprise here – of an impossible, chaste love between the young wife of the Count Orgel and a certain François de Séryuse, who discovers a new 'worldliness'. Both novels map out almost clinically the geometry of desire and the incapacity of one lover ever truly to love, yet Radiguet's working method was also stunningly compact: 1. copy in order to give yourself a foundation; 2. prove yourself only when it becomes impossible to copy. In this case his model was Madame de Lafayette's *The Princess of Cleves*. During this ideal summer of mutually creative stimulation, Radiguet was showing Cocteau how to read and Cocteau was showing Radiguet how to write. Cocteau's constant refrain was that *Count Orgel's Ball* should be trimmed down, for this was his baby too now. Just how far could the two ultimately go?

10

Annus Mirabilis / Annus Miserabilis

In artistic terms 1922 was an *annus mirabilis* for Cocteau. With the
winning combination of summer sun and the presiding calm of
Radiguet at Le Lavandou, he wrote not only *Plain-Chant* but also
two novels, *Thomas the Impostor* and *The Miscreant* (the first completed in one and a half months, the second, which he also illustrated, in just three weeks). Other works produced include one of
Cocteau's most moving stories, a three-act *complainte* entitled *Le
Pauvre matelot* (intended to be performed with music by Milhaud)
and an adaptation of *Antigone*, Cocteau's first 'serious' play, which
received its premiere in December at Charles Dullin's Théâtre de
l'Atelier. The performance of the latter, which included music by
Honegger and costumes by Coco Chanel, was again disrupted
by a group of Surrealists, and through a hole in the back-curtain
Cocteau, as the invisible Chorus armed with a megaphone, directed
his sharp tongue at the demonstrators. So successful was the
production, however, that it ran for more than 100 nights. The
character of Antigone, who confronts misfortune uncompromis-
ingly and disobediently, was an obvious source of inspiration for
Cocteau, yet the crucial aspect of this particular adaptation was its
formal composition. This was really Sophocles speeded up and
abridged with everything pared down to the bare essentials and
conveyed through a rapid delivery of lines sometimes just a phrase
long. Whatever the specific merits of Cocteau's first foray into the
classics (Gide for one considered the play flippant and lacking the

appropriate Sophoclean aura), it would mark a historical turning point in the Paris stage, which gradually turned its attention back to classical drama and, with further works by Cocteau as well as Giraudoux, Gide, Anouilh and later Sartre, radically modernized itself in the process.

Yet 1922 was also the year of Proust's death. On 18 November Cocteau was admitted to view the corpse, and in his later description of the death-bed scene talked memorably of the pages of Proust's *magnum opus* lying in a pile 'like watches ticking on the wrists of dead soldiers'. In a short but affectionate eulogy for the *Nouvelle Revue française* Cocteau celebrated Proust's unique voice, which came as if from the depths of his being and soul. Choosing to omit the long personal story of 'le petit' Marcel's alternating flattery and petty reproaches, Cocteau reclaimed the marvellous fun and worldliness of 'our friend'. This was a vital distinction for Cocteau to make, for although he had taken it upon himself to find a publisher for *Swann's Way*, he had never really been fully convinced of Proust's literary worth. In his original review of the novel in *L'Excelsior* in 1913, he had described it in terms of 'a gigantic miniature, full of mirages'. Perhaps he took too much to heart Proust's thinly veiled portrait of him as Octave, the brilliant but ultimately perplexing young upstart and lazy, vulgar dandy, even though it is finally revealed by the narrator that Octave had become 'a writer whose works created in contemporary art "a revolution at least equal to that achieved by the Ballets Russes"'. If Cocteau never regarded Proust as a literary model it was more because of the very nature of Proust's practice, specifically his approach to the relations between lived experience and art. Cocteau believed that Proust was simply misguided in his wish to put his life on hold for the sake of a masterpiece. Moreover, since, in his opinion, Proust had never really experienced or understood real love and intimacy, he could not write about it other than cynically. In this respect Proust exactly mirrored his narrative namesake Marcel, and there was therefore no ironic distance. Hence, despite its magisterial analysis of the workings of desire, fantasy and perversion, Proust's work was fundamentally frigid. Further, in Cocteau's eyes Proust betrayed the integrity and friendship of all those he frequented in order to mint his novelistic gold since the original models could barely recognize themselves, so total was Proust's travesty of the real. In a letter to Jacob he talked of Proust's 'hypocrisy' with regard to Albertine and homosexuality, and much later in his diary from 1952 referred to the novel's 'monstrous absurdities'. This critique of Proust on ethico-aesthetic grounds culminated in *Diary of an Unknown*, in which Cocteau dismissed him in a one-sentence paragraph as a writer who set himself up as a judge and yet whose maniacal jealousy never shed any real light 'on us' (read: 'us gay men').[1] While never articulating it in so many words, Cocteau saw himself and his new partner-in-arms Radiguet as working *contra* Proust for the very nature and soul of French gay modernism.

What then of Cocteau's own two new novels? Cocteau was extremely proud of the fact that, through the sixteen-year-old character of Guillaume in *Thomas the Impostor*, he was able to talk about himself so accurately and convincingly in the realistic context of war with its sufferings and horror. Guillaume is really an extreme version of Cocteau: he indulges in games of make-believe and self-transformation to the point of becoming an impostor; he belongs to 'a race apart' and feels entrapped like a child with a growing sense of dread. The one stable element in his life is his inabilty to accept reality, and it is paradoxically only when he becomes drunk that he encounters the real world. It is inevitable that he starts to love the naive Henriette just as her real image fades and she becomes a figment of his imagination. The novel is governed by death from the outset, and once unmasked Guillaume can only die. *The Miscreant* offered a still deeper glimpse into Cocteau's constitutional void. The original title, *Le Grand écart*,

Cocteau with Radiguet at Le Piquey, early 1920s.

denotes the splits on stage and thus relates to an act of performance, with the word *écart* carrying additional resonances, such as a sudden change of direction, the separation and distance between a woman of experience and a naive young man, and the playing card that a cheat hides up his sleeve. Set in contemporary Paris, the novel is the tale of Jacques Forestier, a handsome yet parasitic dilettante who struggles to find joy during his adolescence, which he battles with every day. Like his creator he is tormented by a split personality, at once melancholy and humorous, elegant and sloppy, hypocritical and sincere, and always nervous. At times, he could also suddenly become demoralized by a word and weep profusely. To appear as authentic as possible he resorts to artifice, and ten times a day 'deserves to be guillotined'. Add to this the presence of a mother searching to understand and a self-effacing father struck by a 'demon analogous to that tormenting Jacques', and Cocteau's Oedipal past flashes back vividly alive. There is the clear suggestion, too, that Jacques, while he admires beautiful bodies of either sex, is essentially gay on account of his powerful identification with the female object of his love, Germaine, although in the interests of the plot Cocteau carefully modified the real and psychological facts, turning another character Petitcopain (literally 'little friend'), into Jacques's *alter ego* who flatters Stopwell and is spurned by a man at once flawless and beautifully cruel (echoes here of Radiguet). All the characters, in fact, are splintered and narcissistic and thus really projections of Jacques himself.

Overall, *The Miscreant* reads like a concentrate of biographical fact not completely transformed by Cocteau's imagination, recalling both the vicissitudes of his early affair with Madeleine Carlier and his liaison with Jeanne Reynette at the Eldorado in 1906 (including the latter's putative gay relationship with the actress Berthe). As occurred with Carlier (or so we are led to believe), Jacques loves a girl whom he takes to the threshold of penetration before 'withdrawing' ('withdrawn like a knife from the wound' is how Cocteau once described the 'real' incident). As if to reassure his mother, Cocteau explained in a letter in July 1922 that Jacques was not exactly himself but 'resembled' him in many ways because similarly rich and pure of heart, torn between laughter and melancholy and possessing a few ties to the *bas-monde*.[2] Yet like *Thomas the Impostor*, *The Miscreant* pulls no punches about the extreme febrility of its male protagonist, who feels a sense of inadequacy and self-alienation and is pushed to the point of suicide with an overdose of cocaine. This is a brave and compelling self-portrayal by Cocteau that touches to the very core of his

personality. Emblazoned across the novel like a warning for all his
real relationships with men, where identification becomes a by-
word for appropriation, is the idea that Jacques needed to be *like*
those he finds beautiful yet not to be loved by them. The final
summation – 'He [Jacques] realised that to live in the world he
should have to follow its ways, and that his heart would not bear
it'[3] – would hang heavy throughout all Cocteau's negotiations with
reality whenever it fell short of fantasized ideals.

Both *The Miscreant* and *Thomas the Impostor* failed to impress
the public or critics when published in the autumn of 1923. The
first, written like a quick sketch in a tightly economic and allusive
style with intense images, was considered a bold, if rather crude,
reaction to the 'false Sublime' of Cocteau's earlier influences and
one that bore the all-too-obvious hallmarks of the collage techniques of Cubism. Shorn of all romantic and naturalistic
tendencies and narrated in an objective and unsentimental
manner, it was alleviated only by the humorous names of its
puppet-like characters (Mme Supplice, Stopwell, Petit Copain,
etc.). *Thomas the Impostor* was similarly damned for its showy
'brilliance' and deemed by some a perverse desire on Cocteau's
part to insult the memory of the soldiers of the Great War. Critics
failed to appreciate that the disturbing disparity between real
events and the ironically flippant manner in which they were
recounted served to intensify still further the pervasive, other-
worldly horror (wounded soldiers compared to El Greco's 'thin
monks', real wounds 'to which gangrene added its black music',
etc.). Even friends at Le Boeuf were unable to grasp the seriousness of Cocteau's unremittingly stark depiction of the human
condition and the existential malaise affecting his characters.
They whispered that Cocteau was not really on the mark: the style
was too forced, the framework weak, the characters insufficiently
fleshed out. In a move that would soon become familiar, Cocteau
felt compelled to defend publicly his two novels – and thus himself

– in a long and fascinating article in *Nouvelles littéraires* in October where he declared that the key is always to 'to be quick and sharp enough to traverse laughter and tears in a single stride', an ideal that defines all Cocteau's finest work.

The reception of Radiguet's first novel in early 1923 could not have been more different. *The Devil in the Flesh* had been launched in a flood of publicity that included three filmed sequences on Gaumont newsreels in which Radiguet was pictured in Grasset's office signing a contract for two novels, something unheard of then in French publishing. Cocteau took a hands-on role as Radiguet's agent, personally organizing the promotion and stoking up the hype (flyers were distributed declaring that Radiguet had written his novel at the age of just seventeen). The book sold 46,000 copies in its first month, overcoming any initial distaste that Radiguet was simply deriding the seriousness of war and military heroism. A love story stripped to the very bone, ruthless in its directness and lack of narratorial indulgence (it takes the form of a retrospective and apparently cynical confession), this 'false autobiography' was in Cocteau's elliptical style of short, rapid sentences, only more so. In Cocteau's eyes it made the new look as though it had been there all the time (he talked of Radiguet scrubbing down rusty clichés and polishing up commonplaces). In May the book won the Prix du Nouveau-Monde (Cocteau was on the jury) and overnight Radiguet became France's first literary media star. Cocteau was exultant, yet Radiguet as usual remained impassive (it was, in truth, only Cocteau who was actually calling him a genius). Radiguet enjoyed a brief fling with Beatrice Hastings, a bisexual English eccentric twenty years his senior, before moving still further away from Cocteau's orbit to the Hôtel Foyot that fronted the Luxembourg gardens. He was becoming more inebriated with his new drinking companion, the former aviator and writer Joseph Kessel. He still went to Le Boeuf but in the arms now of a young Polish girl, Bronya Perlmutter, whom, he declared to the world, he was planning to marry if only to avoid becoming 'Madame Jean Cocteau'. It seemed that having now outgrown Cocteau, Radiguet was forcing the very fruits of his success into his face. Yet in a familiar Cocteau paradox, the more Radiguet appeared dismissive, even contemptuous, towards him, the more Cocteau considered him utterly unique and pure. When in February 1923 the two travelled first to London then Harrow (to visit Reginald Bridgeman) and finally on to Oxford, they behaved more like master and slave: each found the other indispensable but also cloying, and each served to confirm the other's loneliness.

Following one of de Beaumont's fancy-dress balls in late May 1923, Radiguet left Paris for Le Piquey to resume work on *Count Orgel's Ball*. It was an inauspicious start to a summer marked by tensions with Cocteau and a series of disturbing incidents, including a narrow escape from death by drowning and a barber cutting into his right ear. His debts, together with his intake of alcohol and insomnia, were all starting to take their toll and he talked now of feeling totally spent. In April, during a table-tapping *séance* at the Hugos in the Camargue with Cocteau and Auric, death was predicted for Radiguet during a dialogue recorded with an unseen Presence. Later that summer he suddenly exhibited a new passion for personal order and self-discipline and started to replace alcohol with milk. The end of *The Devil in the Flesh* had included the line: 'A disorderly man who is about to die but doesn't yet suspect it often tidies the world around him. His life changes. He files his papers.' And so it was that Radiguet met his publisher Bernard Grasset, gave him his scarf as 'a souvenir' and classified all his files containing ideas for the new book. It was then, after dining at a restaurant in Bordeaux, that Radiguet contracted typhoid – almost certainly from eating oysters. Upon his return to Paris he attempted to complete *Count Orgel's Ball* and was eventually hospitalized, but it was too late (Cocteau's ever-unreliable doctor Capmas had diagnosed flu). By 9 December Radiguet knew that he would very soon die. If Cocteau remonstrated against this prophecy, Radiguet simply replied: 'The order has been given. I heard it.' Radiguet's frail, alcohol-saturated body soon succumbed to the fever and he perished as he had predicted, on 12 December, alone and in terrible suffering in his hospital room. An excruciating expression remained etched on his face. Having regained consciousness during the night and finding himself alone, he must have been utterly appalled by the discovery that this was indeed the end.

Plunged into complete emotional turmoil, Cocteau withdrew entirely from circulation, leaving Chanel to pay for the funeral and all remaining medical expenses. He would neither visit Radiguet's dead body nor, on the day of the funeral, join the long procession in pouring rain to Père-Lachaise. Nor did he attend the service at the church of Saint-Honoré D'Eylau. In fact, while *le Tout Paris* gathered to pay their last respects to Radiguet in the white catafalque adorned with a single bouquet of red flowers (he had not yet reached the age of 21 and was still considered a minor), Cocteau remained alone in his bedroom consumed by thoughts of suicide. As he had freely admitted during a talk given earlier in May at the Collège de France in which he laid the basis for the Radiguet legend (the object of his devotion was present in the audience), he had staked his entire fortune on 'the Radiguet number'. Radiguet had now returned to the heavens as unpredictably as he had arrived, and Cocteau sensed that he himself might now become a thing of the past. In fact, the early deaths of Cocteau's lovers and *protégés* were already embalming his twenties and early thirties. From now on he would always be focused on the past, left to mourn, regret and somehow preserve a Golden Age he had served to create. Indeed, he would spend the rest of his life celebrating the legacy of Radiguet as the embodiment of artistic freedom. Yet the hardest thing of all remained to do: to live without him. It would constitute Cocteau's daily trauma for many long years to come.

11

Lost in the Wilderness

With the sudden tumultuous loss of Radiguet, Cocteau suffered an emotional breakdown. A period of mourning that lasted effectively three years produced in the first instance an almost total creative block. Cocteau wrote to friends of having lost his 'son', yet he had also lost a partner and virtual spouse. He had chosen Radiguet to create a literary masterpiece and together they had forged a unique bond for the greater glory of art. On this point Cocteau was never less than honest: 'I formed Radiguet to bring about, through him, what I could not do myself'.[1] Having now lost his one absolute sense of legitimacy and identity he felt he was back at square one: alone, incomplete and insubstantial. And guilt quickly set in. Had he not personally been responsible for the meteoric rise yet also horrific eclipse of Radiguet, an 'operation performed without chloroform' as he put it? Holding the moral rights to Radiguet's œuvre, all he could do to lessen the pain was to help publish Radiguet's miscellaneous writings, beginning with the unfinished *Count Orgel's Ball*, which he edited in one last painful act of collaboration (significantly the erotic poems 'Vers libres' and 'Jeux innocents', which appeared to confirm Radiguet as defiantly heterosexual, were left in the drawer). Having earlier been viewed and dismissed by some as 'le bluff sur le moi' (a play on both the spectacle and the bar), Cocteau was now renamed by his enemies 'Le Veuf sur le toit' (the widower on the roof). Part of the problem, of course, was that he was now in his mid-thirties, yet he was still clinging tenaciously to the idea that he was a young luminary, even though Les Six had now dispersed, Cendrars had fled to South America and Picasso was associating himself closely with the Surrealists. How could he escape the merciless march of time? The ever compassionate and vigilant Max Jacob enjoined Cocteau to re-engage with his Catholic roots and return to prayer. In time Cocteau would do just that. For now, there was still some temporary comfort to be derived from the joys (albeit much reduced) of collaboration for the stage, including an adaptation of Shakespeare's *Romeo and Juliet* in which he himself played the role of Mercutio, and the dance operetta *Le Train bleu*, his last collaboration with Diaghilev featuring the dancer Anton Dollin, but which he knew himself to be rather slight, even daft. There was also, for the first real time in his life, opium.

It was in Monte Carlo in January 1924 that Cocteau made the acquaintance of the musicologist Louis Laloy, music critic of *Comoedia* and secretary-general of the Paris Opera, who would now make opium readily available to him (Laloy was the author of *Le Livre de la fumée* [1913], a very fashionable and influential manual on opium-smoking). It was a drug Cocteau had certainly sampled while at the Front during the war – and possibly also with Radiguet himself – and following his return to Paris, where Laloy had his own *fumerie* in Bellevue, it would become an all-consuming habit. His beginnings in opium, however, were not particularly propitious. Typically, he had tried to rush things in order to obtain immediate relief (as he later put it, opium is a living substance and does not like to be hurried). But he persevered, and through association with Laloy, as well as with Auric and Poulenc, who were now his main company, he became part of what Satie outrageously referred to in one article in *Paris-journal* in February 1924 as 'a band of sex, non-sex and emetics' (a statement that widened still further the rift between the two men). Cocteau settled down to the drug with Marcelle George, a former partner of Roland Garros. His entire body began slowly to change, becoming softer round the edges yet also more emaciated and hollowed out as his nose became more pointed. Opium was a new, artificial form of existence for Cocteau that seemed to relieve him of his constant need to be brilliant and loved. By creating a neutral and atemporal state (what Apollinaire once famously described as a 'soft and chaste poison'), opium appeared to stem the void and offer a buffer against the world. It also appealed to Cocteau's ritualistic side, his preferred method of smoking being the traditional bamboo. His first drawings inspired by the drug picture him in intimate close-up with friends, a mildly erotic yet also diffuse figure lacking any real definition. Over time, and with the experience of successive cures and relapses, Cocteau would consistently redefine and nuance his thoughts and feelings on the drug, for which he became one of the most eloquent (and objective) spokesmen.

It was at this point that Cocteau came into contact with a new flock of younger men who, with the obstacle of Radiguet lifted, turned up at the rue d'Anjou to pay tribute to Cocteau and offer their services and favours. The first of these new *jeunes* was the seventeen-year-old Maurice Sachs (real name Ettinghausen), whom Cocteau employed as a part-time secretary and errand boy. Dark-haired, rather podgy and verging at times on the hysterical, Sachs was not really Cocteau's type at all and patently no Radiguet. That said, he was not devoid of charm and Cocteau signed him up for the role of pageboy Ségur in *Roméo et Juliette*. Having just overcome an infatuation with Gide, Sachs sought a different type of fusion and possession with the now almost oriental-looking Cocteau, who appeared to him an oracle and prophet. Cocteau was more than happy at first to serve as a combination of father, mother and tutor for Sachs. The problem, however, was that Sachs was also a born con-man and wracked by seething self-hatred (among his formative experiences was reading Sade at the age of twelve). He would contrive to live off Cocteau like a parasite for a number of years, although for now he busied himself by adopting Cocteau's dress, forging his signature whenever possible and positively fawning upon Cocteau's mother.

Another troubled *jeune* to enter Cocteau's life was Jean Bourgoint, a tall, blue-eyed nineteen-year-old Greek god, bound like a spiritual twin to his equally beautiful sister Jeanne, with whom he still lived. Like Sachs, Bourgoint was impecunious and not at all practical, yet he possessed a cute face and handsome physique and displayed a real potential for love. Cocteau met him just before going to hospital for his first cure and planted a kiss on his cheeks with a whiff of opium – a fatal kiss as it turned out, since Bourgoint immediately fell under the spell of both the drug and Cocteau and the two men ended up sleeping together. If Sachs is to be cast as an obvious villain in the Cocteau story, Bourgoint must fall instead under the category of victim, one of those charming and fragile young men who idolized Cocteau and ultimately paid the price, either by irreversibly corrupting themselves or else being unceremoniously dropped. There are always two sides of the coin, of course, and it is an undeniable fact that these often volatile young men knew exactly what they were letting themselves in for with Cocteau and perhaps had a personal bent for self-destruction. Like Sachs, Bourgoint was also parasitic. By nature lazy and inept, he possessed no personal ambition other than to feature somehow in Cocteau's life, and if that was not possible then to be eternalized by Cocteau's work.

In the summer of 1924 Cocteau went with Auric to the small and still relatively unknown fishing town of Villefranche-sur-Mer on the Mediterranean coast near Nice. He then stayed on alone until October in a small quayside inn called the Hôtel Welcome, sat at his bedside table, stared at himself in the wardrobe mirror and drew himself over and over again, covering these drawings with captions and notes or 'monologues'. The result was a portfolio of 33 drawings later published in 1925 in a small facsimile edition under the title *Le Mystère de Jean l'Oiseleur: monologues* (The Mystery of Jean the Bird-Catcher: Monologues). The volume opens with a bleak and ominous one-page introduction that includes the following:

> the things that permit men to act, form allegiances, engage their gears, have sunk into my vague depths and taken there the place of whatever directs my life, condemning me to solitude. I am not proud of it. . . . I am inhabiting death.

The handwritten mini-texts in the margins represent Cocteau's first serious attempt to write after Radiguet's death. He had, of course, executed self-portraits before in the early to mid-1910s, but those were mainly anonymous and Cubist-like in style, shorn of all features. Now Cocteau was scrutinizing himself directly in the mirror, naked and all too real, and this would provide, as always with his drawings, beneficial side-effects due to the complex processes of identification they entailed (as he put it later: '[drawing] is my only therapy against the illnesses of the soul. While drawing I forget everything. I become the thing I'm drawing').[2] Cocteau was serving finally as his own model while playing out different personae and self-images, for each drawing, a marvel of fine lines and draughtsmanship, represents a different Cocteau: angel, pontiff, poet, geomancer, drug addict, etc. The result in each case was an experiment, a fresh and distinctive configuration of text and image. The theme of the *oiseleur*, or bird-catcher, had been glimpsed already in *The Miscreant* and it is linked formally here to the Italian Renaissance painter Uccello, whose name signifies 'bird'. If Cocteau as author is a bird-tamer, it is because the birds hover in his notes like so many treasures of his unconscious, to be trapped and plucked out of the confusion of opium. Yet 'bird-catcher' also carries other potential gay meanings, since *oiseau* in slang means phallus. Hence, this work should be viewed as essentially a gay self-portrait, with Cocteau bringing together a host of exotic angels and masculine

Self-portrait as 'Jean l'Oiseleur' ('Jean the Bird-catcher'), from *Le Mystère de Jean l'Oiseleur: monologues*, 1925.

objects of love, above all Radiguet (one of the illustrations is entitled: 'I keep my angel').

The effects of Cocteau's opium-taking were all too plain to see. His face had caved in and harsh lines were chiselled into his skin in stark, geometrical formation. For all the signs of the familiar (bowler hat, bow tie, rose, etc.), this was a kind of reverse self-image (literally so on account of the mirror), offset only by the largely neat and legible textual fragments written backwards that range from just one phrase, like 'Jean l'Oiseleur', to short paragraphs that include passing insights into the nature of literary and cultural worth, the music hall, Gide, 'Cocteau' as an artist and his personal list of 'starred friends' (Ronsard, Mozart, Picasso, Radiguet, etc.). Also mentioned here are Cocteau's first impressions of the 24-year-old American trapeze artist and female impersonator Barbette (real name Vander Clyde), who starred at the Casino de Paris and inspired in Cocteau an aesthetics of the high wire.[3] There is a supreme self-consciousness to this modernist act of self-exposure, since Cocteau knew only too well the stakes involved in this process of self-dramatization. One sentence reads: 'I know better than anyone the ridicule you expose yourself to in sitting down between a mirror and a stenographer'. And later, even more self-laceratingly: 'This unreal reality disfigures most of my actions'. He declares finally with astonishing frankness and resignation:

> As for whatever relationship may exist between the words and the faces, whatever confessions and poetry may be expressed in the lines, they must be interpreted as signs of the illness that for nearly twelve years now has forced me to strain my will to the utmost.

Twelve years before corresponds, of course, to the year of Diaghilev's imperious command 'Astonish me!', which had served to dispel Cocteau's childhood nightmare about his father as an indiscriminate parrot. It is as if now, in retrospect, the reprieve had been merely illusory and that his art was actually less an antidote to the pain than a symptom. Had his artistic ambitions simply been one glorious exercise in self-deception that had changed absolutely nothing and even carried within it the seeds of a profound illness? Again, Cocteau's capacity to put himself so explicitly into question here is both impressive and disturbing. He was always intelligent enough to acknowledge the quiddity of his behaviour; the problem came in trying to change it. And this, to return to the title of the work, would always be the mystery of Jean Cocteau.

Cocteau's searing performance in *Le Mystère de Jean l'Oiseleur: monologues* was made possible by opium, which had opened him up directly to his unconscious, equipping him with a new set of biorhythms that enabled him to tap further into subterranean Orphic and Promethean themes. This was not the surrealist Unknown, of course, since Cocteau favoured the waking dream over Breton's vulgarization of sleep that puritanically eschewed the use of drugs. Yet like Breton with the dream-work, Cocteau was romantically obsessed with the absolute presence of the One that he beheld in the crystalline substance and revered with near-fetishistic awe (he even made a collection of crystal paper-weights in which he contemplated an 'intersection of infinities'). In the current intellectual battle for the unconscious Cocteau was not interested in the decoding of Freudian primal scenes, perhaps because he feared that psychoanalysis would tamper with his own neurotic state and hinder his re-emerging creativity. The cruel irony, of course, is that while serving to expand his rich fantasy world, opium was also making Cocteau sick and impotent. In early 1925 he decided to check into a private hospital, the Thermes Urbains, to begin his first major treatment for drugs. Max Jacob participated in the arrangements and Chanel almost certainly covered the expenses, as was now her role. Cocteau's account of the cure to the Hugos was of a strange and atrocious 'suffering without suffering' whereby '10,000 people in my legs are waiting for the opening of the desks that don't open'. The drawings produced during this treatment (later published in a collection euphem-istically entitled *Maison de santé*) are genuinely harrowing. Identified by a day of the week or else signed simply 'l'Oiseleur', they present Cocteau naked in different stages of raw physical pain. 'J'ai mal' is one brutal title, and the festoons of electrodes in another drawing reflect the hospital's regime of needle showers and electric baths. Hands are splayed out in wild desperation and Cocteau's back is riddled with grotesque marks and blotches. All the drawings relate to the eyes and vision, in particular the pinpoint pupils of addicts, as well as to blood and veins. Again, there is a visceral emphasis on the oral (in one image Cocteau is eating a raw fish), and phallic symbols abound, giving the impression at times of a sadomasochistic sexual experience (the captions include the plea: 'my angels, come and help me'). When

Cocteau finally left the Thermes Urbains in the last week of April he felt that his sexual appetite had returned, yet ironically he now viewed Bourgoint through new eyes as a rather oafish clod with no sexual appeal whatsoever and as the probable cause of his writing block. Bourgoint was devastated, and night after night for several months reportedly waved sad farewells with a white handkerchief. It was with thoughts of saving Bourgoint while salving his own conscience (he claimed that up to six boys had already killed themselves on his account!) that Cocteau now entered a new phase in his life, one of the most perplexing, to be sure, but one that he genuinely hoped would deliver him from the new devil of opium and transport him back safely to his archangel, Radiguet.

12

An Ass Bearing the Lord

In early July 1924 Cocteau and Auric stayed at the cottage of Jacques and Raïssa Maritain in the Paris suburb of Meudon, where the couple had their own religious chapter. The Maritains were high-society Catholic converts and proselytizers. The imposing Jacques, a neo-Thomist philosopher and professor at the Institut Catholique, displayed a genuine interest in the avant-garde, in particular those artists and writers who offered vaguely spiritual and accessible messages, such as Georges Rouault, Marc Chagall and Paul Claudel. Maritain was aware of Gide and others of the *Nouvelle Revue française*, but not impressed by their agnostic and Left-leaning vision of modernism. The naturally Right-leaning Cocteau, on the other hand, represented a far more attractive proposition, and Maritain's *Art et scolastique* of 1919, had cited approvingly several of Cocteau's aphorisms from *Cock and Harlequin*. Cocteau was impressed in turn by Maritain's negative stand on Breton, and even more so by his recognition of the value of Radiguet's work. It was thus perhaps inevitable that the two should finally meet. Cocteau immediately felt comfortable in the warm and soft family bosom of the Maritains and was soon confident that his recent experience with Radiguet, including his own original high hopes and ideals, would in time be understood and honoured, a belief inspired by his sense that Radiguet had been sent by God to help better the world. Cocteau explained to the Catholic literary journalist Henry Massis: 'For five years I renounced *myself*, trying through Radiguet to carry out an experiment which I could never have accomplished alone with my own fouled instruments', adding that together he and Radiguet had been 'trying to create something "invisible", "heavenly"'.[1]

The subtle and intelligent Maritain operated like a professional analyst. Listening patiently to Cocteau's inner torment, he subtly proposed a tangible alternative to the 'artificial paradises' of opium and hashish with their inexorable downward spiral. For Cocteau, who was naturally interested in any possibilities for change and transformation, a return to the faith also meant a return to the paradise of childhood, and while in Villefranche during the summer he began re-reading the saints' lives, including the mystic Anne Catherine Emmerich's *Life of Jesus*. In March 1925 he also began to participate in the editing of a journal founded by Maritain, *Le Roseau d'or*. About to leave Meudon one evening after a dinner to discuss the project, he suddenly encountered for the first time Père Charles Henrion, a dashing friend and disciple of the Maritains who had made his name evangelizing among the tribes of the Sahara, whence he had just returned. The missionary was a tall tanned figure in a white burnous. Embroidered on the breast of his robe was the dramatic, not to say melodramatic, device of a crimson cross above a heart designed to rivet the eyes of any poor infidel. Had Henrion's spectacular arrival been stage-managed by the Maritains? Cocteau suspected as much and he was probably right, but he was also utterly seduced and hypnotized by the experience. He found the handsome Henrion to be of simple, elegant grace and blessed with the rare gift of telling stories. It was as if Radiguet were calling to him from the heavens. In a sense Henrion carried the same shock-value as Cocteau's earlier mentors Stravinsky and Picasso, and he possessed a similar stature and presence. For Cocteau this was a decisive artistic-spiritual event of enormous implications. Maritain sighed gushingly: 'We knew that Charles had come only for you.'

With a confession on 18 June 1925 and communion the day after (the feast of the Sacred Heart), Cocteau had finally returned at speed to the sacraments. In fact, fast-track conversion and religious revival were very much the order of the day. In addition to Claudel, new believers included Jacques Copeau of the *Nouvelle Revue française*, Pierre Reverdy, Gide's former lover Henri Ghéon and Charles-Ferdinand Ramuz. Even the Protestant Gide himself was rumoured to be on the way! Soon even the young aesthetes at Le Boeuf sur le Toit who fashioned themselves on Cocteau, from the style of his dress to his speech, were rushing to become penitents. The vogue conspired ironically to bring together both the rarefied young men hovering around 10, rue d'Anjou and the super-virile and militant young Catholics who clustered around Charles Maurras, a staunch supporter of the Church (although himself agnostic) and founding member of the extreme-right Action Française. As for Max Jacob, he considered Cocteau's return to the fold to be the epitome of Christian virtue, and the two began to develop a deeper friendship, styling themselves as 'neo-romantics' on account of their shared fondness for *pierrots*, children and angels. Sachs initially thought that Cocteau had committed a betrayal, but he, too, soon fell under the spell. Cocteau sent him to Meudon and within just six weeks Sachs, still only eighteen, had converted and recanted 'the errors of the Jews' (he was baptized on 29 August). On Christmas Eve 1925 Cocteau received communion at Meudon with his two new 'god-sons', Sachs and Bourgoint. Sachs went even one better than his model, however, and a week later entered a Carmelite seminary in Paris, acquiring a cassock that he chose to wear everywhere, including the beach at Villefranche. Was Cocteau perhaps obliging Sachs, who continued to live with the Maritains, to act as a kind of leader in order to ensure his own correct spiritual path? Certainly, Cocteau thought that strength lay in numbers and that his newly restored faith would eventually bring him closer – not to Sachs, of course, but to Radiguet.

Cocteau was now Maritain's big hope, and his desire was for Cocteau to become a spokesman for his generation by promoting a new Christian brand of modernism. What was clearly needed was some type of major public declaration to trump Breton's highly influential *Manifesto of Surrealism* of the year before. Much was therefore riding on Cocteau's next literary work, which he now began to prepare, buoyed by the simple idea that poetry = love = faith. Cocteau never regarded himself as a Catholic writer, even at this point, and whatever faith he possessed would remain a highly private affair. What, therefore, was the language of home-style Catholic modernism? Cocteau's answer, *Lettre à Jacques Maritain*, was characteristically rapid, hatched in Villefranche within a matter of weeks. A 40-page text rounded off by a 'Post-scriptum' in thirteen parts, *Lettre à Jacques Maritain* was intended to celebrate the joys of an artist's detoxification and return to the sacraments, thereby encouraging other artists to return to the fold and escape the pernicious atheistic influence of the Surrealists. In fact, everything is thrown up in the air very quickly in this biographically leaning work, which reads at times more like a public confession. Reviewing and reinventing his life and career since 1912, Cocteau bombards the reader with colourful yet not always convincing aspects of his nature and behaviour, including the need for voluntary isolation ('I do everything to avoid public places', he asserts.). There are assorted references to his drug treatment, the arrival of Henrion, Jacob, Satie, the 'angel' Radiguet, even the Russian Revolution, plus a series of slogans along the lines: 'I should adopt your [Maritain's] motto – "I am an ass who is bearing the Lord".' On the subject of opium, Cocteau revealed the confusion in his mind at this time: he defends the drug if taken properly, yet relegates it to the role of mere 'illusionist' in comparison with Jesus, all but admitting by this that opium was not an attempt to live life but rather a form of evasion ('My flight into opium is Freud's Flight into Sickness'). Cocteau positions himself in close proximity to God ('We are His poets') and even assigns himself retroactively a scriptural career, for God, it now transpires, was a nameless intuition he had been carefully harbouring since the age of 23. If he has cut a lonely and scandalous figure, hadn't Christ? Indeed, at the root of all his previous lifestyle of addiction and pederasty lay, miracle of miracles, a saintly 'love for love'. All his vices had simply been the deficiencies of a virtue, and now God, like opium before, was gently slowing him down, revising his metabolism and allowing him to be truly human. Hence, he proposed to establish a 'school of undesirables' whose leader he would be, and a new 'art for God's sake'.

In short, *Lettre à Jacques Maritain* unfolds as an almost shameless exercise in self-justification, an extreme manifestation of Cocteau's endemic need for both recognition and acquittal. Not unsurprisingly, the work was poorly received. There were odd pious expressions of joy in Catholic magazines that welcomed Cocteau back as a prodigal son and brother and invoked his child-like soul, yet the major Catholic writers like François Mauriac, as well as agnostics such as Paul Morand, suspected that Cocteau's conversion was neither fully

Cocteau smoking opium, 1937.

fledged nor serious. There was a feeling that he had simply waltzed again into new territory to appropriate a ready stock of angels as if they were androgynous trapeze artists. Even those who admired Cocteau as a unique poetic force deplored his scurrying back to the Church, the traditional repository of spiritual comfort. Anna de Noailles in particular viewed it as an embarrassing *volte-face*. Judged as too literary and too heterodox by the Catholic Right, *Lettre à Jacques Maritain* was tarred with insincerity by the Left and became an obvious object of scorn for the Surrealists, who attacked both Cocteau and Claudel as errant counter-revolutionary 'authors of vile patriotic poems' profiting ignominiously from the current regime. Cocteau later claimed he had intended his Letter as a 'bomb' to shatter the pretty painted and plaster-sainted aspects of French Catholicism in order to restore the Church's lost virtues. What had actually transpired, however, was that the Church, and Maritain in particular with his immediate and somewhat pallid *Réponse à Jean Cocteau*, had simply 'defused' his brilliant bomb by failing to grasp its contents. Cocteau finally acknowledged that *Lettre à Jacques Maritain* had proved all but useless, like a 'sword-stroke in the water', and that it had even been a great mistake. Maritain recognized, too, that Cocteau was probably, in purely practical terms, of little benefit now for the cause. But the truth of the matter was that Maritain also wanted Cocteau to abandon his gay sensibility and inclinations. Cocteau may have felt rather ambivalent now about his alleged 'vice', yet he was still enough of Jean Cocteau the poet-magician to think that even in this new climate of increasing public persecution against him his very solitude and ill luck would eventually provide the key to his salvation, and that he and Radiguet would find each other again.

Yet Cocteau was also having to face up to some unpalatable personal facts. His trusty alternative family was now fast disappearing. The Morands were sailing round the world, Les Six were breaking up, and Satie had just died (however strained their relationship had been, Cocteau celebrated him fulsomely in *L'Exemple d'Erik Satie* (1925) as a 'Master of Wisdom', artistically free and unencumbered). Closer to home, Bourgoint was now waiting to join up, and Sachs, after his intense religious experience, was starting seriously to doubt whether his master was his idol after all. Among the Villefranche set Glenway Wescott regarded Cocteau as a fallen angel and in particular his *Lettre à Jacques Maritain* as the height of hypocrisy, since he had personally witnessed Cocteau smoking opium while correcting the proofs of the work, which preached abstinence from drugs as the precondition for a return to the sacraments. Reinstalled in Room 25 at the Hôtel Welcome in the summer of 1926, Cocteau was soon back to smoking ten pipes a day. By now, of course, Villefranche was becoming a magnet for all kinds of gay bohemia, washed-up European aristocracy and English eccentrics, and it was here that Cocteau met for the first time the artist and future stage designer Christian Bérard, who would become a vital friend and collaborator. All the while Cocteau continued to present himself as a kind of martyr – to opium, to melancholy, to love – though how much this was really a pose was not always easy to determine. He declared he loved simply for the sake of loving, yet this invariably proved a hopeless and thankless task. In the case of the writer Marcel Jouhandeau, Cocteau's innocent wish to look out for him as a Christian neighbour during a time of need was woefully misread and Jouhandeau began to make unwelcome advances. Desiring now to be fiercely secular (relations between Cocteau and God were by this stage entirely mutual: 'I disgust God, He abandons me', Cocteau railed), he nevertheless briefly tried his hand with the fashionable Hindu guru Varma-Yoghi, yet to no avail. In fact, although Cocteau was trying to pump himself up with any type of new experience following his Catholic *chinoiseries*, he felt profoundly that he had reached an impasse. He admitted dejectedly to Jacob: 'My life is limping now', and found himself starting to absorb the very hate he was provoking. He was no longer unique and rare, perhaps nothing more even than a scapegoat for the Surrealists. It was doubtlessly a catch-22 of his making, for there were now in circulation too many true–false Cocteaus, too many false starts, too many false selves, each one proving still more unpopular. Since he could not bear to be disliked he started taking bitter pleasure in his own sufferings, his lack of self-esteem tipping over at times into pure self-loathing (he would later even go out of his way to praise Breton's novel of 1928, *Nadja*).

One might choose to view the whole episode of Cocteau's brief conversion in purely careerist terms, especially since embracing the Father had become such an important avant-garde pastime. Yet Cocteau's re-engagement with Catholicism was extremely formative, and he learned from it a vital artistic lesson: that it was an error, indeed a sacrilege, to assume like the Maritains that one could ever reconcile literature (the true sacred) with conventional religion. Literature demanded its own mortal ceremonies and rituals and brooked no comparison or compromise. Cocteau claimed that even Père Charles had advised him to 'remain free' because he knew that a true artist could never remain in the fold. As for his disciple Bourgoint, who loved him in a way he could never reciprocate, he was cared for in 1932 by Jean Hugo at the latter's country house in Mas-la-Fourques, where he remained for almost the next fifteen years. He then relinquished his name and, after entrusting Cocteau with all his worldly possessions, entered a Trappist monastery in Burgundy to become Brother Pascal, serving for a while as a lay missionary in a leper colony in North Cameroon. His long vow of silence was broken only by a remarkable and entirely unsolicited tribute to Cocteau following his death, in which he celebrated Cocteau's 'royal kindness'.[2]

13

Miracle or Simulacrum?

The debacle with Maritain reignited Cocteau's appetite for work.
He produced illustrations for a new edition of *Thomas the Impostor*;
a libretto for Stravinsky's new work *Oedipus Rex*, adapted from
Sophocles (over which the two again fell out due to mutual suspicion); and a number of poems that would eventually form the
collection *Opéra, 1925–7*, presented as the work of a self-confessed
opium-eater. Cocteau considered *Opéra* as the first set of poems to
capture his real essence, and we get a sense of just how far Radiguet's
death has transformed his imaginary universe. The poet is now a
visionary and his poetry a mystical activity with existential stakes.
If poetry had always been for Cocteau a matter of showing the
existence of a reality hidden behind the appearances of daily life
and thus rendering the invisible visible, he now provided clear
theoretical lines to justify the idea, as in the opening poem 'Par
lui-même': 'Accidents of mystery and errors of celestial/ Calculation,
I've profited from them, I admit./ All my poetry is there: I trace
the invisible (invisible to you)'. The atmosphere in which all this
is generated is theatrical and tragic, for poetry is now a dangerous
activity, a 'boulevard of crime', drawing together both the detective
and the criminal. Cocteau introduced here a motley crew of
ancient and mythological characters that would nourish all his
future work, including the Sphinx, the pharaohs, a man in
Oedipus costume surrounded by laughter, Orpheus, Titus and
Berenice, and a myopic Venus de Milo. Some poems pursue opium

fantasies with a certain light giddiness, others convey grief with detachment and restraint. In 'Le Paquet rouge', however, which turns leprosy into a metaphor to depict self-disintegration, and in which Cocteau suggests once again that he is not simply different and alien but an impostor and artistic fraud, there is a violent sense of shame:

> I am leprous . . . I am uneducated, a dunce. I know no figures, no dates, no names of rivers, no language living or dead . . . Moreover, I stole the id of a certain J. C. born in M. L. on the . . . dead at 18 after a brilliant career in poetry . . . Let me be locked away and lynched.

Another poem, 'La Mort du Poète', shows the narrator dying because 'you, France, you've insulted, ridiculed, ruined me . . . I'm dead'. But there will be revenge: 'I'll strangle you with delights. I will not die alone.' The title of another poem says it all: 'No man's land'. Needless to say, such dramatic and tortuous self-examination was not particularly well understood or appreciated by critics, who also berated Cocteau's excessive word play.

A far more accessible and positive result of the immediate post-Maritain period, however, and one that harks back to the previous summer that Cocteau spent at Villefranche, was the play *Orpheus* (*Orphée*), produced by the famous acting/directing pair the Pitoëffs in June 1926 at the Théâtre des Arts in Paris, with sets by Jean Hugo and costumes again by Chanel. A short 'tragedy in one act and one interval' (essentially thirteen short scenes), *Orpheus* was Cocteau's first really serious dramatic work containing both comic and tragic elements, and he was meticulous in his notes for the decor and staging. Set in a modern apartment where common objects like mirrors become ritualistic symbols, the play retained several of the major episodes of the ancient myth of Orpheus (notably the double death of Eurydice and the crossing of the

Underworld that gives rise to an ellipsis – the interval of the title). Cocteau, however, transformed the Thracian poet into an irritable, indecisive writer beset not by fabulous monsters but by inner demons, producing a major crisis of inspiration. Orpheus begins to rely on a strange, inverted form of Centaur played on stage by an actor with a horse's head. In appearance a pantomime animal performing the familiar music-hall routine of nodding its head and tapping its hoof to spell out messages, it becomes Orpheus' hobby horse or 'dada', and thus a caustic visual pun on Dada. Because of the horse's evil influence, Orpheus is 'petrified' (*médusé*) and decapitated by the Bacchantes for being a disrespectful poet. When finally reunited with Eurydice and the benign winged angel Heurtebise, Orpheus addresses a prayer to God, declaring that inspiration is 'the devil in the form of a horse'. As the set rises into the sky reflecting their experience of personal change, the three figures form an ostensibly chaste and touching *ménage à trois*. This religious and rather conservative conclusion reflects Cocteau's brief reversion to Catholicism, and indeed the transformation of a Surrealist poet into an eloquent and seemingly 'normal' believer delighted Maritain. Cocteau himself spoke of the play as containing many miracles and *trucs* (Heurtebise, for example, is suspended one moment in mid-air), but it also features other elements of his own recent personal experience: the diabolical horse recalls the portentous table-tapping with Radiguet at the Hugos, while the tribunal of the Bacchantes has its origins in Dada's attempted censure of Cocteau.

Orpheus was manifestly a gay author's imaginative deformation of a classical legend, and Cocteau even claimed that the very beautiful woman he found to play Death had been inspired by the transvestite performer Barbette. Does the guardian angel figure of Heurtebise perpetuate Radiguet? Possibly. He is, after all, love and salvation and can suddenly vanish (as when accused of murdering the poet). He is also clearly linked to the Heurtebise of 'L'ange

Cocteau as Heurtebise in a staging of *Orpheus*, Paris, 1927.

Heurtebise', one of the longest and most successful poems of *Opéra*, which described the at once spiritual and violent homo-erotic fantasy of possession by a 'heavy male sceptre', both a violent creative spirit and a young male lover. (It included the arresting lines: 'The angel Heurtebise, with an unbelievable/ brutality jumps on to me. Out of grace/ Do not jump so hard/ Bestial boy, flower of high/ Stature', and: 'How ugly is the happiness one desires'.) Perhaps, too, Heurtebise loves – and is loved by – Orpheus through the intermediary of Eurydice. On this point the play remains less than clear, as if Cocteau were still searching in the dark for some kind of spiritual unity. Certainly with the high-profile and lavish production of *Orpheus*, which trades in innuendo, verbal razzle-dazzle and irreverent jokes for a knowing in-crowd (one of the horse's aphorisms is 'Madame Eurydice reviendra des enfers', the first letters of each word spelling 'MERDE' [SHIT]), Cocteau was catering very much now to a gay audience and laying claim to a new status as a popular gay artist. When the police inspector questions the disembodied head of the dead Orpheus, he even flaunts his own birthplace and Paris address like a calling card. Cocteau's apartment in the rue d'Anjou duly became overrun by young men who each wanted a piece of this 'new' Cocteau, compelling him at one point to detail the loss of certain possessions, such as inscribed editions in a letter to the publisher Roland Saucier. Cocteau, of course, provided lustre for this roving gay milieu that traded in intrigue and half-open secrets, although he was caught a trap of his own making on one occasion when he launched a campaign against one of Diaghilev's regular composers, Vladimir Dukelsky. When Dukelsky ranted one night against 'decadent Parisian *musiquette*', Cocteau, a past master at one-upmanship and ever impulsive, retorted: 'Dima, we Parisians send you a load of shit.' When Cocteau proceeded to deliver a blatantly anti-Russian harangue, Dukelsky immediately challenged him to a duel and slapped him humiliatingly in his own home. In typical style Cocteau wrote to Diaghilev the next day to excuse himself, suggesting that it was Dukelsky who was the coward.

It was during the following Christmas, shortly after a major exhibition in Paris of his unusual hybrid sculptures and collage constructions (*objets-poèmes*) called *Poésie plastique*, that Cocteau met a young man who ushered in a completely new phase of his life. Wearing naval uniform because he was on military service as a land-based sailor in the Naval Ministry on the Place de la Concorde, Jean Desbordes was a softly spoken youth of twenty with classic high cheekbones and feline, sensual looks reminiscent of Radiguet. There was nothing especially distinctive about him (from one angle his short, slight build even lent him the demeanour of a bank clerk), and he may have lacked real intelligence or personality. Yet he was manifestly kind and gentle, emotional without being in any way effeminate, and, as he would later prove,

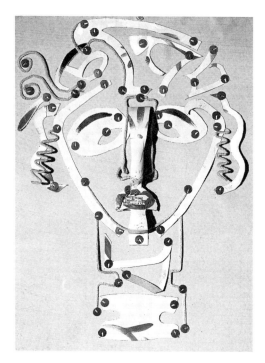

Cocteau, *Tête aux punaises* ('Drawing-pin head'), 1926, mixed media. 'Poème-objet dit "Poésie Plastique" (objet no. 8).'

fundamentally decent and honest. For Cocteau their meeting was of the order of a miracle. Was Desbordes, who had also brought with him that day a typewritten manuscript, a reincarnation of Radiguet? Cocteau chose to believe so, although he quickly revised that opinion when he read the manuscript, which was really a mass of formless utterances with periodic dream sequences about another world. Cocteau detected in it, however, odd signs of genius and decided to teach Desbordes how to exploit his reveries rather than leave them to chance. He soon became infatuated by Desbordes, re-naming him 'Jean-Jean' to differentiate him from Bourgoint (now in barracks in the Ruhr). He also installed him in the nearby Hôtel de la Madeleine (in the very room once occupied by Radiguet) and together they settled into a routine of opium.

In the many drawings he made of Desbordes, Cocteau depicted him with a mixture of tenderness and desire in poses echoing the sleeping figure of Radiguet in 1922. The effect was now far more overtly gay and homoerotic, however, because of Desbordes' sailor uniform, his seductively pursed lips and the simple fact that he really *was* Cocteau's lover.

It was a measure of Cocteau's influence and standing that he was able to secure Desbordes' early release from military service. Hence Desbordes continued to write as well as produce eulogies of Cocteau's works, such as *Lettre à Jacques Maritain*. Yet for many the relationship could not be taken seriously. The very name Desbordes, pronounced like the second-person singular of the present tense of the verb *déborder* (to overflow), epitomized this playboy writer whose prose poured forth in a way Cocteau found so refreshing. The overall effect was a virtual parody of Cocteau's ideal collaboration with the severe Radiguet, and it is symptomatic that Desbordes, unlike his predecessor, was on extremely good terms with Cocteau's mother and would often write to her expressing his gratitude to her son for teaching him 'the necessary things'. Eventually, there were enough of Desbordes' pieces for a volume, and *J'adore*, a collection of intense effusions, was launched in June 1928 with a major advertising campaign conceived by Cocteau. Posters of Desbordes in his sailor costume were posted up in bookstores carrying Cocteau's imprimatur. Cocteau also wrote a fulsome preface to the novel in which he addressed the youth of France and presented Desbordes as Antigone's little brother, describing also in frank terms his own personal and professional involvement with Desbordes. The novel itself was a no-holds-barred pantheistic paean to universal love, a series of pagan Georgics written by a Protestant clearly influenced by Gide's *The Fruits of the Earth*. It offered raw sexual and emotive phrases of the kind: 'My heart is full of love, my limbs are filled with sap', and, even more graphically:

When I think of nothing, I listen to love rising. I sense my sex at the lightest touch of a hand . . . I take love from everything. I can sense every drop of sperm in the air, and I never fail to transform it. Everything fertilizes me.

Cocteau praised *J'adore* for its 'limpid streams' and 'burning ejaculations', presenting Desbordes as an incarnation of the innocent and primitive. For Cocteau, such physical love governed by the heart constituted a new anarchy, that of loving God without limits, and through typical identification he began to fancy himself now as a kind of noble savage.

For Maritain, who was explicitly invoked in the novel only to be negated, *J'adore* was a flagrantly false Christian monologue intended to provoke him. Along with many other Catholics he immediately denounced Desbordes as the devil in disguise, writing

Drawing by Cocteau of his lover Jean Desbordes, 1928, pen and ink on paper.

in *Le Roseau d'or* of a total betrayal of Christ: 'They [i.e. Desbordes and Cocteau, but perhaps all gay writers] adore, do they! God, and the genitals (and the printed page)'. By way of response Cocteau declared simply: 'No, Jean is love.' Cocteau, of course, had already pre-empted such criticism with a statement in his preface: 'I judge only from the heart.' He knew that he was putting himself on the line, but it could not be any other way: the personal and artistic were inextricably linked, and the natural risk for an out-gay writer was always public confusion and misunderstanding, if not scandal. He now conducted a campaign to try to influence every gay Catholic he knew, as well as every sympathetic literary journalist and critic, although with little effect.

Cocteau and Desbordes spent the summer of 1927 together first at Chantilly then Nice, and finally, towards the end of the year, in Chablis, where Cocteau wrote *The White Book*. This short auto-biographical novel incorporates elements of his boyhood escapade to Marseilles (here Toulon), as well as the more recent stories of Radiguet's death (the mysterious writer 'H', who dies early from tuberculosis), the Bourgoints' and Sachs' conversion. It was his first avowedly gay work, conceived of as a kind of companion piece to *J'adore*. Yet while it reproduces Desbordes' peculiar mix of sensual confidences and religiosity, it also reveals considerable *pudeur* in its accounts of gay love as a natural component of the general disarray of youth and innocence. The anti-heroic narrator tells of his love for boys and young men, relays a few incidents from his childhood, mentions his father's latent homosexuality and then describes his own unhappy affairs, one with a girl's pimp and another with the girl's brother. Each episode ends in death or painful separation: the wondrously endowed school vamp Dargelos dies from angina in hospital; the pimp Alfred is abandoned sobbing on the pavement; 'Pas de Chance' is deserted in a hotel bedroom; and Mademoiselle de S's brother shoots himself. That gay love is doomed to failure and disappointment, even death, is inescapable, yet there is no sense here of this being a social punishment for sinful sexuality, although by the end the narrator feels that even the monastery has rejected him and attempts to drown himself.

The White Book was published first anonymously and clandestinely through Sachs in 1928, then two years later by the Editions du Signe with 'illustrations by the author'. The manner of the book's publication has always dictated its critical reception. Indeed, far too much ink has been spilt on questioning Cocteau's desire not to acknowledge authorship, even though the book contains unmistakable proof of its creator's hand. Certainly, Cocteau stretches the levels of coyness and obfuscation when he states at the start of the second edition that he is happy to 'approve' by means of such images 'this anonymous effort towards clearing a terrain [i.e. homosexuality] that has remained too long uncultivated' (the title *The White Book* refers in both French and English to an official parliamentary document or white paper. Yet the text's further value is that of a fiction articulating some of Cocteau's deepest feelings and character traits. Through the narrator's account of his 'tortures', Cocteau offers a brilliantly concise breakdown of his own psychological and emotional condition and the sad fact that he is doomed always to lose in matters of the heart:

> I am ravaged by love. Even when I am at peace I shrink with fear that this peace will cease, and this anxiety prevents me from taking any pleasure in it . . . Waiting is torture; possession is another, for fear of losing what I have.[1]

In one of the most potent identifications between narrator and creator – the graphic scene in the bathhouse where a man makes love to his own reflection unaware of the onlooker behind the mirror – we see vividly how Cocteau can transform pure erotic fantasy into poetic reality. For this reason, *The White Book* may be viewed as a belated artistic response to Gide's *Corydon*, a major defence of homosexuality also first published anonymously in 1911. Unlike *Corydon*, however, Cocteau's self-consciously ludic and libidinous text celebrating gay sexuality as 'the fair sex' harbours no major claims to influence social or sexual mores. Nevertheless, its final defiant message of refusing mere tolerance opens out on to the more general question of the relations between life and art and thus leads the way in ethico-erotic terms. Troping on Rimbaud, the narrator states powerfully that 'the young would have done better to retain the phrase: *Love is to be reinvented*. Society accepts dangerous experiences in the realm of art because it doesn't take art seriously, but it condemns them in real life' (emphasis original).[2] Like all Cocteau's best work, *The White Book* bespeaks the translation of the gay real into art and actively contests the lazy and ultimately homophobic assertion that gay life and gay art should be kept separate and smoothed out clean.

By the spring of 1928 Cocteau had became Coco Chanel's official houseguest at her private mansion in the rue du Faubourg Saint-Honoré. She was now effectively sponsoring his smoking habits, although things went typically awry when Sachs misused funds intended by Chanel for assembling her new library. As for Desbordes, he was beginning now to withdraw from circulation and would soon undergo treatment for opium addiction under the care of his sister. In December, claiming he wanted to set a good example to Desbordes, Cocteau checked himself into a fashionable clinic run by a certain Dr Sollier in the wealthy suburb of Saint-Cloud in order to begin his second major cure. This would last more than three months and constitute one of the most formative and productive stages of his life-project.

14

Body and Blood of a Poet

Within a week of his arrival at the clinic in Saint-Cloud, Cocteau was already charting his experiences in a notebook that would eventually be published as *Opium: Diary of a Cure* (*Opium: journal d'une désintoxication*). It was formally dedicated to Desbordes, who, according to Cocteau, exhibited naturally 'that *profound lightness* that opium can imitate a little' (original emphasis). Running to more than 100 pages and couched midway between the romanticism of Thomas de Quincey and the later realism of William Burroughs, this highly personal chronicle-cum-essay is really another White Paper, for Cocteau is putting on the table all the documents for and against opium. He explains that initially under the drug's spell he had lived some of his finest hours, during which he opened himself up to the deepest layers of his being and experienced feelings of euphoria. But opium was a 'living substance' and like all drugs exacts a price. The opium-eater is, as he puts it, eventually eaten by opium. Cocteau's accompanying drawings are dramatic and harrowing, half-phantasmatic and tortured in appearance, but always clear and sharp like shards of broken coral. Entire figures are composed of phallic, tube-like shapes resembling opium pipes and presented as 'cries of suffering in slow-motion' (the treatment is 'a wound in slow-motion').[1] There are frightening images of physical torture too: a naked body stretched out on a dissection table with smashed pupils removed from their orbits, screaming mouths, decapitated bodies and eyes protruding on stalks as though electrocuted with gauzes of black ink.

Opium is a totally original and uncompromising modern work bursting with typical Cocteau exaggerations, fantasies, coincidences and self-projections, yet also extremely sound in its medical observations, providing a dispassionate and disabused account of addiction and drug use in general. In an ever-expanding mushroom of penetrating wisdom, Cocteau declares that opium possesses the slow speed of silk and nourishes a half-dream. To smoke it is to 'leave the express train of life heading towards death'. So clear and controlled is the text that one wonders at times how and why Cocteau is not in even greater disarray, given the visceral extremity of the experience he is relating – the scattering of consciousness – and his 'nervous disequilibrium'. *Opium* unfolds instead miraculously like a slow-motion film providing luminous insights on the deep associations between life and creativity and the relations between aesthetics and ethics. Despite its multiple personal and artistic references (Proust, Gide, Moysès, Eisenstein, Buñuel, Wilde, Rousseau, Bergson, Mallarmé, Rilke, etc.), the style is ruthlessly pared down and stark, for Cocteau's stated wish here is to arrive at a form of 'numbers' beyond literature. This means in practice staccato sentences, apparent non sequiturs and jerky aphorisms interrupted only by smoother, semi-narrative passages. Interwoven in this pell-mell of assertions and speculations are personal anecdotes and frank confessions, updates on treatment, bouts of apparent free association, notes on dreams, continuous self-commentary and self-archiving (he talks already of his 'periods'), and what Cocteau calls *reportage* on the drug *du jour* that may serve as a guide to novices who do not recognize in opium's slowness one of the most dangerous forms of speed. The bubbling, cross-pollinating phrases and ideas of *Opium* will constitute a dynamic seedbed for all Cocteau's future work on the self, the body and dreams.

The curious irony of Cocteau's second detoxification is that things were now going rather well for him, and despite polite suggestions by Chanel, who was paying for the treatment, he did

Cocteau with pipe-cleaner figure. Photo by Man Ray, 1926.

not wish to leave the clinic. The pre-Surrealist author Raymond Roussel was also a co-resident, and figures like Gide were now paying him regular visits. Above all, the experience was laying the basis for a whole new set of works, beginning with a novel that was already starting to consume him. The closing part of *Opium* is really an advertisement for *Les Enfants terribles*, which he claimed was dictated to him by his 'unconscious self' at a rate of seven pages a day and which he needed just seventeen days to transcribe (the Cocteau publicity machine never took a day off!). With its tale of incestuous love and jealousy between a young, angelic Paul and his beautiful delinquent sister, *Les Enfants terribles* is clearly inspired by the Bourgoints, Jean and Jeanne, yet Cocteau also incorporates vital autobiographical ingredients accrued over the previous 40 years, including the image of a revolver with gushing blood, the school bully Dargelos engaged in a snowball fight in the Cité Monthiers, and an eternally cluttered bedroom. He also conveys an insulated, tree-house atmosphere suspended above time and space that characterized all the hotel rooms and apartments he resided in. In this adult-free sanctuary a group of four children become the initiates of their own secret society, founded on talismans, myths, whispers and innuendoes. Together with the collusion of their friends Gérard and Agathe, Paul and Elisabeth create a state of 'half-consciousness' and 'play' by requisitioning objects into their private mythology. Presented more as opposing instincts than developed characters, the two siblings become like actors performing 'their own masterpiece', observing a mysterious rhythm akin to the hallucinations of an opium-smoker. In taut, highly compressed prose, Cocteau brilliantly captures this intense, hermetic world of rituals, fetishes and theatricality, as well as the slip and tug of disgust, revolt, baiting narcissism and egotism. The infernally possessive and matriarchal Elisabeth, an 'iron virgin' in her white dress demanding, like the Sphinx, total submission, desires union with her weak brother and fantasizes his death, waiting for the moment when they will belong to each other completely. Their twin act of death unlocks the series of narrative double-binds and, with the final falling away of the bedroom screen, childhood is terminated. The apparent transfiguration of the closing moments, when the dying Paul imagines he is glimpsing Dargelos' 'immense gesture', suggests that Cocteau is trying yet again to exorcize the wound of his departed male lovers and companions.

When *Les Enfants terribles* was published in 1929 it met with immediate and almost unanimous critical and popular success, even hailed as a masterpiece by the *Nouvelle Revue française*. It would quickly become one of the crucial points of reference for the new generation precisely for celebrating the individuality, innocence and freedom of youth over the anonymity of society. Yet we are reminded once again of how success always came at a cost for Cocteau, so powerfully rooted is his work in personal reality. For Jean Bourgoint was now himself in a clinic due to drug abuse, while his sister had morphed from an elegant model into a virtual prostitute (rumours circulated of abortion, alcohol, narcotics, cures, a male lover's suicide). She would kill herself the following Christmas, probably from poisoning, on the night of a ball given by the wealthy Princesse Violette Murat, a purveyor of opium whom Cocteau once described as an obese monster. He now found himself accused in some quarters of influencing events with his portrayal of Elisabeth (although Cocteau wisely chose never to comment publicly on Jeanne's death).

When he finally emerged from the clinic he headed first to a hotel in the rue Bonaparte then settled into a small apartment at 9, rue Vignon behind the Madeleine. With this short and simple move he had finally broken away from his mother after a period of forty years. He also felt severely depressed and daunted, however, at the prospect of confronting the cold face of reality without the ready buffer of opium. Looking deathly pale he travelled with Desbordes down to Villefranche for the summer, but this quickly turned into a series of now familiar scenes of jealousy and reconciliation. Desbordes was indulging in escapades with companions of both sexes and finally smashed the car Cocteau had provided into a wall.

In November Cocteau set to work rehearsing Berthe Bovy for her solo role in *The Human Voice* (*La Voix humaine*), the third work he had been engaged on while at the clinic and presented at the end of *Opium* as a 'non-aesthetic act'. It was, in fact, a one-act monologue directly inspired by his frustrating experience with Desbordes. A woman on the verge of despair is speaking on the telephone to her long-term male lover with whom she is still infatuated, but who is due to be married the next day to someone else. This is their act of farewell. The lover pretends to be alone, yet he is actually with his fiancée, his deceit motivated in equal measure by cowardice and kindness. Cocteau conveys brilliantly the fatal inevitability and bleak horror of the drama, which is heightened by the idiosyncrasies of the modern telephone. Divested of his usual stage tricks and dislocating strategies, *The Human Voice* is perhaps Cocteau's most deeply moving and human play. During the first preview at the Comédie-Française in February 1930, however, no sooner had Bovy begun her monologue in her nightgown and negligée on the heavily draped set designed by Christian Bérard than someone in a box cried out: 'It's obscene! Enough! Enough! It's Desbordes on the other end of the line!' The perpetrator was Paul Eluard, who found himself instantly set upon by Cocteau groupies and evicted from the theatre (the scandal was eventually resolved amicably in the administrator's office). The outburst can be accounted for certainly in terms of artistic jealousy: like other Surrealists Eluard thought that Cocteau was now far too successful and had entered the theatrical establishment. Indeed, the play was a great hit both critically and commercially, and henceforth Cocteau would increasingly surround himself with actors and singers from the entertainment as opposed to literary world. But there was also a highly personal aspect to the affair, for Eluard had by now become the partner of Valentine Hugo, who had separated from her husband. Valentine became immediately a constant object of tension and rivalry between Eluard and Cocteau. She had effectively chosen the Surrealists over Cocteau, whom she reproached for personal ingratitude and even refused him entry into her flat, which lay directly above his at 9, rue Vignon. Cocteau took the break-up very badly indeed, since Valentine was the one woman since *Parade* to whom he had been close, with the exception of his mother. Perhaps part of the problem for Eluard watching *The Human Voice* – and in

this he was not alone – was the degree of acceptance and understanding imputed by Cocteau to the abandoned woman, a fact not
entirely plausible in the heterosexual context portrayed (Cocteau
himself acknowledged it was difficult to grasp). In fact, the play
must be read as a thinly disguised account of a real gay relationship,
where the confines of institutionalized marriage were not (at least
during that period) an issue.

Towards the end of *Opium* Cocteau had signalled that his next
major work would be a film, and again he was true to his word.
He had already made in 1925 a slapstick-style short entitled *Jean
Cocteau fait du cinéma*. This had been inspired in part by the young
actor Fabien Haziza, who starred in it and was also possibly for
a brief moment his lover (like the film itself, which was almost
immediately lost, precise details about this relationship are lacking). Cocteau's absolute faith in cinema as the tenth muse and a
vehicle for pure poetry and source of epiphanic power would now
summon from him all his talents. The result was the first multi-
media film, *The Blood of a Poet* (*Le Sang d'un poète*). Reworking
familiar themes that had already begun to congeal into the Cocteau
legend, the film charts the trials and tribulations of a Poet, the
influence of his childhood and the transformations he must undergo in order to achieve immortality. The work's genesis is the stuff
of film legend: the rich aristocratic and film-loving patrons, the
Vicomte Charles de Noailles and his adventurous wife Marie-Laure,
gave Cocteau, like Luis Buñuel, a million francs to make a short
film (the result in Buñuel's case was the Surrealist classic, *L'Age
d'or*). It featured a largely non-professional cast, including the
Chilean playboy Enrique Rivero as the Poet, Desbordes as the
Poet's friend in Louis xv costume, the American model Lee Miller
as the human statue, the black jazz dancer Féral Benga as the
guardian angel, and Barbette as a member of the audience. The
hermaphrodite was played by Francis Rose, a member of Cocteau's
Villefranche set, and the novice cameraman Georges Périnal was

chosen virtually at random. Auric composed the music and the final editing was executed by Cocteau himself.

I have explored at length elsewhere both the troubled production and the artistic and technical innovations of this mesmerizing black-and-white short, one of the first sound films produced in France and in which Cocteau experimented with the full potential of the medium.[2] When at the very start Cocteau as the masked Author draws back his open arm he effectively becomes a Master of Ceremonies, welcoming the viewer into his private club, the Hôtel des Folies-dramatiques, where the various theatrical follies, 'pantomime' effects, cinematic tricks (slow and reverse motion, superimpositions, etc.) and 'tragic gags' will unfold like a series of happenings. *The Blood of a Poet* is a veritable cinema of the senses and at times lushly queer. The assorted effects of disembodied lips bubbling in the palm of the Poet's hand, the visceral contact between human flesh and the cold dingy wall, the close-up of Dargelos wetting his lips in oral satisfaction during the orgiastic riot, the sound of blood oozing out of the mouth of his prey like sexual moaning, the rolling of bare muscles in a male back caked in sweat, together with other elemental images of opium, snow and slush, are all physically sensuous and erotic. Further, Cocteau loads the image with movements, sounds and sensations in one dense, composite frame in order to transform it into a dazzling ideogram with multiple textures and calibrations. The pace is often excruciatingly slow as if itself 'under the influence', a fact that bewildered many in the initial audience, who scrambled to make sense of its highly personal allegories. Indeed, with so many traces of Cocteau's own life in play here, including the suicide of his father, flying lessons with Roland Garros and opium, critics then and now have elaborated vast theories. For some, the Poet's suicide by revolver during a game of cards is to be interpreted as his response to failing at the heterosexual game of love, since in an earlier sequence he had lost his ace of hearts to a young boy. For others, the film

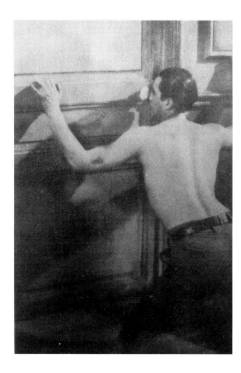

'The Poet' (Enrique
Rivero) peering
through the keyhole in
the Hôtel des Folies-
dramatiques. A still
from *Le Sang d'un poète*
(1932).

represents more a sublimation of the unrealized love that Cocteau
felt for intimate friends such as Radiguet, the final episode in particular appearing to offer an apotheosis of the gay artist by revealing
how the image of one adolescent's power over another – the wound
of homosexual attraction and its 'fatal' consequences – can coalesce
with the image of the mysterious creative force that traumatizes the
Poet from youth (the two images are expressed through the single
symbol of the angel). For the critic Milorad, who knew Cocteau
personally, the primary issue was the (symbolic) death of the child
and the (real) death of the father: all Cocteau's work, he argued,
replaces a real complex – the Oedipal murder of the father – and
represents an attempt to redeem the Oedipal crime. Cocteau
himself refrained from ever offering a full interpretation, though

mischievously suggested that Freud had devoted a whole article to the film.

How did all this relate to Cocteau's personal relationship with Desbordes? In June 1930 Cocteau stayed with Desbordes and Bérard in Toulon, first at the Villa Blanche of the playwright Edouard Bourdet and his wife Denise. With the arrival of the recently married Auric it was a time for talking theatre, playing poker and *bilboquet*, and indulging in transvestite skits and naked *divertisse-ments*. But Cocteau's relations with Desbordes degenerated after he himself formed a liaison with a 26-year-old sailor known as 'Pas-de-Chance' (literally 'No Luck') (real name Henri Fefeu), with whom he was often seen frolicking about in Toulon while he paraded his newly adopted Malagasy pet monkey Petit-Crû. It was a strange sight: Pas-de-Chance with his open tattooed chest, Cocteau dressed in a white bicycle costume combined with a black collar and tie. Cocteau could play the slut too if he wished! Their brief affair ended abruptly when Pas-de-Chance lived up to his name and was arrested for petty thieving. This served only to plunge Cocteau further into the *bas-fonds* of seaboard society, where he would now smoke up to 30 pipes of opium a day. In September 1931 he was struck down by typhoid and spent a week in hospital before convalescing at the Villa Blanche, the loggia of which he decorated out of gratitude a year later with drawings of sailors. Desbordes, meanwhile, was settling down with an older woman. The problem for Cocteau was not just that there was a lack of reciprocity in their love, but that Desbordes fell so lamentably short of Radiguet. No real creative intensity had existed between the two that could be transmuted into artistic symbols, a fact underlined by the self-enclosed world of *The Human Voice*. They parted ways in 1933.

Significantly, Cocteau never wrote much, if at all, about Desbordes in later life. What had begun so promisingly as his first fully fledged gay relationship never constituted one of his *grandes amitiés* and left him instead feeling a profound sense of personal

Cocteau with his pet monkey, Petit-Crû, in Toulon, 1931.

and artistic disappointment. Desbordes continued to write, producing during the early 1930s several novels and plays, as well as a study of the Marquis de Sade, and he married a pharmacist in 1937, for no other reason perhaps than to have direct access to a regular supply of drugs. But it was World War Two, when he entered the Polish Resistance as 'Duroc', that brought out the best in him. At the start of July 1944 he was arrested and eventually murdered after being tortured at the hands of the Gestapo and the French militia for refusing to divulge military secrets. For Cocteau, who did not learn of these facts until much later, Desbordes had finally redeemed himself and was reborn as a national hero.

15

Tripping Across the World

The deteriorating relationship with Desbordes, who was drifting ever more towards the opposite sex, was just one reason for Cocteau's troubled start to the new decade. Valentine Hugo still contrived to avoid him even at 9, rue Vignon, and from 1934 onwards he would stay for short periods in nearby hotels such as the Madeleine-Palace Hôtel and the Hôtel de Castille in the rue Cambon. He was also trying to maintain a healthy distance from Sachs, who had fleeced him of money by selling his letters (notably from Proust) and other personal documents. Such, however, was the brazen effrontery of these acts that they actually re-endeared Sachs to Cocteau, who never sought prosecution. As for Jean Bourgoint, who had just been dumped by a rich Egyptian and was on the verge of suicide, Cocteau now rarely saw him. Meanwhile, Cocteau's ageing mother was becoming progressively more pious, supplementing daily Mass with classes in religious instruction. Finally, his other original soul-sister, Anna de Noailles, with whom he continued to share an uneasy relationship, died in 1933. Having been effectively shunned by avant-garde intellectual circles, who remained highly suspicious of the *beau monde* with which he was still associated, Cocteau still made it his business to be in regular contact with high society figures such as Marie-Laure de Noailles, Etienne de Beaumont and Lady Diana Cooper, wife of the British ambassador. Yet as the world slid into financial and political crisis provoked by the Wall Street crash and its aftermath, Cocteau retreated further into his own private grotto with its opium-induced time warp. His face had become irreversibly gaunt with a yellow cast, and he started again to receive guests in bed, even dining there. This was the Depression Cocteau-style.

A bizarre experience occurred in 1932, however, that left him feeling all the more disconnected: his improbable affair with Princess Natalie Paley, grand-niece of the Tsar Alexander III. Although married to the eminent couturier Lucien Lelong, the elegant and cinema-loving Paley began to visit Cocteau alone in the rue Vignon in the winter of 1932 and to partake of opium served by his Chinese 'boy', Biou. He proclaimed a wish to marry her and even father a son (a son with a suitably royal pedigree to boot), even though he had been made virtually impotent through opium. There was much gossip (Cocteau was still with Desbordes, at least nominally) and Paley's husband immediately sued for divorce. She travelled to Switzerland to reflect on the situation (Cocteau claimed it was to have an abortion) and her final answer was a resounding no. Throughout most of this saga Cocteau became a laughing stock of Paris society, yet he clearly experienced real feelings for Paley and suffered once again the acute pain of rejection. It provoked from him some ugly misogyny, as when he remarked that women were 'the killers of poets' children', later referring to Paley as the Princess Fafner after the legendary Norse ogre. He also took pleasure in backing a photograph of Paley with a larger-than-life depiction of male fellatio carrying the caption: 'Indecency is *our* heroism' (emphasis original). All sorted then! In truth, Cocteau took a long while to recover from the collapse of his paternal hopes and claimed henceforth always to be looking for his 'lost son'.

Much of 1933 was taken up by renewed attempts at self-recovery, including summer health-spa treatments first in Paris, then in Nantes, before he checked in at the end of the year to the Salem clinic to begin his third cure. He intended now to work through his double grief over Desbordes and Paley. It was with typical resourcefulness, however, that at the same time he took on a new, 22-year-old secretary called Marcel Khill, the son of an Algerian soldier and a Norman peasant whom he had been admiring on the beach at Toulon. Cocteau had managed to entice Khill away from his finder, a French naval officer called Tranchant Lunel, who had plucked him from a road gang and had been maintaining him at his home, where, in Arab costume, he supplied opium pipes and performed other domestic duties. When Lunel died that year, Cocteau immediately stepped in and took Khill back to the rue Vignon, much to the fury of Desbordes and another long-time intimate and aspiring favourite of Cocteau, the tall, muscled and elegant Franz Thomassin. (Thomassin managed to befriend Khill and thus retain close contact with his appointed prince, although – and we are reminded again of how Cocteau attracted volatile youths like moths to a light bulb – he soon had a breakdown and cut off one of his fingers in despair, which he sent to Cocteau.) Although uneducated, Khill was a strong and lively personality, witty and cheeky like a clever elf and possessing a fine temperament. He was also extremely handsome and swarthily masculine, or, as Cocteau liked to put it, 'possessing feminine beauty without being effeminate'. For the first time in a long while Cocteau experienced the pure pleasures of the skin and happily allowed himself to be distracted by Khill, who enjoyed a good time out on the town dancing and driving and mixing with the crowds. In most of the line drawings that Cocteau produced of Khill he appears stunningly sensual with his feline features, moody eyes and wise, intelligent air. One drawing of Khill naked while smoking opium could not be more warm and direct, and it can be likened to photographs taken by Cecil Beaton in 1935 in which he is portrayed smoking and cavorting with Cocteau in a kind of mutual shadow play with no hint of inhibition or shame on either side.

Uncomplicated by any literary pretensions on Khill's part, a solid friendship soon developed between the two men and it was perhaps the most genuinely erotic of Cocteau's entire life, certainly the most physically charged. Khill could swing either way sexually so long as he assumed the dominant role, yet he was never simply a wild *fauve* for Cocteau, whatever some people may have wished to believe. He was actively encouraged by his older lover to paint and draw and write, although this did not stop Cocteau from tattooing Khill's bust and face with a pencil for a photograph taken by George Platt Lynes in 1936, as if Khill were his own literary creation. And Khill was more than content to be directed by Cocteau, as when he performed a small role as a messenger from Corinth in Cocteau's new play, *The Infernal Machine*, which premiered in Paris in April 1934. The production, for which Bérard provided costumes and dramatic decor, featured not only renowned actors such as Jean-Pierre Aumont and Louis Jouvet (who produced it) but also, in a highly ironic piece of casting, Paley as the Sphinx. Ploughing the furrow initiated by *Orpheus*, *The Infernal Machine* transported high classical legend to the level of a situation comedy set on a rich estate in the Midi with

The premiere of *The Infernal Machine* in Paris, April 1934. The actors include Cocteau's then lover Marcel Khill, second from right.

Cocteau with Edith Piaf. Photo by Serge Lido, *c*. 1938.

elements of satire and farce sustained by gimmicks, shocks and repeated double entendres (the soldiers are kitted in contemporary uniform, speak slang and play jazz music). The central message, as always for Cocteau, was that nature is a vast and incomprehensible machine devised by the infernal gods to ensnare man. The untrained Khill survived just four nights.

The Infernal Machine achieved relative critical success and even the conservative press appreciated its good taste and bravura, especially regarding the theme of incest, yet it failed to attract the general public that Cocteau was counting on. For Cocteau had finally registered that, with fascism sweeping across Europe and the birth of a new Leftist Popular Front in France that was transforming Surrealists like Eluard and Aragon into Communists, the artistic tide was now turning back towards realism. He suddenly wished to have direct contact with contemporary popular culture, however implausible such a prospect might seem due to his timeless status as a Poet. Indeed, his ghostly and emaciated state seemed to preclude any possible identification with the hearty goodness

Cocteau with his lover Marcel Khill (back) and the costume and set designer Christian Bérard in 1938.

of *le peuple*. He became fascinated, however, by Kurt Weill and Marlene Dietrich, and soon began to write songs for the *chanteuse* Suzy Solidor, a lesbian idol from Montmartre, as well as for the Berlin singer Marianne Oswald, an exponent of 'existential' blues who sang – or rather 'spoke' – the monologues he composed for her, such as *Anna la Bonne* and *La Dame de Monte-Carlo*. For the actress Arletty he wrote a radio script called *L'Ecole des veuves* (The School for Widows), while for Edith Piaf he would later write a new version of *The Human Voice* called *Le Bel Indifférent*. Cocteau was still an avid connoisseur of the music hall, but it was now the working-class Bobigny variety that excited him. He was genuinely moving forwards in his work, a fact also confirmed by his meeting in 1934 with the new poet and novelist Louise de Vilmorin, about whom he wrote that she was a kind of marvel, 'a woman who invents illustrious things . . . new, fresh, comic, poetic, fierce, and miraculously light'.[1] De Vilmorin was a beautiful free spirit blessed with a powerful imagination who wrote expressly about lost love, childhood and death. She quickly became Cocteau's new confidante and spiritual sister, and he wrote that were he rich (and presumably heterosexual) he would marry his 'Loulou' and they would live together (instead, she chalked up a list of illustrious lovers that included André Malraux).

It was after reading Cocteau's affectionate and witty new book of memoirs *Portraits-Souvenir* (*Paris Album, 1900–1914*), in particular his recollections of the original Paris stage version of *Around the World in 80 Days*, that Khill proposed to his lover that they attempt the same feat for themselves. Cocteau, who had just turned 47, was thrilled by the epic potential of such a project and sold the idea to *Paris-soir* of a series of regular despatches charting the trip's progress (the instalments were later collected in a book entitled *Round the World Again in 80 Days* (*Mon premier voyage: tour du monde en 80 jours*). Gleefully assuming the role of Dr Phileas Fogg, Cocteau left Paris on 29 March 1936 with Khill as his trusty French valet Passepartout. Written in a direct first-person, the text is a hybrid of reportage and cultural and anthropological instruction, with Cocteau/Fogg imparting to Khill/Passepartout his knowledge and wisdom. The recounting of fantastic tales and marvellous sights is intercut with slices of dialogue between the two, and Cocteau is never less than professional in his attention to the telling detail and image. Yet how much did Cocteau actually see? New York, for example, is compressed into a set of very selective highlights: Harlem, Coney Island and Minsky's Burlesque. Carrying his opium cloud around with him, Cocteau did not so much engage with the Other, even in the skewed exoticist terms of Pierre Loti or Victor Segalen, as simply find himself the Same wherever he went, thereby making the trip more an exercise in self-extension and self-promotion according to the rhythms and *longueurs* of opium. On the positive side, he engaged like a pioneer with the 'counter-time' of opium and its 'immobile speed', which he insisted was the only way to gain access to both the world of the Invisible and that of one's own individual rhythm. The downside, however, was that although alert to the colonial contradictions of the

Cocteau as Phileas Fogg on the liner Ile de France, 1936.

places he visited, notably the eastern/western paradoxes of Japan, which was then still under martial law, Cocteau blithely reduced the world to a mass of speechless ceremonies, improbable anecdotes and accounts of meetings 'written in the stars'. He gives the game away himself at one moment when he declares: 'My function was to colonize the unknown, to learn its patois'. Happy to deceive himself like any other globetrotter that he was encountering real people in their native lands when dining with the 'coolies' in China, he also indulged in all kinds of self-regarding poses, at one point in Japan even projecting himself as a womanizer with a young geisha (Why? Two other geishas were at the same time apparently fighting over Khill).

The trip included other sorts of missed encounters too, notably on 11 May with Charlie Chaplin and his wife Paulette Godard on the ship crossing the Pacific to the United States. Two versions of the event exist: for Chaplin the first meeting was over-intense and exhausting; for Cocteau it was a pure delight of conversation born of instant respect between two poets. Either way, it proved awkward for both men and thereafter they deliberately avoided each other, resorting to excuses of sickness. The return to France in mid-June provoked in Cocteau one of his less impressive natural defaults: nationalism. France, he concluded, was 'the most admirable land-scape of all we had seen on our way round the globe', and once Paris, 'a city built to man's measure, a city of human emotions', had restored its natural sense of 'rhythm and ceremonial', it would 'emit once again those phosphorescent gleams, that dazzle and mystify mankind'.[2]

A marathon trip across the world was not the only remarkable feat that Khill conjured out of Cocteau. One day in early 1937 he brought home a completely new type of challenge: the boxer 'Panama' Al Brown. Brown had once been the first Hispanic bantamweight champion of the world, but two years before had lost his crown to the Italian Balthazar Sangchili in Valencia. He was now, at the age of just 35, a down-and-out sax player in a Pigalle nightclub, forlorn, demoralized and wracked by a lethal combina-tion of opium, champagne, syphilis, painkillers and young boys. Cocteau naturally recognized himself in this naive, lost and perse-cuted figure who, when performing, somehow transmogrified himself and became as if airborne. Improbably, but as always spon-taneously and with unfathomed energy, Cocteau decided on the spot to become Brown's manager and assist in his return to the ring and then recovery of his title. Cocteau was motivated to do this by a number of factors, most obviously the sheer novelty of the project and Brown's tall, muscled body and athletic grace (it appears that Brown was willing to reciprocate Cocteau's sexual attentions and at one point they shared a hotel room together). Brown's triumph over his sceptics and persecutors would, Cocteau believed, also offer ultimate proof of his own unique poetic ingenuity. And so it proved. He immediately ensured that Brown was not expelled from France by writing directly to the President, and Chanel stepped in yet again to pay for the boxer's drug rehabilitation treatment. Cocteau then put Brown through a rigorous training regime, including solitary confinement for a month at the Sainte-Anne asylum and a training camp in Aubigny. Under his exclusive and unstinting care (Cocteau did nothing by half measures when suitably inspired), 'Panama' Brown finally stepped back into the ring in September. Six months later, on 4 March 1938, at a re-run match in Paris at the Palais des Sports attended by invited members of the show-business world (actors such as Jean Gabin, Raimu and Robert Toutain), Brown finally won back his world crown from Sangchili. Having already written extensively about Brown in a series of newspaper articles in which he celebrated 'the poetry of boxing', Cocteau now published an 'Open Letter' advising him to quit while ahead. Brown eventually did stop fighting in 1942, and Cocteau was on hand at the Cirque Médrano to choreograph a shadow-boxing dance act based on a scene from his own *Antigone* with a jazz accompaniment by black musicians. In a show-stopping number that he took on tour with the Cirque Amar, Brown would enter the stage in the same long dressing gown he had worn on the night of the comeback fight and suddenly throw it off to reveal an elegant white tail-suit. It did not all work out as planned, however. Exhausted by this nightly performance, Brown eventually returned to Harlem, where he was reduced to working as a dish-washer and doing the odd sparring. He died penniless of tuberculosis three years later at the age of 48.

As for Cocteau, although his mounting hotel bills continued to be met by Chanel, he found himself reduced to writing journalism, giving public lectures and even selling off personal possessions to finance his drug habit. And all the while opium continued to

Cocteau (holding the umbrella) with the boxer 'Panama' Al Brown and others, 1937.

deplete his energies and stamina and exacerbate his increasing propensity to mythomania. His artistic project appeared derailed. Yet Cocteau was also now engaging successfully with some of the rising stars of French popular culture and collaborating on the communist daily evening paper *Ce soir* founded by Aragon, even penning a column from March to June 1937. He also began to sign petitions and produced his own equivalent of *Guernica* in support of Spanish refugees: a huge charcoal drawing, entitled *La Peur donnant des ailes au courage*, of five semi-naked and lubricious raw figures spattered with blood on a bed sheet. As for Khill, he was now becoming increasingly undone by opium and turning more fractious, so desperate was he to escape the tentacles of Cocteau's custodianship. It was rumoured that out of frustration he was starting to begin quarrels with his older lover and even inflict body blows. Like Radiguet and Desbordes before him, Khill eventually reverted to the heterosexual model and took up with an actress. His fate was sealed by a similarly tragic turn of events: he died in 1940 from a stray German bullet while serving with the French army in Alsace. The event occurred just a few hours after Pétain had signed the Armistice, the proclamation of which had been delayed in Khill's military sector. Cocteau would be informed of the full details only a year later.

16

Enter Apollo

It was in the room at the Hôtel Castille which Cocteau shared in 1937 with Al Brown and Marcel Khill that a dashingly handsome man half his age (an 'Antinoüs sprung from the people', as Cocteau later put it) came to hear him read aloud from his new play, *Oedipe roi*. Cocteau had first set eyes on Jean Marais at a casting session, yet he claimed he had been drawing him well before, proof that their meeting was preordained, or rather that Marais corresponded exactly to his pre-established idea of beauty incarnate, with his athletic build, perfectly chiselled face, blond hair, blue eyes and brilliant smile (the clichés roll out all too quickly with Marais). Marais, an aspiring actor and consummate opportunist, had managed to gatecrash the session, and Cocteau was immediately drawn by his winning combination of erotic presence and slight awkwardness. Cocteau chose him to play Oedipus, although other members of the cast promptly ensured that he gave Marais the minor – and completely silent – role of Chorus. Three weeks later, Cocteau ordered Marais to come urgently to the Hôtel Castille, where, as the legend goes, he told him: 'I am in love with you'. 'I am in love with you too' was Marais' automatic response, a lie. In rehearsals Cocteau was already imagining him naked in strips of cloth to maximize his raw physicality and instinctive sensuality, and this proved a scandalous touch in performance at the Théâtre Antoine, accentuated by Marais' rather mediocre acting. Booing ensued, yet Marais prevailed, and Cocteau respected his fortitude.

Shortly after he read aloud to Marais the first act of another play, *Les Chevaliers de la table ronde* (*The Knights of the Round Table*), a piece of cardboard cut-out medieval imaginary based on the theme of the Grail, which became in Cocteau's hands a personal symbol of the impossible, that is, harmony and self-equilibrium. At the Théâtre de l'Oeuvre in October 1937 Marais triumphed in the starring role of Galahad, for which he sported a ripped tunic revealing his bare breast. So began a long and exceptional collaboration between Cocteau and Marais that included not only their extensive work together on stage and screen, but also their many texts, poems and drawings, on, about and for each other.

Cocteau had started the year in desperate straits, not only physically weak but also extremely vulnerable mentally. He now saw himself spectacularly rejuvenated by this new boy-man. Marais, nicknamed 'Jeannot', was always of the order of a miracle for Cocteau, linked in mysterious ways with *le merveilleux* and possessing a quasi-religious dimension. The fact that Marais came from a poor Cherbourg family raised in the art of deception (his mother was a kleptomaniac) only increased Cocteau's fascination. In early 1938 the two stayed for a while at the Hôtel de la Poste in Montargis, near the small village of Saint-Benoît-sur-Loire, where Max Jacob now lived in a presbytery. Later that spring they moved into a small apartment together at 9, Place de la Madeleine, before then leaving for Toulon and the villa at Pramousquier where Cocteau had spent the summer of 1922 with Radiguet. It was here that Cocteau inducted Marais into his artistic world and compiled lists of writers for him to read (number one, of course, Radiguet). The young actor began now to discover new things while displaying in Cocteau's dazzled eyes every kind of virtue, kindness and practical or moral sense. For Cocteau had fallen completely in love with Jeannot, who seemed also to want the best for him. As well as penning some highly lyrical poetry about Marais, Cocteau drew him obsessively, establishing in his work a whole

Jean Marais as the Chorus in Cocteau's *Oedipe Roi*, Paris, 1937.

new tradition of rather artificial 'Greco-Marais' profiles. Their relationship was initially physical and they behaved like a couple of young lovers, for the good-natured Marais was more than happy to be intimate with Cocteau. Yet Cocteau soon began to doubt that Jeannot spontaneously desired him, surmising that if the young Eros was struggling to give himself to him at night it was because he wished to reserve for others his 'blond strength'. Since Cocteau could not actually prevent Marais from going out, his only option was to demean the other young men whom Marais was meeting. Slowly but surely, Marais deserted Cocteau's bed and Cocteau rationalized the situation by admitting that it was probably better to be deceived by a few men 'passing through' than to enter into full-scale rivalry with a woman. He now felt impelled to write

elegiac poems, which he placed under Marais' door at night to
be read on his return. In fact, Marais soon established his own
bachelor pad elsewhere and sometimes returned to embrace
Cocteau for the sole benefit of the photographers. The noble knight
was gradually morphing into an executioner, yet it never deterred
Cocteau as Marais' self-appointed mentor and impresario from
pursuing his sacred artistic duty of grooming him for success on
the Paris stage.

Marais, to repeat, was not an actor blessed with psychological
depth and he appeared destined for mainly physical roles. Moreover, having failed to enter the Paris Conservatoire, he had never
received formal training, apart from some odd acting classes with
Charles Dullin. But this meant, theoretically at least, that he was
totally malleable, and Cocteau took it upon himself to transform
his *jeune premier* from a middling actor into a living idol of the Paris
stage. Marais' performance in 1938 in *Les Parents terribles* was to
prove historic for them both. Cocteau had written the play according to Jeannot's express requirements. Fearing typecasting as an
action hero, he wished to play a nervous and confused man, not
obviously attractive and even prone to tears. At times the stress
reached unbearable proportions as Cocteau pushed still further
the oppressive, impossible relationship between Michael and his
mother Yvonne (partly based on Marais' own mother, Rosalie).
With Cocteau's full support and in front of his eclectic 'family'
who attended the final dress rehearsal on 14 November 1938 at the
Théâtre des Ambassadeurs (Khill, Desbordes, Maritain, Picasso,
etc.), Marais threw all caution to the wind and broke away from
the contemporary 'modern' acting style imposed by the dictates
of cinema. His was a totally new dramatic method focused on the
body in action and, in the words of Cocteau, 'without taste'. It
shocked those in the audience who perceived only bluff and insolence, but seduced and disarmed the majority. Describing Marais
as an 'amalgam' of different acting elements and styles, rather than

perfection itself, Cocteau emphasized the young man's natural 'fire' and excess, his professional honesty, his capacity for self-criticism and his total investment in a role. He also ascribed Marais' hypnotic charisma and magnetic hold over spectators of both sexes not to his evident sensuality but to the childhood that 'inhabited' him. As for Marais, he regarded his Apollonian looks more as a natural curse than a blessing, and this certainly helps to explain his desire to take on very different and 'unnatural' roles under Cocteau's aegis, most brilliantly in the film *La Belle et la bête*.

Buoyed by the artistic and commercial success of *Les Parents terribles*, Marais returned to the Place de la Madeleine to live with Cocteau. When he fell seriously ill Cocteau looked after him and would not let him out of his sight, earning in the process the respect of Marais' still suspicious mother. But no sooner had Cocteau re-established 'normal' relations with Jeannot than the young man fell head over heels for Denham Foots, an American dandy who also dabbled in the theatre. Once again, Marais began to stray from the conjugal bedroom, leaving Cocteau traumatized to the point of taking it out on himself. And the threat of personal scandal loomed when, in Toulon in July 1938, in the company of Marais (who did not smoke opium), Cocteau was busted for drugs and taken for questioning. At the trial seven months later, with his ever-loyal young courtier Franz Thomassin supporting him in the public gallery, he escaped astonishingly with only a fine.

In the spring of 1939 Cocteau headed south-west to Dax, where he produced an unexpected sequel to *Le Potomak* entitled *La Fin du Potomak*, a humorous yet unsure and darkly disturbing novel (his last as it would turn out) comprising 'anecdotes' of his own life and work since 1914. Cocteau then travelled with Marais and a young acolyte, Roger Lannes, to Le Piquey, where together they created another version of happy family life: Cocteau wrote while Jeannot drove and painted and Lannes read. Marais would continue to spend his weekends with Foots, and all Cocteau could do

Cocteau with a bust of himself by Apelles Fenosa, 1939.

was to make Marais agree that whatever happened he (Cocteau) was his sole confidant. He proclaimed to the world that their relationship was 'absolutely pure': his ephebe had become his son whose development he would continue to supervise and who, in return, would help him try to live like a saint. Marais, meanwhile, declared privately to friends that he felt only 'affectionate feelings' for Cocteau, who physically was now becoming increasingly grey and wan, like a spectre haunting his own destiny. In fact, Cocteau, who had all the while been wishing to *live his work*, now felt that his work was eating him whole ('Jean Cocteau is dead and lives to frighten you' was the caption he gave to one new painting). Yet Cocteau was not going to kill himself over this. Under the right

Cocteau with his bust of Marais as a faun, 1951.

lights he could, after all, muster just about enough energy still to smooth out his wizened face and become again 'Cocteau'.

When France suddenly declared war on Germany on 3 September 1939, Cocteau found himself in Saint-Tropez with Marais, who was mobilized as a reservist and sent to the Somme. Cocteau returned home to Paris and 'slummed' it at the Ritz at Chanel's invitation. He was determined during this honeymoon period of Franco-German cooperation to continue his artistic projects undisturbed by daily political and military events. Hence, with the aid of opium, which allowed him to indulge in fantasies of universal creative harmony extending beyond the borders of geography or politics, he focused on his most crucial concern, Jeannot, a large bronze bust of whom he was now completing that represented Marais as half-god and Adonis, a faun-like apparition with glowing hair and large, stag-like eyes. He fretted about Marais' well-being and safety, of course, but with the *drôle de guerre* quickly over followed by the signing of the Armistice, Marais was demobbed and returned to Paris. Together, the two would now spend the war in the relative peace and security of the small apartment at 36, rue de Montpensier in the Palais-Royal, which Cocteau started to rent in the spring of 1940, just across the way from Colette, who became one of his closest female friends. The routine and calm was interrupted only by Cocteau's brief exodus that summer from Paris to Perpignan when the French government decamped to Bordeaux (he duly returned like thousands of other Parisians in September). Having signed up in the early stages of the war to fight the Germans, Marais had initially wished to join the Resistance, but this was denied on the grounds that his relationship with Cocteau would constitute a security risk (it was feared – correctly – that Cocteau would talk too much).

In June 1940 Cocteau entered into a different type of arrange-ment with Marais when Marais' new lover, Paul Morihien, moved in with them with Cocteau's full consent. How could Cocteau have refused the personal wishes of his young god Jeannot? Since they were no longer lovers in the physical sense, he did not wish to deprive Marais of any happiness, which, in Cocteau's particular romantic way of thinking, was also his own. Moreover, the straight-seeming and athletic Morihien was an all-round nice guy, at once respectful and prudent, and he immediately slotted into the role of Cocteau's official secretary. Together the trio functioned like a small inseparable family (although this did not prevent Marais from continuing to seek sex on the side). In the harsh opinion of some, then and now, Cocteau's relationship with Marais was that of a *faux couple*, in the same way that Cocteau's own life and career had been intrinsically false. Yet despite the complicated relations between them involving other men, Cocteau and Marais enjoyed a

Cocteau with Marais and his dog Moulouk, early 1940s.

strong and caring friendship that cannot be relegated to the category of *faux amour*. And for all the lingering problems of insecurity, hurt and jealousy that Cocteau experienced, their working and affective relations provided them both with a degree of artistic stability and continuity that, for Cocteau, was always the bottom line. It would reap full rewards a few years later with the film scripted (and part directed) by Cocteau, *The Eternal Return* (*L'Eternel retour*), which transformed Marais in the leading role as the beautiful doomed lover Patrice into one of French cinema's first male heart-throbs. On its release in October 1943, Marais' heraldic Jacquard sweater created a tidal wave in men's fashion, and crowds of young women began to besiege the apartment building. The film's extraordinary success, which also featured Marais' dog Moulouk, had a powerful effect on the public perception of the relationship between the two. Marais was now extremely eager to be seen with Cocteau, for it was a kind of implicit avowal of their unique relationship, at once half-brotherly and half-conjugal, and imbued with the mythic aura of the finally transcendent couple of *The Eternal Return*. Whatever the precise status of their private life, and despite their mutual reserve when out together in public (Cocteau could tone up or down his slightly effeminate and artfully campish gestures to suit the occasion), they became the first out-gay artistic couple to achieve popular celebrity in France and were even championed in the pages of *Vogue*. Whilst never claiming to be a gay figure-head or 'sublime national queen', as the writer Angelo Rinaldi later wryly put it, Cocteau helped to project a confident gay sensi-bility, actively supporting after the war the first official gay asso-ciation, Arcadie.

The relations between Cocteau's life and art were arguably at their most successful and productive in the films on which Marais collaborated. It was Marais, after all, who encouraged Cocteau to return to the cinema as a director after their spectacular success together with *The Eternal Return*, resulting in such remarkable films during the mid-to-late 1940s as *La Belle et la bête*, *Les Parents terribles* and *The Eagle with Two Heads* (*L'Aigle à deux têtes*). The last, written first as a play by Cocteau in 1943 in a manor in Brittany while Marais painted and Morihien cut wood (domestic bliss personified), was created like *Les Parents terribles* according to Marais' express wishes: to be silent in Act I, cry with joy in Act II and fall backwards down a set of stairs in Act III. In this tale of political and romantic intrigue a young poet-cum-anarchist Stanislas breaks into the royal apartment of Queen Natasha on a mission to kill her; they both end up dead because of the impossible nature of their absolute love. Offered by Cocteau as a Christmas present to Marais, the play reflects the intensity but also the pathos and frustration of their relationship in some of the explosive exchanges between the Queen and Stanislas, who is left helpless and alone and suffocating in love.

Despite Marais' diligence, hard work and genuine awe of Cocteau (he always declared that he owed everything to Cocteau, a father figure who both formed and transformed him), there was actually a constant tension to their collaboration. In later interviews Marais explained that he had struggled against Cocteau in early stage productions such as *The Knights of the Round Table* precisely because he did not wish to become a mere cog in Cocteau's artistic machine. He made the point repeatedly that the collaborative process with Cocteau proved easier in the cinema because he was mature enough – and by implication humble enough – to receive Cocteau's directions and interpret them in his own fashion. By the time of *Orphée* he was able to wax lyrical about Cocteau's direction, or rather lack of it, celebrating in the process an ideal Coctelian harmony of life and work: 'His [Cocteau's] method is different: to live, speak, look at beautiful things together, to cultivate the soul without thinking of art – which in his eyes is no more than a margin of life.'[1] As for Cocteau, in his book of 1951 entitled simply *Jean Marais*, a comprehensive and admiring but also impressively objective portrait of Marais' life and artistic activities (including poetry and painting) he acknowledged the young man's natural defensiveness towards him. He also, however, revealed how Marais usually came round to his point of view in such a way that he never betrayed his own and miraculously ended up unifying both. Theirs was a unique meeting of styles or 'strong lines', and Cocteau celebrated in particular the moral aspects of a collaboration that both shaped their friendship together and served to fine-tune his own artistic practice. Even as late as 1960 Cocteau still regarded Jeannot as indispensable to the correct interpretation and promulgation of his work. In return, until his own death in 1998, Marais powerfully defended Cocteau's work against detractors and continued to act in revivals of his plays. He even produced successful stage shows about their professional relationship such as *Cocteau–Marais*, first performed in Paris in 1983. In so doing Marais ensured that he, too, would remain a living legend.

17

World War Redux

How different Cocteau's second experience of war was from the clear certainties of the first, when he personally defended the national cause! Now was a period of interminable crisis and paradox not just for Cocteau but for France itself with its major ideological fault-lines pushed to new extremes. As a self-confessed man of nuance, Cocteau came into his own, yet not always for his own good. Indeed, during this time he exposed himself cruelly to the dangers and pitfalls that can occur when a self-styled 'timeless art' rubs up against the brute politics of the Real.

Installed since June 1940 in his small cubby-hole in the Palais-Royal, Cocteau felt as if he were living in a small village within the city, rather lifeless and melancholy at first glance, especially during the night-time curfews, yet alive with personal memories from the past and cushioned from the unpredictable terrors of the Occupation. At Marais' instigation, towards the end of 1940 he began a new cure at the Lyautey clinic. After all, he could not afford to be dependent on opium during this time of rations and increased policing. Marais took a hands-on role in his treatment and by early 1941 Cocteau had checked out, believing himself finally cured after more than twenty years of drug dependency. Apart from the daily toils of wartime and the fact that Marais continued to be his own boss in matters of sex and desire, forcing Cocteau into the by now standard position of patient martyr, this was a period of relative stability for Cocteau. Indeed, he never lacked for comfort since

Cocteau at his blackboard in the rue de Montpensier, Paris, early 1940s.

Morihien and Marais' other 'side-lovers' ensured a steady stream of black-market goods. He also happily accepted from the German authorities a *laissez-passer* to move around Paris virtually at will. He continued to write regularly for the daily *Comoedia* and produced articles on the theatre and music that essentially elided the war and depicted a Paris outside time. A little later, in the spring of 1942, he began for the first time to keep a private diary and started to write film-scripts and dialogues to raise money, revelling in the atmosphere of the Studios de Joinville with its camaraderie that afforded relief from the austerity of occupied Paris. In one film for which he wrote the screenplay, Serge de Poligny's *Le Baron Fantôme*, he even played the small eponymous role. On more personal matters he experienced a temporary *rapprochement* with Valentine Hugo as well as Picasso, through whom he linked up with some of his former Surrealist enemies, notably Paul Eluard, now heavily involved in the Resistance. Other young men and disciples in Cocteau's entourage also joined the Resistance, including Franz Thomassin, Pierre Herbart and Roger Stéphane, and Cocteau felt with some justification that his personal world was vanishing. It was, however, the death in January 1943 of his mother, his one eternal lady-love, in the Paris convent where she had spent the last four years, that most rocked Cocteau's universe. She had, in truth, been deteriorating since 1939 and was an ailing absent figure, to the point that Cocteau had virtually become *her* mother. As with Radiguet, though, he declined to mourn her publicly and instead devoted to her memory one of his best and most lyrical and melodious autobiographical poems, *Léone*.

When the first concrete anti-Jewish measures came into force, such as the enforced wearing of a yellow star, Cocteau was on hand to help his Jewish friends, informing them in advance whenever he could of potential danger. He espoused an absolute revulsion towards racism, a fact all the more significant in view of his family's ingrained anti-Semitism as displayed during the Dreyfus affair of the 1890s. In May 1940, one month before France's ignominious defeat, he signed a petition of the Ligue Internationale contre l'Antisémitisme (LICA) and made a clear stand of solidarity against racism in its organ, *Le Droit de vivre*. Upon hearing this, the rabidly anti-Semitic writer Louis-Ferdinand Céline condemned Cocteau outright, fulminating in a letter published in *Je suis partout* in November 1941: 'Cocteau decadent? That's one thing. Cocteau in the League? Liquidate him.' Céline even began to promulgate the idea that Cocteau had been brainwashed by Jews. This, of course, was a familiar taunt of the far Right aimed not only at Cocteau but also at other 'ambivalent' writers such as Gide, who, in the new era of the Révolution Nationale based on the professed values of 'Travail, Famille, Patrie', all came under suspicion and were branded immoral 'individualists', responsible like the Jews, freemasons, communists, Gypsies and others for sapping French moral fibre.

Cocteau was singled out in particular because he seemed to incarnate most the decadence and abjection of the Third Republic. Collaborationist and right-wing writers and critics such as Robert Brasillach, Lucien Rebatet (aka François Vinneuil) and Alain Laubreaux engaged in a concerted anti-Cocteau campaign, vilifying him as anti-French and a 'Jewified' lover of 'negroids' ('Panama' Al Brown was defamed by association as 'la pédale noire' with its ugly connotations of pederasty). The insults were not only verbal. One of Cocteau's most disturbing self-portraits is a drawing of his obscured face with a black eye entitled *Souvenir du compère Doriot*, produced the day after he had been beaten up by Jacques Doriot's Ligue des Volontaires Français (or 'gardes françaises') on 27 August 1943. The reason? For not donning his hat in front of the French flag brandished by the troupe as it paraded down the Champs-Elysées in German uniform. *Je suis partout* used this event to persecute Cocteau still further as a 'notorious Gaullist' and 'fanatical Semite-lover'.

Cocteau eventually resolved to find protection in the hands of the Occupiers themselves, at least those he considered Francophile, cultured and influential enough. They included Otto Abetz, the German ambassador and former professor of drawing, Lieutenant Heller, who had studied in Toulouse; Bernard Radermacher, the artistic and personal representative of Goebbels; and the writer Ernst Jünger, who acknowledged Cocteau as the most important contemporary French literary figure in Germany. Jünger immediately warmed to Cocteau, even if he considered him 'tormented like a man residing in his own particular hell, yet comfortable'. Jünger was a relative pacifist within the Nazi regime and, like Cocteau, believed himself to be beyond politics and historical actuality, that is to say, *inactuel*. He was similarly curious about drugs and spent evenings in the rue de Montpensier enthralled by Cocteau's monologues, which transported his listeners to Proust's bedroom, among other rarefied places. Cocteau made additional contact with a circle of German intellectuals with whom he felt safe and who reassured him that they, too, found Céline's racist outpourings distasteful. He wrote in his diary, without any trace of embarrassment or irony: 'A homeland is a meeting of men who immediately find themselves to be on the same level.' Cocteau's fraternizings with the Occupier were not untypical of other French intellectuals at this time, of course, nor were they without a measure of risk and danger. Putting aside the thorny moral question of whether such activities constituted in themselves a form of collaboration, there were crucial moments in Cocteau's second war that brought his universalizing artistic practice into direct conflict with the politics of the time.

In a deliberately incendiary article in *Je suis partout* in April 1941 called 'Marais et marécage' (literally, 'Marais and marsh'), Laubreaux attacked Cocteau's play *The Typewriter*, which had been successfully submitted to the censor and was directed at the Théâtre des Arts by Jacques Hébertot. The terms used were crudely homophobic ('invert theatre', 'degenerate Jocrisse', etc.), and were matched by equally insulting and demonizing reviews in *La Gerbe* and *Le Pilori*. Cocteau the pederast was a sexual and 'jewified' *youppin*, and the play a 'demoralizing' series of moral turpitudes. The German authorities forbade its performance, although the ban was eventually lifted in the name of artistic freedom. Cocteau was compelled to write to the theatre to say that he had not sought German support for staging *The Typewriter*, yet he also declared it lamentable that artistic justice was to be found at the hands of the Occupier and not the French themselves. The story did not end there. In June 1941 Marais punched the loathsome Laubreaux to the ground outside a restaurant on the Boulevard des Batignolles after leaving the Hébertot theatre with Cocteau. This rash action by Marais succeeded in silencing the collaborationist press for a while and the German authorities never pursued the matter, yet Laubreaux swore to exact revenge and it was not long in coming.

He had, after all, in November 1938 already mounted an extremely virulent attack on Cocteau's play *Les Parents terribles* on account of its purported immorality, specifically its unsavoury portrayal of family relations.[1] When the same play was reprised at the end of October 1941 at a different theatre, it caused outrage in the right-wing press and was forced physically off the stage when, with Laubreaux's active encouragement, members of Doriot's militant Parti Populaire Français threw tear gas and ink jets at the actors. The production was soon banned altogether by the Germans. *Les Parents terribles* was a shocking satire against the sham world of bourgeois respectability and the abuse of innocents, in particular with its themes of incest and obsessive love. In his preface to the play Cocteau presented his 'dysfunctional family' in his by now standard terms of (impure) order vs. (pure) disorder, terms that were massively loaded during the Vichy period. The idea still persisted that Cocteau was a corruptor of youth, and Laubreaux himself regarded the play as embodying all the worst clichés of the 'Jewish theatre of [Henry] Bernstein'. Turning to Jünger as a kind of intermediary with the German authorities, Cocteau was successful in having *Les Parents terribles* reauthorized, and the production resumed in mid-December. Again it was attacked by the ultra-Right in the form of Jean Filliol, a *cagoulard* (literally 'hooded one'), who 'with his fellow members of the Comité Secret d'Action Révolutionnaire (CSAR)' laid siege to the stage with firebombs. The production was suspended, and Cocteau's theatrical project found itself consigned to the dark (his next play *Renaud et Armide* in Alexandrine verse was rejected altogether by the Comédie-Française and would have to wait until the following April to receive its successful premiere).

Despite all this, with his rivals like Breton and Gide having fled the capital and even the country, Cocteau began to see himself as finally legitimated. The year 1943 would even be a golden one, with the successful revival of *Antigone* and a recital of *Plain-chant* in

Scene from *The Eternal Return* between Patrice (Jean Marais) and Nathalie/Isolde (Madeleine Sologne), 1943.

which Serge Lifar danced as Apollo. The most spectacular instance of Cocteau's sixth sense for the cultural Zeitgeist, however, and proof that he had finally reached *le peuple* by answering its need for escapism, was his first major feature film, *The Eternal Return*, an adaptation of the medieval legend of Tristan and Isolde produced in collaboration with the commercial director Jean Delannoy. Even right-wing critics normally hostile to Cocteau approved of his brand of poetic realism, succumbing to the plastic beauty of Roger Hubert's cinematography, Georges Wakhévitch's sweeping sets and Auric's haunting, atmospheric score. In *Echo de la France* Brasillach praised the film for its 'delicacy' and 'good taste', in particular Marais' interpretation of Patrice as the magnificently handsome but naive Tristan wounded emotionally and physically by his fatal love for another 'child of the sea', Nathalie / Isolde (Madeleine Sologne). Similarly, in *Je suis partout* Rebatet celebrated Cocteau's 'fairy-tale' style of visual poetry. *The Eternal Return* has, in fact, the dubious privilege of being the most Aryan-looking work of French cinema during the Occupation, especially with the lovers' ultra-blond hair and statuesque poses. Cocteau had talked in the screenplay of marrying the real with the unreal, yet as one critic has persuasively argued, Cocteau wished ultimately to transcend the political altogether. In this most quintessential of romantic myths set in an indeterminate never-land, the fantastic death of the two lovers and their expulsion from the world of the quotidian serves as the very guarantee of their authenticity. Pure art, after all, requires death and persecution, and Patrice is martyred in the name of Art as much as love.[2]

Cocteau considered Marais' physiognomy in *The Eternal Return* as itself compatible with one of the sculptures he so highly praised in a notorious article he wrote on the German sculptor Arno Breker, a friend from the days of Le Boeuf sur le Toit and now Hitler's favourite artist (one wonders even whether the background image in the film's opening credits – the close-up of a sculptured hand – is a sample of Breker's work). Cocteau's burst of purple prose entitled 'Salut à Breker', published on the front page of *Comœdia* on 23 May 1942, was a stunningly naive and entirely uncalled-for eulogy of Breker's exhibition of hyper-muscular, testosterone-fuelled, neo-Grecian male figures that opened at the Jeu de Paume in May 1942. It was not that Cocteau especially sought to celebrate the heroic virility of the sculptures. Rather he felt a genuine wish to impress upon the French media and intelligentsia that a German could also be a fine sculptor. Indeed, he felt it was vital in the name of art to be personally 'brave' by honouring even such an officially sanctioned artist as Breker. His article, which reads on one level as merely sycophantic, was designed therefore as a liberationist plea to disregard the imposition of any artificial barriers in art. The response, even from Cocteau's friends and admirers, was uniform dismay. In a blunt letter in early July 1942 Eluard declared that Cocteau had effectively changed sides

Cocteau with the German sculptor Arno Breker in Paris, 1943.

from the *interdits* to the *censeurs*. Significantly, Cocteau placed together in his diary a couple of press cuttings about what became known as 'the Breker Affair' and wrote alongside them (citing Nietzsche): 'Woe is me, I'm all nuance.' Although he declined Breker's invitation to go to Berlin (Marais resolutely forbade him), he later tried to justify his article by saying that Breker had helped machine operators in the film industry to escape the Service du Travail Obligatoire (STO) in Germany, as if Breker were a thoroughly decent guy really. Perhaps Cocteau had further personal reasons to say this since Breker had once given him a mysterious Berlin phone number to call in the event of an emergency (was it this perhaps that saved Marais during the Laubreaux Affair?). Breker, meanwhile, was happily indulging his own mythomaniac tendencies, choosing to believe that the former artist Adolf Hitler was actually a pacifist and wanted to save France. He briefly convinced Cocteau of this woefully absurd idea, and again in his diary Cocteau privately accused France of disrespect and ingratitude towards the Führer who loved the arts and all artists! He even harboured the illusion that Hitler, still unmarried, might be gay and thus a man who had nobly sublimated his sexuality by nurturing such artists as Breker. The public repercussions of 'Salut à Breker' would be felt by Cocteau for a very long time, and it was primarily on account of this dreadful error of judgement that Cocteau found himself at the beginning of 1944 branded even by the BBC as a collaborator.

The last days of the war took a real toll on Cocteau. Max Jacob died from pneumonia on 4 March 1944 after a month's internment at the transit camp for Jews in Drancy. Cocteau had exerted what pressure he could on Otto Abetz by formulating a petition on Jacob's behalf, as well as on friends such as Georges Prades, who had contact with key Germans in the deportation process. The petition was in the hands of the Germans when Jacob perished. Cocteau was appalled by this tragic turn of events and was forever haunted by his inability to save his dear friend. Yet when at last Paris was liberated in July 1944 Cocteau joined the throngs to witness de Gaulle descend in triumph down the Champs-Elysées. Indeed, so keen was he to witness these momentous events from the Hôtel Crillon that he almost had himself killed by a sniper. Very soon he was back to hobnobbing with Lady Diana Cooper, wife of the British ambassador, and her 'Comus band' that also included Bérard, the Aurics, Louise de Vilmorin and Cecil Beaton. His sense of elation quickly turned to dread, however, as the spectre of purification loomed. With Marais away on duty in the Alsace, Cocteau now found himself alone facing two of the many committees assembled for this purpose, one for writers, the other for workers in the film industry. As an object of suspicion on all political sides during the war he knew he had not been a courageous resister, but he also believed profoundly that he had committed no wrong. Like everyone else he now sported the rosette (a *tricolore coq*) of the resistant French Forces of the Interior (FFI). He also published a poem entitled '25 Août 1944' in *Les Nouvelles Littéraires* and produced drawings of Marianne in a Liberty Cap, one of which was adopted by the new Fourth Republic as its 20 centimes stamp. Hence, he saw no reason at this stage to reinvent any of his past actions or try to present himself in a more favourable light. In the end, Aragon and Eluard intervened on his behalf and he was never 'purged'. Moreover, bearing as usual no trace of personal vengeance, he offered his support to the very people who had been so hostile towards him during the war and now found themselves charged with treachery. He publicly called for the repeal of Brasillach's death-sentence and deplored his execution in 1945, as he would that of Laubreaux a year later. 'My only politics is that of friend-ship', he accurately explained to Mauriac.

18

No Man's Land

In the immediate post-war period of ongoing purges and short-
ages, Cocteau decided, almost perversely, to mount a lavish film
production. Inspired by Madame Leprince de Beaumont's fairy
tale of 1757 of the same name, he began shooting *La Belle et la bête*
in August 1945, using for exteriors a seventeenth-century château
near Tours and the Château de Raray near Senlis, with its bizarre
terrace of animal statuary. Starring Josette Day as Belle and Marais
in the triple role of la Bête, the Prince and Belle's handsome best
friend Avenant (a character added by Cocteau), this black-and-
white film with sumptuous sets and extravagant costumes by
Bérard, together with swirling, sensurround music by Auric, is a
work of utter enchantment. It begins with a direct plea to the viewer
to bring a childlike naivety and suspend disbelief and contains
many truly hypnotic moments, for example, Belle crossing the
threshold of la Bête's grotto in balletic slow motion, then gliding
down a long corridor past white curtains billowing out from the
windows on her left. Here as elsewhere Cocteau makes the viewer
alive to the transformative potential of speed and rhythm. This
trip into a porous world of flux, reversals and metamorphosis
unfolding like a series of tableaux was produced paradoxically
through an extreme, almost documentary commitment to realism,
what Cocteau called 'the impeccable realism of unreality'. It relied
on Henri Alekan's crisp and precise cinematography that emphasized sharp contrasts of light and darkness, unlike traditional

Still from *La Belle et la bête* (1946), featuring Belle (Josette Day) and anonymous arms.

cinematic notions of fantasy that tended to favour haziness and vapour.

What was Cocteau doing with this extraordinary film? In a fascinating diary he kept during the production and which serves as a mirror for the project, he noted in detail the daily struggles and *trouvailles* of the shoot. *Diary of a Film* (*Journal d'un film*) also reveals a melancholic and slightly paranoid Cocteau suspicious of traps being laid by his team of professionals to prevent the unforeseen treasures of the Invisible. Moreover, the film's difficult gestation is directly linked to his own debilitating skin ailments, such as anthrax, impetigo and eczema, which even necessitated a spell in hospital. The story of the 'good' monster whose beauty is finally unveiled is clearly a screen for – and reversal of – his own physical ugliness. 'The more ugly we become with age, the more beautiful our work should be, reflecting us like the child we resemble', he writes.[1] But Cocteau goes even further. The state of his film and his own health is associated with that of France itself, since the sick poet in search of his art is also the failing citizen who wishes to affirm his patriotic feelings. In short, the double mask of suffering allows Cocteau to redefine his film as an allegory of the bond between Poet and Nation. Due to his physical and artistic pain (he

On the shoot of
La Belle et la bête
in 1945.

considered himself the victim of a *bête méchante*), Cocteau believed
he could atone both for his own passivity and the collective humiliation of his countrymen and thereby *après coup* his own – and
France's – resistance against *la peste brune*. According to his own
elaborate ratiocinations larded with Christian imagery, the miracle
of resurrection, whereby France rediscovered its natural goodness
and capacity for wonder after suffering the evil spell of the
Occupation, was possible *only* through the difficult work of art.

Cocteau was certainly right to claim that *La Belle et la bête*
embodied both a national and personal mythology, for his cultural
and aesthetic re-envisioning of de Beaumont's fairy story enabled
him to re-present himself as a new type of film poet and virtual saviour of French cinema. His exceptional ability to use art to construct
both his public and self-image, together with his unique capacity to

remember *and to forget*, are what ensured his survival through trial after trial, and it would serve him well as he prepared to forge a new life post-war. Things did now seem to be swinging a little in his favour. In November 1945 Roger Lannes published the first monograph on Cocteau in a prestigious new collection by Seghers, and a year later work began on a projected eleven-volume edition of his Collected Works by the Swiss publisher Marguerat. Written with rather wide eyes and sometimes lacking the full facts, Lannes' *Jean Cocteau* was a direct riposte to Claude Mauriac, son of the novelist François, whom Cocteau had befriended and who had just published a hatchet-job venomously titled *Jean Cocteau; ou, la vérité du mensonge*, heavily influenced by the bitchy and frequently damning opinions of Gide. Cocteau believed he had been completely betrayed, although characteristically chose to delude himself that the vindictiveness of Mauriac *fils* had little to do with himself personally and was more the result of the young man's private disillusionment, which could thus always be reversed. Cocteau thought the same, of course, of Maurice Sachs, who, in early 1941, out of pure revenge and perceived injustice, had deliberately sought to harm him in the new moral climate by publishing an article entitled 'Contre Jean Cocteau'. Yet still Cocteau could not bring himself to hate him. Revelling in war, Sachs was eventually killed in Germany after enlisting as a spy with the Gestapo, yet he would not so easily be silenced, his bile continuing to be published posthumously well into the 1950s in works such as *La Chronique joyeuse et scandaleuse*, where he damned the unreciprocating Cocteau.

As for Jean Genet, whom Cocteau had first met in early 1943 and whose brilliant first novel, *Our Lady of the Flowers*, he succeeded in getting published clandestinely through Paul Morihien, personal relations had always been complex. Although he had been inspired by his earlier readings of Cocteau, Genet was now already defining himself as a kind of 'anti-Cocteau' and would make it his personal business and pleasure to put all Cocteau's benign sailors and saints and acrobats into the joint services of theft, betrayal and abjection. This did not stop him, of course, from seeking Cocteau's help when he was rearrested for stealing from a Paris bookshop and sent back to prison, imperiously demanding the safe transfer of his possessions from Villefranche (a task for which Cocteau was barely thanked). Why did Cocteau choose to put up with Genet's ungratefulness and arrogance, especially since, as he later acknowledged in his diary, Genet attached no real importance to what mattered most to him, i.e., the act of friendship? For Cocteau it was simple: Genet was a genius; geniuses had their own sacred prerogatives; thus he could never do anything truly wrong. Cocteau arranged for Genet to be defended by the celebrated lawyer Maurice Garçon and he personally testified in Genet's favour during the hearing in July 1943, invoking the case of Rimbaud to prove that art exceeded the bounds of morality. The judge was seduced by Cocteau's elevated logic and Genet received just three months and a day at the Santé prison (he could have been sentenced for many years).

With Genet becoming ever more unsure about the nature of his own notoriety, which Cocteau had so assiduously helped to forge, the personal relationship between the two deteriorated into a series of mutual recriminations fuelled by artistic rivalry and petty jealousies over various protégés. Nevertheless, during the winter of 1944 Genet hailed Cocteau as the greatest living poet and wrote a preface to the new edition of *The Infernal Machine* (he would later pen a fulsome tribute to Cocteau in which he celebrated the raw intelligence and limpid purity of his work).[2] And despite Genet's scornful treatment of him, Cocteau always remained loyal to Genet as an exceptional artistic and even *moral* 'hero'. He illustrated *Querelle of Brest* (1947) with a series of wonderfully raunchy, if slightly morose, images of heaving, super-sexed sailors, and supervised Genet's filmic paean to masturbation, *Un chant d'amour* (1950). Yet the Existentialist love-in with Genet that was sweeping through the Left Bank was also making Cocteau feel distinctly *démodé*, even though he was a frequent visitor to the Café de Flore in Genet's very presence and enjoyed good personal relations with the main players of Saint-Germain-des-Prés, Sartre and de Beauvoir, whom he positively entranced with his flamboyant wit and conversation (although typically he over-extended himself on one occasion and found himself placed thereafter at a respectful distance). Sartre in particular sought his advice on the manuscript of his 1947 play, *Les Mains sales* (which Cocteau helped successfully to stage in 1948), and gratefully acknowledged his letters of support while engaged on his monumental sanctification of Genet entitled *Saint Genet: comédien et martyr*, which directly cites Cocteau. Although he viewed *Saint Genet* as really an inflated projection of Sartre himself (a touch of sour grapes perhaps, since Sartre had effectively dispossessed him of one of his own literary discoveries), nevertheless Cocteau appreciated Sartre's 'warm heart and noble soul' and saw in him a vital ally against François Mauriac. In July 1948, when Genet was again threatened with a long prison sentence, the two came together to address a letter to the French president, as a result of which Genet's crimes were expunged, although he was never fully amnestied.

Following the success of *La Belle et la bête*, Cocteau finally agreed to take some proper time off and convalesced in the monastic solitude of Morzine in the Haute-Savoie, where he began to collect his thoughts for what would become his most important collection of biographical essays, *The Difficulty of Being*. In it Cocteau took full stock of his life as an artist and man now past his mid-fifties. Each chapter is a short essay in the moralist style of Montaigne, probing universal themes such as pain, dreams, laughter, beauty and death (the book's title is borrowed from the eighteenth-century French polymath and *philosophe* Fontenelle, who declared to his doctor while on the point of dying: 'I feel a certain difficulty of being'). Interspersed are fresh accounts of Cocteau's own life and childhood as well as portraits of the usual suspects (Radiguet, Nijinsky, Apollinaire, etc.). Freed from any need to dazzle or mystify, he criticizes unsparingly his lack of political concern or insight and acknowledges his human frailty ('Since birth I've had a badly stowed cargo. I've never been balanced'). The level of self-analysis ranges characteristically from the ostensibly superficial (he returns repeatedly to his face and physical demeanour) to the profound (the workings of the unconscious). He confesses that he diverts himself too easily in the present moment and that he probably had a direct part to play in the creation of all the false, 'absurd' legends about him. In a remarkably honest chapter on friendship, in which he underlines his fundamental need for human contact ('I love others and exist only through them'), he explains why he cultivates friendship more than love, which is based on purely temporary 'spasms'. He also presents himself in disarmingly humble terms as an 'inventor' of sons who is educated by younger men rather than the other way round. Indeed, he disclaims here any idea of analytical mastery or authority in favour of a materialist sense of natural disorder, depicting his aging constitution as a 'factory' with a 'confused head' and 'lively instinct'. In the final brilliant chapter on responsibility he reveals how much the pulse of his body beats in the very ink of his work, for he is always searching for a primary connection with his reader's 'heat'. The best he can hope for is an intertextual exchange or 'entanglement' between Self and Other, and to be, as it were, resuscitated in very moment of reading. 'To write is an act of love. If it's not that, it's only writing', he famously declares.

The Difficulty of Being is one of Cocteau's most compelling literary performances, a unique evocation of haunted and fractured being, and its only false note is struck at the end, where he presents himself as belonging with Genet to the *race maudite*, as if he were still marginal and *hors-la-loi*. Yet this goes hand in hand with a sweeping avowal of personal failure: 'I reproach myself for having said too many things to be said and not enough things not to be said.' And this being Cocteau, he doen't just leave it there but rebukes himself in almost grotesque fashion:

> [w]hen I happen to read some article attacking me I believe that I would hit the target better, that the lance would enter right to the hilt, and that all I could do would be to fold my legs, pull out my tongue and kneel down in the arena.

In an astonishingly brutal 'Postface' he dismisses whatever therapeutic function his writing may have had before plunging into self-disgust: 'Go ahead, unashamed and stupid. Risk being at the very limit.' We catch a raw glimpse here of the troubled and fomenting underbelly of Cocteau's life-project.

Yet 1947 also marked the beginning of a far more positive period for Cocteau. In July a handsome, muscled 22-year-old amateur painter called Edouard Dermithe strolled into his life. This son of immigrant workers from Slovenia had worked in the iron mines of the Lorraine before suffering an accident to his finger. Having escaped to Paris, he was now eager to meet the director of *La Belle et la bête*. Cocteau immediately recognized in him a natural kindness and candour and asked him there and then to live with him in the large historic house he had just purchased with Jeannot (largely to escape the hordes of Marais' fans), which lay in a small village on the edge of the Fontainebleau forest south of Paris called Milly-la-forêt. Dermithe explained this was not practically possible, but six months later he turned up, to be greeted by Cocteau's open offer: 'Here's your home' (the financial corporation formed by Cocteau and Marais to purchase the house was soon dissolved and Marais went to live on a canal boat moored on the Seine). Dermithe was spellbound by Cocteau's act of generosity and his complete confidence in him from the start. Yet, of course, Dermithe had also come to work, and since he could not be employed as a private secretary (he lacked full literacy), he was assigned to tend the garden and groom the horses. With earnest dedication he quickly progressed through a series of odd jobs before ending up preparing opium for the still helplessly addicted Cocteau. Inevitably, he also succumbed to the drug and became even more docile than he already was by nature, absorbed by a new dream world he now rarely left.

With his penchant for diminutive first names Cocteau called Dermithe 'Doudou' and referred to him as his 'adopted son', although this status would never successfully be made legal. He even took the liberty of lopping off the final two letters, '-he', of Dermithe's surname to make him appear both more of an artist and a thoroughbred Frenchman (another instance of Cocteau's latent nationalistic tendencies). Doudou loved with simple devotion the man who had chosen him and to whom he now owed everything, and Cocteau loved him even more in return, although he stressed at an entirely sublimated level. For Cocteau's sexual abstention had by now become a matter of personal pride. As he put it in *The Difficulty of Being*, after a certain age sexual 'things' can risk becoming risible 'turpitudes' and prevent real exchange, whatever gender is involved. Doudou became therefore Cocteau's inseparable companion. Their hearts belonged totally to each other, and as relationships go it was safe and straightforward, one might almost say (advisedly) 'straight'. While Doudou lovingly refined the extensive garden divided into oblongs like a medieval herbarium, Cocteau decorated his first real home with assorted *objets*, predominantly Victorian but also Regency and neo-Baroque. In addition to its Louis XIII-style façade and turrets, the house now acquired two stone sphinxes flaunting the entrance, a large portrait of Cocteau's mother in the foyer, Bérard's large canvas of Oedipus and the Sphinx floating amid Art Nouveau wallpaper, and in the centre of the main room a gigantic narwhal tusk. A menagerie of bronze deer and stuffed owls contributed to the rather stultifying

Cocteau drawing
Doudou drawing
Cocteau in the rue
de Montpensier,
late 1940s.

overall effect. It was in such surroundings that Cocteau would occasionally stage private parties, although in truth Milly always functioned more as a museum where he posed for photographs than as a true home.

The late 1940s and '50s were really the 'Dermit years', and since they also corresponded to Cocteau's major work in the cinema it was perhaps inevitable that Cocteau's next film took its baroque inspiration directly from Milly. *The Eagle with Two Heads* featured costumes and majestic sets by Bérard and Georges Wakhévitch, and along with members of the original cast of the play (Marais as Stanislas, Edwige Feuillère as the Queen) featured Dermit in a small role as a young waltzing member of the guard. He was effectively cast as himself, earnest, all but mute, and given to rather stiff, abrupt movements. This determinedly theatrical film, which has a visual exorbitance all of its own, matched by an excessive number of angle shots as well as subjective point-of-view shots (a technique usually avoided by Cocteau, who never pretended to penetrate to the psychological core of his characters), becomes by the end a slightly awkward and kitsch melodrama-cum-tragedy. It met with much criticism precisely because of its decorative artificiality and over-theatricality, although it offers some stupendous

sequences brimming with phallic propensities, such as the knife
standing erect in the Queen's back, the many statues of naked men
and the Queen's super-virile activities (she uses her library both as
a firing range and a circus ring for trapezing). *Les Parents terribles*,
shot immediately afterwards in May–June 1948, was Cocteau's
artistic counter-response: a 'hypotheatre' that 'de-theatricalized'
his original play while remaining utterly faithful to its theatrical
'mechanism'. Cocteau re-employed Marais for the part of Michel
and included the great stage actress Yvonne de Bray (whom Marais
admired with almost filial awe) as his diabetic mother Yvonne,
together with Marcel André as the feckless father Georges, Josette
Day as the young girlfriend Madeleine, and Gabrielle Dorziat as his
scheming aunt Léo. The result is a work of calculated voyeuristic
fascination as we observe in keyhole detail every movement and
twitch of the characters, who, although blessed with the potential
for free will, are also creatures of squirming organic matter. Almost
every frame in the film becomes like a cage squeezing them ever
tighter in their sealed tragic world.

Following the successful release of *Les Parents terribles*, Cocteau
embarked in December 1948 on a short trip to America to promote
The Eagle with Two Heads (the original play starring Tallulah Bank-
head had been badly translated and poorly received on Broadway).
He was shepherded around New York variously by the French consul,
the actor Jean-Pierre Aumont and the art historian and critic of the
Museum of Modern Art, Monroe Wheeler, and he made brief contact
with assorted stars and celebrities, such as Marlene Dietrich, Greta
Garbo and 'Panama' Al Brown. Except while on stage presenting his
work or in the company of friends, Cocteau played the part of the
rude and condescending Parisian and ostentatiously declined to
speak English. He found time, however, to execute some dazzlingly
homoerotic photo sessions for *Life* magazine with the photographer
Philippe Halsman featuring the black dancer Leo Coleman. One
series of these 'living paintings', where Cocteau as the Poet brings an

Cocteau with the cast and crew (minus Dermit) of *The Eagle with Two Heads* in 1947.

image to life, was never published because it exposed Coleman's nipple. In another Cocteau portrayed himself as a multi-talented monster-magician with three pairs of hands smoking, drawing and reading. On the overnight flight back to France in mid-January 1949 he dashed off an essay entitled *Lettre aux Américains*. This was not one of his finest moments, for he is often here at his incorrigible worst, at once snobbish, arch and withering. Believing that his twenty days in New York gave him the right to speak about all Americans, he indulged in some truly warped clichés about a nation founded exclusively on material success and scientism. If only 'you Americans' had the capacity for self-criticism and experimentation, he admonishes, you could learn sometimes that two plus two can equal five! Act more like who you are, a people of intuitive, childlike heroes, for once you have saved yourselves you will then be able to achieve your preordained mission of preserving the dignity of all mankind. The saving grace in all of this is yet again Cocteau's mordant self-deprecation. He can say all this because he is, after all, just a relic of old Europe, or more specifically that 'old French farmyard', a land of dupery that still possessed some genius. We observe once again that whenever Cocteau returns to France from abroad it is always to re-evaluate his homeland and with it his own identity. The French, he asserts, are strong in their weakness and thus have contempt for their own products, otherwise they would be terribly vain. And whereas Americans are not really free, and worse, do not even know it since they are afraid to open themselves up to their dreams and the unconscious, 'I' – that is to say, the unique Jean Cocteau – am a bastion of authentic freedom and 'disorder', a true individual with an 'agile mind'. This smug self-declaration provokes some personal home-truths, however, that reveal Cocteau's own inner insecurities. He may be one of the world's last free men but he is also one of the most alone: 'I'm speaking of those like me who always expect to get hit', he rues. Such frank admissions are hardly convincing publicity for the superior happiness and grounded universal values of Old World liberty and individualism.

A few months later Cocteau undertook with both Dermit and Marais another major trip, this time a four-month theatrical tour of the Middle East, which had the air of a semi-official government mission promoting French culture, and featured mainly Cocteau's own plays and adaptations. He kept an irregular diary of the experience and the resulting text (subsequently published as *Maalesh: A Theatrical Tour in the Middle-East*) is an uneven mix of sometimes thrilling accounts of the performances of the troupe, nuggets of local history, obligatory references to Loti, Gide and Proust, assorted trivia dressed up in extended images and aphorisms (by now standard Cocteau output about dreams, visibility and invisibility, etc.), and world-weary private feelings, underlined in the English edition of 1956 by a frontispiece photograph of Cocteau as a slightly fusty academic in tie and jumper. Both the tour and the book hung heavy with the news from the start of the year of Christian Bérard's sudden death at the age of just 47 during a rehearsal. For Cocteau, Bérard was an immortal, a fact symbolized by the 'still burning flame' of his shocking red beard, and he was laid to rest beside Radiguet at Père-Lachaise cemetery. The book has a familiar narrative: Cocteau must leave Paris due to Bérard's death, yet because he is constantly reflecting on Bérard he enters into a process of almost total identification with him, the dangers of which he becomes fully aware ('I had adopted his personality to the point of fearing to speak of him lest I should seem to speak of myself'). And just as in *Round the World Again in 80 Days* Cocteau pulls off a rather embarrassing patriotic ending, where his identification with Bébé is replaced first by Paris and then more generally by France, which is brilliantly quixotic like himself. The latter point has become by now such a commonplace that Cocteau does not even feel the need to spell it out here, leaving it for his trained reader to infer and applaud (or not).

19

Club Santo-Sospir

In early summer 1949 Cocteau began shooting a major new film, *Orphée*. It was a project marred by misfortune from the start on account of Bérard's sudden death and the fact that, despite Cocteau's strong track record and undisputed prestige in French cinema, he was unable to find adequate financial backing. In fact, producers kept well away, regarding the script as even a little sinister, and he was compelled to form his own company, Les Films du Palais-Royal. Cocteau's disappointment set the tone for the film, one of the first lines of which reads: 'I [Orphée] have had a drink, it was rather bitter.' We are worlds away from the frivolity of Cocteau's earlier tragi-farce of the same name. Moreover, *Orphée* represents his long-delayed engagement with historical reality, although in a typical Cocteau paradox he resurrects it here within the framework of fiction. The fantastical 'Zone', the name of which is charged with French military and political echoes, was filmed in the bombed-out ruins of the Saint-Cyr military academy outside Paris and thus presents a direct image of recent historical anguish (other traces include the car-radio messages inspired by the coded signals of the Resistance transmitted from London, the begoggled motorcyclists dressed fascistically in black operating as an independent militia, and the atmosphere of denunciation and inquisition in the tribunal scenes where three backroom men dispense summary judgement). Above all, however, *Orphée* is a scathing self-portrait reflecting the general state of Cocteau during the post-war period,

Transporting the freshly killed Cégeste (Edouard Dermit) in *Orphée*, 1950.

when he was trying to work through his self-doubts as an artist now turning 60 while facing widespread critical indifference from the Paris intelligentsia, a fact he regarded as nothing less than persecution. He had just found himself excluded from Gaëton Picon's important *Panorama de la nouvelle littérature française*, because deemed passé in the new age of political engagement (Picon referred to Cocteau very unkindly as 'the grand couturier of French literature'). The degree of personal self-derision on display in the form of the weak protagonist Orphée, a successful yet universally despised middle-aged poet haunted by the baggage of Cocteau's own past, betrayed his genuine fear that he was steadily becoming irrelevant (not helped by the fact that during the making of the film he was made a Knight of the Legion of Honour).

The personal and creative stakes of *Orphée* were thus extremely high, and Cocteau's very survival depended on his capacity to regenerate himself artistically. By inviting the *chanteuse* Juliette Gréco, a new icon of Paris night-life, to play the part of Algaonice, he was clearly attempting to retain some kind of contact with the

Heurtebise (François Périer) and Cégeste inflict death on the already dead Orphée under the command of la Princesse (Maria Casarès) in *Orphée*, 1950.

new generation, although some critics, mindful of the representation of the Bacchantes as humourless and vindictive troublemakers, regarded this more negatively as a form of revenge on Cocteau's part (in another ironic, not to say masochistic, piece of casting, the young man acting as a witness against Orphée is none other than Claude Mauriac). I have explored at length elsewhere the formal steps that Cocteau takes to reassert his artistic potency and stamp his seal of authorship in *Orphée*, in particular his extraordinary representation of the Zone and the brilliant setpieces of reverse motion photography.[1] Made 'of the memories of men and the ruins of their habits', the Zone becomes a highly ambivalent theatrical space of inversion composed of the most incontrovertible historical real (war) and the strangest unreality (fantasy), where human time does not pass or even exist.

As Cocteau put it in his published notes to the film, '[the Zone] is a margin of life. A no-man's land between life and death, where one is neither fully dead nor truly alive.' The final result, obtained with a typically mathematical precision and rigour, is a kind of hyper-real that offers a heightened vision – indeed, a virtual case-study – of some of Cocteau's most personal desires and drives, notably his obsession with oral and anal eroticism. In the process the true meaning of the Zone as 'a site of ruination of men's habits' is fully revealed. For Cocteau's dazzling array of phallic shapes and forms – the bread and butter of his personal symbolic of resurrection and proof of his poetic gloss and phallic lift – constitutes here little more than a customized ornamental frame for those other far more unusual and enticing filmic pleasures of reverse and slow motion produced internally within the camera and externally between men. All this is happening under our very eyes in a commercial feature film that deliberately cultivates mystery and undecidability through mirrors, enigmas, numbers and secrets, as well as a con-tinual shifting of genres (from quasi-*reportage* to crime mystery, secret agent / spy thriller, melodrama, romantic comedy and tragedy). This exemplifies the subversive thrust of Cocteau, working as always from within, almost unnoticed and invisible, to undermine the castratory clarity of normative structures of identity and representation (i.e., the phallic economy of 1940s and '50s French cinema), and in so doing generate new images and sensations *for our eyes only*.

For these reasons *Orphée* is not a completely dark or melancholy work. Indeed, the film illustrates another use of lived experience for Cocteau: as a source of artistic self-amusement and contempla-tion. The highly graphic process of replacement of one poet (the established Orphée) by another (the arrogant young upstart Cégeste played by Dermit) is a highly self-conscious playing out of Dermit's supplanting of Marais in Cocteau's affections, although in reverse (in the film the two poets become sworn rivals for the hand of the Princess, whilst in real life Marais welcomed the arrival of Dermit, who in turn regarded him as an older brother). Yet *Orphée* remains a brooding, complex and disturbing masterpiece devoid of real optimism. The obvious 'happy end' – the reuniting of Orphée with Eurydice (Marie Déa) – rings deliberately hollow, and when the Princess (Maria Casarès) and Heurtebise (François Périer) are taken away by her own henchmen in the last magnificent tableau the viewer is left in an interpretive limbo (the Princess had already explained that the transcendent and elusive entity of Death presumed to reside at the bottom of the film's infinite abyss occupied, in fact, nowhere). Although it did reasonably well at the box-office and was acclaimed in many quarters (it took the International Critics' Prize at Venice), *Orphée* never proved the popular hit that Cocteau was counting on, a fact that served to aggravate still further his increasing sense of isolation.

While still involved in the post-production of *Orphée*, Cocteau worked quickly on an adaptation of *Les Enfants terribles* for the relatively untried director Jean-Pierre Melville. He insisted on two conditions to which Melville reluctantly agreed: that Dermit be cast in the male lead, and that the setting be updated to the contemporary period. The project developed inevitably into a power struggle between Melville and Cocteau, who was in the end formally credited only as 'co-adaptor', even though he had filmed the brief location shots at Montmorency when Melville became ill (according to Melville, Cocteau even secretly hoped that he [Melville] would die so that he [Cocteau] could complete the film). The excessive number of Cocteau voice-overs, which often merely duplicate what is shown, constitute his belated attempt to compensate for the loss of authority he felt over the film, which, although generally successful, also scaled down the novel's gay undertones. When it was released in the spring of 1950, the film received generally positive reviews, although much to Cocteau's chagrin Doudou's brave but rather wan performance was universally panned.

Cocteau with
Doudou and
Francine
(Weisweiller),
early 1950s.

It was, however, midway through the filming of *Les Enfants terribles* that Cocteau first met Francine Weisweiller (*née* Worms), a cousin by marriage to the outstanding female lead, Nicole Stéphane (born de Rothschild). She immediately invited Cocteau and Melville to contact her if they needed any financial assistance with the film. They did, and Cocteau approached her unilaterally (some of the scenes were even shot in her mansion on the Place des Etats-Unis). Francine was the young and attractive daughter of a well-to-do Jewish family who had recently married the millionaire Alec Weisweiller, immediately inheriting half of a vast fortune gained from Shell Oil. By the late 1940s, however, she was harbouring ambitions to be part of the artistic world of *le Tout Paris*, although she had no particular distinction other than being extraordinarily rich. Cocteau was her obvious ticket. He soon became a regular guest at the Weisweillers' home and grew dependent upon Francine financially (he claimed he was finding it difficult to keep up with hefty post-war taxes). Accompanied by Dermit, he went one weekend to her villa called Santo-Sospir above the hills of Saint-Jean-Cap-Ferrat, near Villefranche-sur-Mer, where they ended up staying for several months as free guests. Cocteau was soon executing frescoes and softly toned decorations, or what he called 'tattoos', over the villa's walls and ceilings (naked sailors, local fishermen, Dionysus, Orpheus, Christ,

Narcissus, Holofernes, Ulysses, etc.). Francine eventually placed her entire fortune at Cocteau's disposal and even arranged for Dermit's family to be brought down from the north and installed as flower growers in nearby Biot. The trappings of this new life of luxury included for Cocteau not only the villa and servants but also the beautiful garden facing the Mediterranean, a yacht called *Orphée II*, and trips across Europe. Cocteau, Doudou and Weisweiller were photographed as a family trio and wore identical triple-banded rings designed by Cocteau (at Francine's expense, naturally).

Edouard Dermit in front of Cocteau's tapestry *Judith et Holopherne* at Milly-la-Forêt, 1948.

We catch a glimpse of this odd but happy *ménage à trois* – Cocteau's new family – in *La Villa Santo-Sospir*, a short home movie that Cocteau made over the course of a week in August 1951 assisted by just one cameraman. With the hyper-theatricality of Cocteau's own performance (this is the first Cocteau film to feature Cocteau as 'Cocteau' and his only foray into colour), *La Villa Santo-Sospir* often stretches the limits of taste and decency, as Cocteau himself later acknowledged when he called it an 'indiscretion'. The tone appears deceptively light, its bright, summery feel enhanced by the fresh, compliant faces of Doudou and Francine, yet this pseudo-documentary elicits no biographical secrets or intimate confessions from Cocteau, either about himself or about Dermit and Weisweiller. With his teasing voice-over delaying the appearance of certain details and promising ever more images, he takes us on a tour of the tattooed villa as if it were a magic grotto of marvels. He also pictures himself in the garden campily mounted on life-size sculptures of animals. Although he talks at length about technical forms and film processes, he never acknowledges the pervasive use of reverse motion photography to which he submits his own body and which produces strange shapes and movements: playing *boules* with and almost 'on to' and 'over' himself, 'peeling back together' petals of flowers, waiting to receive fragments of pottery that fly up into his hand, and so on. As in *Orphée* but even more so, there are moments when it is not clear whether we are watching forward or reverse motion: Cocteau's own arm is pictured dropping down slowly in consecutive shots (but is it actually rising?); waves crash irregularly into themselves (or is it really back on to themselves?). There is no obvious meaning to be read into this playful perversion of cinematic form, although the experiment serves neatly as a kind of advertisement for Cocteau's new fun lifestyle.

From his new base at Santo-Sospir Cocteau found himself again in relative proximity to Picasso, who was now residing on the Côte d'Azur with Jacqueline Roche. It was Picasso who finally chose during this period to renew contact with him and they were photographed together in public, often at the bullring. Yet Picasso was never less than an opportunist when it came to Cocteau. After all, he needed a loyal and intelligent admirer to theorize his aesthetic mutations and present them to a wider audience, a task which Cocteau performed brilliantly again with a lecture on Picasso's work in Rome in 1953. Cocteau's permanent infatuation with the artist, who was at best merely tolerant of him, proved an almost masochistic addiction ('I loved his cruelty', he confessed in 1952). He let himself be reduced to slavish adoration by a ferociously straight man who positioned him homophobically as his posterior, 'a spark in the comet's tail – I [Picasso] am the comet'. Despite Picasso's casually contemptuous behaviour towards him, Cocteau's awe of Picasso the artist never wavered. In countless poems and essays dating from 1917 with *L'Ode à Picasso*, Cocteau celebrated the purest incarnation of Orpheus who belonged to no school and extracted gold from daily life. Such artistic appreciation was entirely one-way traffic, for despite Cocteau's persistent hopes and requests, 'Picasso the untouchable' only ever produced during their 45 years of contact a rather bland and non-committal Ingres-like drawing of him in uniform while on leave in 1916, as well as a purely workmanlike drawing dated Easter 1917.

Picasso was the not the only source of tension during this time, however. On the opening night of Cocteau's eagerly awaited new play, *Bacchus*, at the Théâtre Marigny in December 1951, François Mauriac rose dramatically just as the audience began to applaud and exited ostentatiously. Then, in an 'Open Letter' published a few days later in *Le Figaro littéraire*, he accused Cocteau of being sacrilegious and committing heresy by whipping his venerable Mother, the Church. Was this Mauriac's long-delayed personal revenge for the abortive affair with Cocteau in 1910? Either way, Cocteau published in *France-soir* a response entitled 'J'accuse', in which he complained that Mauriac could never tolerate a friend's success and was nothing less than a hypocrite. 'Adieu!' This ugly public spat, together with the hissing on the first night by students and artists sitting in the galleries (the very people Cocteau was now trying to reach) and the accusation made in some quarters that he had simply pillaged Sartre's contemporary *The Devil and the Good Lord* (a play similarly set in sixteenth-century Germany), was enough to ensure that *Bacchus* quickly closed. Why had this very earnest drama, which Cocteau had dedicated to Francine out of gratitude and respect, generated such a negative scandal? As a *pièce à these* framed against the backdrop of religious war it appeared to mark a new departure in Cocteau's work and a more concise style of realism, although in truth it was a hotchpotch of many of his familiar artistic theories cobbled together with assorted remarks by Radiguet, Picasso and Genet. The play's one obvious major weakness was its lack of plot. Most of the action takes place off-stage and is presented as narration, while onstage there are long, drawn-out and often pretentious discussions based around a fairytale. There was also a basic confusion around the principal themes of freedom and the disorder of youth. The central character, Hans, a village idiot of imposing beauty, tries to show his fellow citizens who have elected him Bacchus in accordance with pagan rituals that their liberty is despised both by the Reformation and the Church. He relieves the peasants of the tithe, sets prisoners free, and is acclaimed by the populace as its saviour, yet strangely, despite such illegal actions, is never prosecuted or ostracized as such. Instead, he is presented by Cocteau as another solitary *poète maudit* merely 'pretending' to be mad. Condemning politics as a masquerade by arguing that morality is always a private and invisible matter, the naive and instinctive Hans refuses on pain of death to accept the hypocrisy and cunning of the Church in the form of Cardinal Zampi, envoy extraordinary of the Holy See. He thus reveals himself ultimately to be a reflection of his creator, Cocteau, who, in the face of a perceived Marxist /

Existentialist tribunal, was clearly seeking here to prove his credentials as an engaged artist with the common touch, certainly not a *bourgeois* maintained by a wealthy *bourgeoise*. Hans promotes love for its own sake, although the townspeople prefer not to accept this and he suffers a martyr's death, impaled by an arrow while declaring 'Free . . . '. The parallels with Cocteau's own mauling at the hands of Mauriac and other critics of the play are hard to escape, and the fact that, by Cocteau's own admission, he had already written 'J'accuse' in the eventuality of trouble encourages the idea that persecution was exactly what he was hoping for. Out of a still smouldering need for some kind of public apotheosis and final redemption? No doubt.

The *Bacchus* affair raged on in Cocteau's head and he took further revenge in *Diary of an Unknown*, his most candid work thus far. The open, personal tone of this book of short essays betrays the fact that he had just resumed his private diary, which would see the light of day posthumously under its intended title *Le Passé défini* (*Past Tense*). Among the many chapters on general themes (invisibility, criminal innocence, the death penalty, translation, memory, distances, etc.) is the innocuous sounding 'On a Purple Passage', in which Cocteau lays into Mauriac, dismissing his 'Open Letter' as 'a purple passage of yellow prose that evinces a complete misreading of the world I [Cocteau] inhabit'.[2] In a typically self-justificatory tone, Cocteau first clarifies his position on *Bacchus* by attempting to prove (not very conclusively) its total difference from Sartre's play, then goes straight for the jugular, attacking Mauriac 'for assuming the rights of a priest and sitting at God's right hand', adding rather bitchily: 'The truth is, Mauriac has always been one of those children who like to mingle with the grown-ups'. Yet having castigated Mauriac's behaviour as 'an act of sabotage', Cocteau suddenly back-pedals and performs a standard manoeuvre of exoneration: Mauriac is not guilty of any serious wrongdoing at all and despite everything remains a friend. Mauriac, he explains, 'was only the tool of those forces which I have been studying, of the shadow's wiles in its fight against the footlights and projectors'.[3]

The rest of *Diary of an Unknown* does not possess such personal bite. When Cocteau does take time out from his over-extended thesis on the double bind of visibility and invisibility (and with it the rather tired hyperbole of being the most famous yet misunderstood of all artists), it is more to offer some not entirely original views on metaphysics, all grounded on a rather superficial knowledge of medicine and recent readings in science fiction (he refers vaguely to mystical concepts and Eisenstein's experiences in Mexico). In customary fashion he makes repeated reference to his peers, in particular Sartre and Stravinsky, and finally chastises his prodigal sons Sachs and Mauriac *fils,* whose appalling behaviour he ascribes to the rashness of youth. He also settles accounts with Gide, who had just died at the age of 82 and who is to be blamed ironically for his 'impossible yearning' for youth (Cocteau had just read the not so flattering parts about himself in Gide's *Journal,* which he dismisses elsewhere as a 'great hoax' and pack of lies). The strongest parts of the book remain as usual those moments when Cocteau focuses in close-up on the artistic process, including a fascinating account of the genesis of 'L'Ange Heurtebise', and develops his cherished notion of friendship as man's greatest invention. Yet overall there is a sense of missed opportunity here, with Cocteau instructing us ever more finely on how to read him, but not really surprising us with anything new to sustain our interest in his project. He never quite manages to break free from his well-rehearsed psychological reflexes tinged with self-hate. In a final 'p.s.' he refers to his 'imprudence' that prevents him from writing 'brave delicious books', offering himself to his readers virtually as an anti-model from whose mistakes we can learn.

The trappings of Club Santo-Sospir were perhaps just that, a trap, for Cocteau's life had become almost too easy: a lazy lifestyle of lunches and cocktails and cruises around the bay believing himself to be a Tibetan sage. If he felt at last supremely comfortable within a new family of his own design, the fundamental question that had haunted him for so long, and which *Orphée* so powerfully articulated, still remained to be addressed, namely what was his real identity now as a man and artist? To answer this Cocteau would need somehow to reverse his downcast vision and kick-start his life-project. Yet after all he had been through, did he have any reserves still left to draw on?

20

The Long Haul

According to the idiosyncratic logic of *Diary of an Unknown*, in order to become fully invisible and unknown and thus truly a Poet Cocteau would need to occupy centre-stage as often as possible. And this he achieved brilliantly throughout the 1950s when he seemed to be everywhere at once, wherever in fact there was a flashlight or lens or microphone. As a celebrity *de luxe* with Francine and Doudou at this side, this natural-born exhibitionist could not have been more available in the public eye if he had tried. Genet had accused him very unkindly of doing nothing but being a star during the 1940s. Now, during the 1950s, as he consolidated his life with the jet set on the Midi in the starry company of Ingrid Bergman, Maria Callas, Juliette Gréco or Fellini, this charge carried real force. He also travelled extensively throughout Europe, in particular Spain (in 1954 he attended his first *corrida* in Seville, which he recounted in taut, breathtaking prose in *La Corrida du 1er mai*). When not being interviewed by the media or celebrating particular bullfights or giving speeches at the International Congress for Sexual Liberty (in 1951) or else dispatching brief missives to all and sundry, he was churning out endless prefaces and introductions to books on practically anything, from Greek epitaphs to tourist Paris to aviation. He continued to work extensively in music and ballet and created a number of international productions, including an oratorio entitled *L'Apocalypse*, the ballet *La Dame à la licorne* and, for the Spoleto Festival of 1959, *Le Poète et sa muse*, with music by Gian-Carlo Menotti. During the late 1950s there were also major revivals of *Oedipus Rex* in Vienna and London, where Cocteau played the role of Chorus as originally intended.

Everything was now proving just a little too predictable, though. It seemed that Cocteau was more content to memorialize his name by rehashing old ideas than to advance his project, which still remained largely impervious to the momentous world events now taking place in this new era of the Cold War. Yet by force of need and habit – call it his *déformation professionnelle* – Cocteau never stopped experimenting with new artistic forms and media. Indeed, over the course of the decade and into the next, he would design a vast range of mosaics, panels, frescoes and stained-glass designs for theatres and chapels, even for the occasional town hall and shop. Of special note are his interior frescoes for the Romanesque chapel of Saint-Pierre at Villefranche-sur-Mer in 1956, the three frescoes dedicated to Mary for the chapel of the Virgin in the newly rebuilt Notre-Dame-de-France church in London in 1960, and the design of twelve stained-glass windows for Saint-Maximin in Metz in 1962. These large-scale graphic projects enabled Cocteau to project himself and his work into new physical and social spaces according to his own bio-rhythms. In the case of his chapel art, which invites immediate comparison with that of Matisse (whose talent Cocteau always disputed), he sought to marry his own iconography with that of sacred art, positioning himself explicitly within the Western tradition of painting that he effectively extended by innovating from within (Cocteau may have been unorthodox, but he was never an iconoclast). So over-determined and self-conscious now was Cocteau's artistic project that the *Crucifixion* scene in the Notre-Dame-de-France fresco even included a self-portrait.

It was also during this period that Cocteau took up oil-painting properly for the first time, as well as pottery and jewellery, and his investment in the decorative arts and interior design would lead him eventually to produce fashion accessories such as scarves and shoes, including the odd design for Elsa Schiaperelli (as a proponent of timeless art he had nevertheless always been fascinated by the transitoriness of fashion). It could be argued that Cocteau's sudden interest in frescoes, gouaches, felt and pastel drawings was simply his way of compensating for the progressive loss of acuity in his vision and hands due to his advancing years. Some of the results were, to be sure, a little crude and clumsy, like the loud and rather garish decor and drawings in bright yellow and orange for the Salle des Mariages at the Town Hall in Menton (1957–8). His religious work for chapels relied similarly on flat, cartoon-like figures sporting the same androgynous features with slightly banal, fey expressions. When it came to easel painting, the style was often derivative of early Cubist painting (or, when figurative, pre-Cubist Picasso) and exposed Cocteau's major shortcomings as a colourist (his instinct, as we have seen, was for the crisp, moving line). The themes were largely religious, Neo-classical and mythological, such as Christ, Eve, Phèdre, and assorted fauns and angels. One large canvas of 1951 entitled *Portrait des tragédiennes* underscored the heaviness of much of Cocteau's painting of this period. His belated engagement with the female form simply lacked the sparkle and fluency of his drawings of young men. That is to say, the true subject of his mythological compositions remained virility, most often naked and 'outsize', for instance, his image of Orpheus of 1958 with an erect penis engaged in 'ancient battle', or his drawing 'Pégase et les Poètes' depicting male forms in profile. Such moments match the turbulent scenes that Cocteau celebrated in the work of El Greco, where the male body bursts forth in a kind of vibrant sexuality or 'explosion of the line'. Of course, Cocteau continued still to produce, mainly for private consumption, extremely erotic drawings of anonymous hunks engaged either alone in ecstatic acts of masturbation or else together in fellatio and rimming. This would culminate in 1961 in his radiantly queer 'Innamorati' series of drawings and pastels inspired by the fishermen of Villefranche.

For all the flurry and hype of Cocteau's new artistic activities, and despite the easy reproducibility of his late style (he was now happy, like Salvador Dalí, to sign off extended print-runs of his work and distribute his 'label'), little was created during this period that was genuinely ground-breaking. This is most manifest in Cocteau's poetry, where he seemed to be going round in ever-decreasing creative circles, proposing in *Appogiatures* (1953), for example, mini-filmscripts with titles such as 'Crime of passion', 'The Skater', 'The Dentist', etc., or else in *Clair-obscur* (1954), where he worshipped the bizarre in essentially generic symbolist fashion, conjuring up the mystical. *Paraprosodies* (1958) represented a more concerted attempt to use music as a model for moving beyond language and 'transmuting figures into numbers', yet it was ultimately rather contrived and half-hearted. One senses in each collection a certain self-restriction and regression in theme concomitant with a lack of genuine innovation on the level of form. Rare now were those instances of direct and unpretentious rhythmic style where Cocteau simply allowed the words to create emotion. Articles on the poetic process ended now on a note of slight desperation, as if he were still searching after all this time for an unbiased reader to understand and embrace him. 'I love others. I love to love. I hate hate', he declares importunately in 'Démarche d'un poète' (1953), one up at least from *Le Chiffre sept* (1952), where, as the eternally suffering and misunderstood poet, he simply presented his own death.

The tangible lack of vision at the heart of all this can be attributed in large part to the fate of Cocteau's film career, which had now effectively stalled following the relative commercial disappointment of *Orphée*. He found himself unable to secure financial backing to make feature-length films, resulting in an expanding catalogue of unrealized scripts, notes and plans for films. It is not that Cocteau lacked for work in the cinema. On the contrary, he was continually solicited and commissioned to write screenplays, voice-overs, prefatory texts, monologues and dialogues, most of which he may have secretly derided but which he rarely refused on account of his financial needs. Moreover, he could deliver to order. From the 1940s onwards he collaborated on more than fifteen different films and acted or appeared in a further six. Many of these were interesting experimental and avant-garde short works, for example, a short sequence called 'Queening the Pawn' for Hans Richter's *8x8* (1952), yet he could also knock off a commentary for a short official film on nuclear power (René Lucot's *A l'aube d'un monde* of 1956). He even found time in 1956 to design a set of Japanese-style house-lights for the auditorium of the historic Studio 28 cinema in Montmartre. All this, however, was in lieu of actually accomplishing a major work in the one medium that promised to integrate all others and which he alone was singularly qualified to take to a new level. With the exception of *La Villa Santo-Sospir* and a few other home-style shorts that never saw the light of day, Cocteau was denied the opportunity to develop his notion of the 'complete' film. This was, therefore, a period of continual frustration and misspent creative energy. An instructive case in point was when, in the spring of 1950, he personally arranged for a cortège of limousines to be waiting at the docks in Le Havre to greet the young American gay filmmaker Kenneth Anger, whose explosive short *Fireworks* of 1947 had so overwhelmed him. Anger decided to shun all the pomp and quietly took the train to Paris instead. Lacking a sense of artistic progress and direction, Cocteau was now effectively on the creative rebound, forced continually to regroup, take painful stock and justify himself yet again to the world as a major artist. Only his unflagging commitment to experimentation, and thus to providing new forms of self-image, ensured a necessary sense of personal progression. Fortunately, there was still a public very keen to view the results whatever the actual quality (during the 1950s retrospectives of his paintings, drawings and ceramics took place across Europe).

The urgency of Cocteau's need for a connection with his audience ('vous') was intensified by his perception of a growing disconnect between himself and the new post-war consumer society with its increasingly vulgar and frivolous consumerism. In 1961 he wrote a short old-fogey piece for the review *Les Oeuvres libres* entitled 'Du Sérieux', in which he inveighed against the lack of genuine seriousness in the modern world, bemoaning both the absence of grammar, style and 'professional secrets' and the presence of too much slang. He was, in fact, becoming decidedly cranky and capricious with the years. When, for example, during the mid-1950s he was first asked his opinion on the young literary prodigy and media star Minou Drouet, he dismissed her publicly with a cruel put-down: 'All nine-year-olds have genius – except Minou Drouet'. Later however, at a book-signing, he bounded up to Drouet and hugged her, instantly winning her over. Cocteau's latent misogyny continued to fester, a fact confirmed by his utterly devoted housekeeper Madeleine Bourret, who acknowledged that he was becoming progressively intolerant. Indeed, for all the greatness of a film like *Orphée*, the female characters there presented only three extreme and rather derisory alternatives: an insipid wife, the embodiment of prosaic reality; a Princess who incarnates the phallic gesture and, as 'Death', verges on sadistic cruelty until she melts not very convincingly in love; and a vicious, man-hating League of Women manipulated by the 'undesirable' Aglaonice. That Cocteau had little to say about women and sexual politics in general was inadvertently exposed in a small volume from around the same time entitled *Reines de la France*, a series of nineteen admiring yet highly schematic 'rapid sketches' of women from the legendary past, such as Mme de Pompadour, Marie-Antoinette and Joan of Arc, as well as more recent artistic figures, high-society women and *demi-mondaines* whom Cocteau had known, including the Empress Eugénie and Anna de Noailles. The collection closed with a kind of mini-survey of 'Tomorrow's woman', Cocteau's only real artistic engagement with contemporary women and where the tone is one of conservative scepticism and mild disdain of the kind he now held for France in general. Women are slaves to fashion and as such remain eternal victims; they are naturally the idols of men and will always function so.

By 1958 Cocteau was writing letters to his friend, the critic Milorad, in which he gave full vent to his disillusionment with the modern world and his sense of feeling both isolated and 'the shadow of a shadow'. Even in the fully achieved domestic bliss of Santo-Sospir, Cocteau behaved like the perpetual malcontent, for he felt he was steadily becoming an 'old, sad gentleman'. An overwhelming sadness was compounded by the incontrovertible fact of his worsening health. While on a visit to Madrid in 1953 for a performance of *Le Bel Indifférent*, he contracted uraemia and almost died from it. A year later in July he suffered his first heart attack while travelling in a car through Paris. He was immediately cared for by France's best cardiologists courtesy of Weisweiler before being taken to the Villa Santo-Sospir to convalesce. From now on he would experience regular attacks of angina. Cocteau was finally paying the price for abusing his body with toxic substances, overwork and emotional stress, and this could not be disguised by his multiple hair dyes, permanent waves and facelifts (one even as late as 1959), which left his face looking even more pinched and stretched. The image comes to mind here of Cocteau as the Baron Carol in Serge de Poligny's film *Le Baron Fantôme*, in which, hidden for decades in his decrepit castle, he is pictured literally wasting away.

As the decade dragged on there was a kind of fatal inevitability to the many national and international awards and honours heaped on Cocteau and which he gratefully accepted, culminating in his elevation in 1961 to Commander of the Legion of Honour. To take just the case of film: in addition to becoming President of the Jury at the Cannes Film Festival in 1953 and 1954, he was made President of the French Scriptwriting Union and Honorary President of the

Cocteau with Francine Weisweiller on the day of his reception into the Académie Française, 20 October 1955.

French Federation of Ciné-Clubs. It was in the world of literature, however, that Cocteau was most spectacularly feted. On 1 October 1955 he took up the Chair of French language and literature at the Belgian Royal Academy, a position made vacant by the death in August 1954 of Colette and previously held by Anna de Noailles (the lines of literary tradition and influence were now coming together almost inexorably). Then on 20 October 1954 he was received into the Académie Française. This was something Cocteau actively campaigned for during the autumn and winter of 1954–5 following the death of Jérôme Tharaud. He sought out an official sponsor, André Maurois, and with Francine, who played the well-rehearsed role of Fairy Godmother, wined and dined and seduced at her mansion all the hoary Academicians who could vote. He was, in fact, a perfect choice for this gentleman's club: the prodigal son who had now visibly come home to roost as a grand bourgeois. His induction in late October 1955 stands as one of his greatest theatrical triumphs, attracting more than 12,000 people to the Quai Conti,

in addition to the select group of artists, movie stars and royalty he
had personally invited. Cocteau insisted on all the pageantry of his
new prestige as Academician and invested much time and friends'
money in creating his own special decorative sword for the occasion.
Manufactured in Spain according to a design by Picasso, the hilt
contained multiple Cocteau symbols: the pommel formed a lyre,
the handle developed into a Greek profile, the haft represented the
Palais-Royal, and the coquille bore his signature in the shape of a
six-pointed star. As for Cocteau's acceptance speech, it hovered
around some of the less savoury aspects of his predecessor before
getting to the point: he accepted this new honour in the name of
all *poètes maudits*! This was a Coctelian paradox if ever there was,
since the likes of Baudelaire and Balzac had never made it into the
Academy (Baudelaire withdrew his candidacy; Balzac was rejected;
Proust and Gide had never cared to apply). Implanted in the very
heart of the Establishment, Cocteau stood now for everything
he had originally claimed to despise. At the reception afterwards he
bounded up to a bemused Georges Auric and exclaimed disingenuously: 'I only did it to make you laugh!'

The real problem, of course, was that Cocteau could never fool
himself for too long that such honours made him feel any more
happy or secure. Leaving aside his alleged status as Grand Master
of the Priory of Sion, he knew he had still to 'arrive' in the elite and
truly immortal company of the great Poets. With this ideal still
eating away inside him he crossed the Channel with Francine and
Doudou in June 1956 to receive an Honorary Doctorate of Letters
from Oxford University. He was given a new name and title:
'Johannes Cocteau, Gallus poeta', and his acceptance speech on the
tried and trusted theme of Poetry and Invisibility, which included
some spicy profundities on art as an 'internal erection beyond our
control' provoked by a 'kind of psychic sexuality', concluded with the
phrase 'Gentlemen, the Queen!', greeted first with mild giggles then
raucous laughter. Cocteau's remarkable run of awards and honours

Cocteau and W. H. Auden receiving honorary degrees at the University of Oxford, 14 June 1956.

would be marred only by his election in June 1960 as Prince of Poets, an informal poet laureateship in Paris. A friend of Cocteau's, Philippe Mas, campaigned on his behalf and obtained enough support to pronounce him the new Prince of Poets, succeeding Paul Fort who had just died. Some figures, however, had not been canvassed and a ten-strong committee, including Cocteau's eternal nemesis André Breton, finally chose Saint-Jean Perse by an overwhelming majority. Cocteau, who by now considered the honour his by right, refused to cooperate. It was an embarrassing fiasco for everyone involved. The one consolation was that Aragon proved his loyalty to Cocteau over Breton, and as a sign of their reconciliation they recorded together a long – though far from riveting – dialogue on the art treasures looted by the Nazis and rescued from the destroyed art museum at Dresden. At Aragon's behest Cocteau also signed an appeal in favour of Spanish refugees and found himself promptly expelled from Franco's Spain, although all was resolved in time-honoured Cocteau fashion by means of a highly contrite formal apology.

In short, the medals of glory bestowed on Cocteau served only to increase his disenchantment with his blocked artistic project. To quote *The Blood of a Poet*, a 'mortal tedium of immortality' had set in, exacerbated by a real sense of his own mortality. In early 1959 he suffered an internal haemorrhaging that confined him to bed for many weeks and obliged him to lie still on his back. The result of this experience was a poetic 'saga' called *Le Requiem*, an extremely long, multiform poem which, with its accumulation of names, places, anecdotes and metaphors grafted together with moments of genuine pathos, provided a kind of codicil to Cocteau's work (it closes with the moving and memorable epitaph: 'Stop pilgrim my voyage/ Was passing from danger to danger/ It's right that I be contemplated/ After having been stared at'). Cocteau staggered on, visiting Jean Hugo occasionally at Mas-la-Fourques and even engaging in correspondence with Valentine Hugo during the period of her mother's fatal illness. As his own family began to pass away – first his sister Marthe in January 1958, then his brother Paul in December 1961 – he found himself called upon to honour the memory of cherished friends and figures from the past, such as Mistinguett in 1956. Some compensation was afforded by the arrival on the scene of new acolytes such as Jacques Perry and Pierre Georgel, who later served to preserve and transmit the official Cocteau legend. However, the conclusive sign of Cocteau's collapse came with the destruction of his adopted family. Francine had simply had enough of playing the role of Queen and benefactress and now wanted out. Or more precisely she wanted Cocteau out of her villa, which had become his own luxury retreat where he could happily have spent the rest of his life with his beloved Doudou. For Francine herself, Santo-Sospir had turned into a kind of limbo and she wished now to be in greater circulation. Cocteau inevitably took this as a personal betrayal and the only possible resolution to their quarrels and ructions was his humiliating exit first to Villefranche, then in the spring of 1960 to Marais' villa at Marnes-la-Coquette outside Paris before his eventual return to Milly-la-Forêt. It would not be too dramatic to say that as Cocteau entered the new decade he felt as good as dead.

21

Jean Cocteau is Dead, Long Live Cocteau!

When death finally came to Cocteau at the age of 74 in Milly-la-forêt on 11 October 1963, he accepted it gladly. He had just heard of the death of Edith Piaf in the morning, had immediately recorded an interview about her for the radio, and was rising to answer a call from Aragon regarding a written tribute when he suffered an attack of pulmonary oedema. Earlier that year, in April, he had managed to survive a second massive heart attack, and heavily dosed up on sedatives and antibiotics had recuperated for a while at Marais' home. On his subsequent return to Milly he had sought to conduct business as usual, proceeding with his diary of personal mementoes and critical reflections, as well as receiving visits from friends, notably Francine who wished for an eleventh-hour reconciliation. Now, however, when the new attack began, he instantly declared to his housekeeper Juliette: 'The boat is finally drowning, you can do nothing more for me. I feel death coming.' With no oxygen tank on hand he coughed up large clots of blood and quickly choked to death. He was embalmed the following day and photographed by Raymond Voinquel in serene sculptural pose in the salon, reconverted now with its shutters closed into a mortuary chamber like a stage-set. Around the neck of his body dressed in black was the red collar of the Legion of Honour, while at his side lay the sword of the Académie Française. The funeral at Milly's parish church took place four days later. The tone was set by an dignified procession led by three administrative officers of the

Cocteau on his deathbed at Milly-la-Forêt, October 1963.

Académie Française followed by nine 'immortals' (including René Clair, Jean Paulhan, Jean Rostand and Marcel Pagnol) and Cocteau's close 'family' of friends: Doudou, Jeannot, Francine, Auric, Genet, Lifar and Picasso's son Paulo (Picasso himself was noticeable by his absence, as was Stravinsky). Bringing up the rear were assorted government ministers and prefects and around 5,000 other mourners. A rather conventional speech was delivered by a fellow Academician, André Chamson, and Cocteau's body was duly laid to rest with a lyre of red roses in the ground behind the small twelfth-century chapel of Saint-Blaise-des-Simples, which he had decorated in 1959 with the theme of medicinal and culinary herbs (the 'simples' of its name). The following April Cocteau's body would be transferred to a site within the chapel itself and interred under a tombstone donated by the Mayor of Menton that bore the inscription: 'Je reste avec vous' ('I remain with you'), emphasizing Cocteau's solidarity not just with his personal friends and beloved public but also with the townspeople of Milly, who had already appointed him in 1953 an honorary citizen. At a later service in the chapel to mark the first anniversary of his death, Clair delivered a rather awkward speech containing no reference to Arno Breker, whose lumbering bronze effigy of Cocteau was unveiled at the same time.

Of course, Cocteau had effectively been preparing for death during much of his life, most obviously with the various chapels he had recently decorated. At the instigation of Denise Bordet, who harked back to the period of the Villa Blanche in Tamaris, he had also published in 1962 the short biographical work *Le Cordon ombilical*, in which he brought together his assorted works and attempted one last time to control their reception. He reeled them off virtually in list-form and proposed yet another critical gloss, suggesting that painting and writing were simply ways of being and that any legendizing of one's characters led to one's own self-mythification. The style here – grand and universal in its claims, seductively casual in its manner – is quintessential Cocteau, and the tone is at once penetrating and self-indulgent. He confesses endearingly at one point that he occasionally loses the plot by attaching himself to those whom he respects rather than to himself. The volume would not be complete without a highly defensive and paranoid counter-attack against the harmful *vous* who hate him for being so dispersed. The following year, in April 1963, Cocteau recorded at Milly an extensive interview with Roger Stéphane that was subsequently broadcast on national television, though did not reveal anything particularly new.

It was a little earlier, however, with his self-consciously valedictory film *The Testament of Orpheus* that Cocteau had prepared most fully for the eventuality of his death. This is one of the most remarkable and honest works that Cocteau ever produced, the culmination of more than fifty years of experimentation and practice, and it marked the first – and last – time that Cocteau took centre stage in his cinema as the Poet. The film is an artistic self-portrait, or

Cocteau with the film director François Truffaut and his young star, Jean-Pierre Léaud, Cannes Film Festival, 1959.

more specifically a confessional portrait of the artist as Orpheus. It is also a stunning act of poetic will and control, the first of its kind in the history of cinema and endowed with a clear function: to bequeath a final self-image to posterity by which Cocteau will be remembered. Funded in large part by the newly famous François Truffaut, who donated the international profits of *The Four Hundred Blows* (for Truffaut and other French New Wave directors of the period, Cocteau was the living embodiment of the complete auteur), *The Testament* presents itself explicitly from the outset as 'the legacy of a poet to the successive groups of people who have always supported him'. The formal ingredients that make up and define Cocteau – documentary truth, fiction, fantasy, self-image, legend – fuse together now almost seamlessly as he leads us in person through a virtual inventory of his life's work, a vast back-catalogue comprising Orpheus, Minerva, the Sphinx, Anubis, Antigone, Tristan and Isolde, Man-Horses, doubles and false doubles, and more. All these various elements serve as figurative mirrors of Cocteau's life and are some of the most potent and iconic images of twentieth-century French art.

The Testament proceeds in the barest linear fashion as a series of extended sketches during which Cocteau is continually on the move 'like a sleepwalker' passing in and out of slow and reverse motion. He is accompanied by phrases culled from his many writings and poetry, as well as references to his films (notably *The Blood of a Poet* and *Orphée*) and his work in the plastic arts. With him are his intimate friends and loyal actors: Doudou as Cégeste, Jeannot as the blinded Orpheus whom the Poet ironically passes by in the final moments, Francine as 'The Distracted Lady', and Maria Casarès and François Périer as the Judges. The death / resurrection scene, in which the Poet rises upright from his death-bed in reverse motion after having been lanced in the back by Minerva, is played out in front of a hybrid group of Gypsies and celebrities positioned as witnesses (Picasso, Lifar, Lucia Bosé, Luis-Miguel Dominguin, Charles Aznavour). So identified now is Cocteau with his chosen medium that, in a series of what he calls 'imaginary acts' arranged according to the mechanism of dreams, his body in reverse motion becomes like that of the film itself, i.e. a fully reversible construct. He emphasizes in his opening voice-over the personal stakes of the work: 'My film is nothing other than a striptease show, consisting of removing my body bit by bit and revealing my soul quite naked.' This, along with his intention that *The Testament* constitute 'a kind of shadow puppet' of his life, underlines the performative nature of Cocteau's entire project, and the film's provocative subtitle, *Ou Ne me demandez pas pourquoi* (*Or Don't Ask Me Why*), signals once again that he is not going to help us to interpret it.

The Testament is concerned explicitly with the creative process and Cocteau defines himself completely by his work and artistic acts. We see paradoxically that it is when the figure of the Poet is incarnated in his very body, and therefore at its most concrete and physical, that his own life is depersonalized and universalized in the wider interests of his project. Moreover, with his sustained experiment into the relativity and reversibility of cinematic time and space, Cocteau provides a temporary resolution of his own personal difficulty of being, which is here transcended – albeit provisionally – by the reversibility of Being itself. For space and time are revealed now as one and the same. An entire early episode where the Poet is lost in 'this frightful entanglement of space-time' is formed of a discussion with the Professor (Henri Crémieux), designed to demonstrate that time is not linear. Unlike the Professor the Poet can 'unwind' time, and even change the course of time, because he has discovered a filmic method for achieving the process of resurrection. Time is thus compressed and distended by reverse motion photography, as well as through narrative devices such as multiple time zones, flashbacks and loops.

By crossing through time and melting away in the image, thereby becoming 'translucid' like Cégeste, the Poet can abolish the emptiness of space and distance that the film insists on through both extreme close-ups of eyes and long shots of colossal caves in which the Poet appears as but a minuscule object. In short, we witness in *The Testament* the complete transformation of the Poet as Self into the Other, that is, the work, producing what Gilbert Adair has aptly described as 'a uniquely Protean projection and dispersal of self-hood'.[1] Liberated from the curse of its overbearing author with his repeated delusions of personal destiny, the work can now finally undergo a critical metamorphosis and be considered on its own artistic merits.

For such a momentous farewell film *The Testament of Orpheus* possesses a rare wit and legerdemain that defies gravity and keeps it alluringly aloft. Its penultimate image of the car carrying off its young passengers into the distance and blowing away the fallen hibiscus flower ensures that the final note is not one of sadness or remorse but joy – that of the material enjoyment of the work, which, combined with the elegance of form, exemplifies the Cocteau ideal. In his final voice-over he declares: 'A joyful wave has just swept through my farewell film. If you didn't like it, I will be sad because I put all my energy into it, as did the humblest worker in my team.' As I have argued in detail elsewhere, part of

Cocteau as the dead Poet moments before his resurrection in *Le Testament d'Orphée* (1960).

the unique power of *The Testament* derives also from its degree of eroticism.[2] I am thinking of the many homoerotic moments of men looking back, like the Poet turning round irresistibly after cruising past the Man-Horse, the constant framings of men's backsides (a virtual reflex in the film) and some totally odd, almost unqualifiable events such as the Man-Horse taking the javelin slowly out of the Poet's stomach (from behind). In the case of the Poet's virtual 'crucifixion' by Cégeste, a kind of anal dissolve back into the bowels of the earth, the gestures that the two men make appear to be a preparation for oral sex, with Cégeste's legs bent down and the Poet's hands outstretched as if on a rack, waiting perhaps like Ganymede with Zeus to be lifted away. Such moments take to a new level the various processes of anal eroticism and sexual ambivalence found throughout all Cocteau's work and bring to the fore his gay aesthetic, as does the extraordinary performance of power relations between the Poet and Cégeste who guides him, like Virgil with Dante, through the quarries of the Val d'Enfer in Baux-de-Provence (the spot where Dante allegedly wrote the *Vita nova*). Cégeste, who performs a series of physical feats and possesses his own powers of resurrection and metamorphosis, magically intuits the rhythms of the Poet's destiny and continually goads him into proving his mastery. As his name, which breaks down phonetically into *ces gestes* (these acts), or *ses gestes* (his acts), suggests, Cégeste provides Cocteau with the perfect means to achieve his aesthetic goal of a *poésie de cinéma*, that is to say, a cinema of pure acts. And it is Cégeste who ensures that Cocteau, as he put it in one interview at the time, is constructively 'turned inside out' by his own film like a glove. By propelling Dermit into such an active artistic role Cocteau is clearly attempting here something new and audacious in his ongoing exploration of the relations between life and work, namely to displace and even undermine some of his own authorial importance. For he is shifting and reversing through art the power dynamic that operated in his life with Doudou and all his male companions-cum-collaborators. Dermit, the man and the actor, was completely formed by Cocteau, a fact alluded to when Cégeste first meets the Poet in the hyper-real gleam of dusk and responds to his surprise exclamation 'Cégeste!' with 'It's you who named me'. As Cocteau's 'adopted son' (a status explicitly mentioned in the film), Doudou would serve after his death, with the blessing of Cocteau's family, as his official heir and literary executor, in short, the guarantor of his futurity. As it turned out, Dermit remained a model of personal allegiance and discretion right up until his own death in May 1995 (even later when married and with children, Dermit still talked of Cocteau steering him through his daily life). Cocteau's supreme confidence in his individual power over Dermit is surely what allowed him to consider divesting himself here of his own directorial authority, an approach that goes hand in hand with his general wish to lay himself open to the mysteries of the cinematographic machine. By facilitating new artistic sites not of power but of powerlessness, Dermit proved to be a unique and vital collaborator for Cocteau, his literal and metaphorical *compagnon de route*, even though they wrote no books on or about each other like Cocteau with Marais.

The Testament marks an important contribution to modernist gay aesthetics in other ways too. By offering essentially a tour of Cocteau's dream factory, a working gallery displaying his multiple artistic activities and personal friendships, the film prefigures another gay and supremely materialist filmmaker, Andy Warhol. As the first multi-media artist to bring together literature, the visual arts, cinema, music, theatre and fashion, Cocteau shone a beacon for the emerging trans-avant-garde of Warhol, who, with his chosen 'family' in his New York Factory, took to vertiginous heights Cocteau's cult of youth, beauty and celebrity and his obsession with death, as well as the notion of mass-production with which Cocteau experimented in later years. The moment in *The Testament* when the young autograph hunters stuff their newly gained booty into the mouth of the tall, Tiresias-like Idol, a 'machine to make anyone famous for a few minutes', is a proleptic parody of Warhol's famous dictum. There is also the fact of the physical resemblance between the two artists, particularly their white hair and rather formal attire, traits which Warhol himself recorded in a series of silk-screen prints of Cocteau during the early 1980s. Cocteau is of major importance to Warhol and other modern gay artists, writers and filmmakers precisely because he sought to transgress and transcend all genres, classifications and taboos in his bid to translate a fully assumed gay real into universal art. This post-Proustian project led Cocteau to stage a dark and sensual adaptation of Tennessee Williams's *A Streetcar Named Desire* in Paris in 1949, just as it encouraged W. H. Auden to translate Cocteau's own play, *The Knights of the Round Table*. An entire study could be devoted to the many chains of Cocteau's gay influence, in film, for example, the work of the French director Jacques Demy, who made a virtual career out of 'remaking' Cocteau, first respectfully with *Le Bel Indifférent* (1959), then more adventurously with the heavily stylized *Peau d'âne* (1970) and *Parking* (1985) (the latter two were based around *Orphée*, although employed Marais in various roles). Cocteau inspired other filmmakers working in totally different cinematic traditions too, including Kenneth Anger, Pier Paolo Pasolini, Derek Jarman and Pedro Almodóvar, to name just a few.

This is not the end of the Cocteau story, of course, for as we have constantly witnessed, he is always oriented towards the future due to his undimmed faith in the creative act, and none more so than in the medium of film. Indeed, he was even more advanced in his preparations for death and the after-life of his work than originally thought. Just a couple of months before his death, in August 1963, he made one last film: a 25-minute short entitled *Jean Cocteau s'adresse à l'an 2000* (*Cocteau addresses the year 2000*). The film comprises one still and highly sober shot of Cocteau facing the camera head-on to address the youth of the future. Once recorded, this spoken message for the 21st century was wrapped up, sealed and posted on the understanding that it would be opened only in the year 2000 (as it turned out, it was discovered and exhumed a few years shy of that date).[3] If in *The Testament* Cocteau portrays himself as a living anachronism, a lonesome classical modernist loitering in space-time in the same buckskin jacket and tie while lost in the spectral light of his memories, here he acknowledges explicitly the irony of his phantom-like state: by the time the viewer sees this image, he, J. C., our saviour Poet, will long be dead. Temporality is typically skewed: speaking from both 1963 and 2000 Cocteau is at once nostalgic for the present that will have passed and prophetic about the future. There is thus both a documentary aspect and projective thrust to the film, another new configuration of 'superior realism' and fantasy enhanced by Cocteau's seamless performance as himself and his now 'immortal' status as a member of the

Cocteau directing *La Belle et la Bête* in 1945.

Académie Française. He reiterates some of his long-standing artistic themes and principles: death is a form of life; poetry is beyond time and a kind of superior mathematics; we are all a procession of others who inhabit us; errors are the true expression of an individual, and so on. The tone is at once speculative and uncompromising, as when Cocteau pours vitriolic scorn on the many awards bestowed upon him, which he calls 'transcendent punishments'. He also revels in the fact that he can say now what he likes with absolute freedom and impunity since he will not be around to suffer the consequences.

The status of *Jean Cocteau s'adresse à l'an 2000* remains ultimately unclear. Is it a new testament or confession, or a heroic demonstration of the need for human endurance, or a pure 'farce of anti-gravitation' as he puts it? Or everything at once? It is entirely characteristic of Cocteau to leave us hanging on this suspended paradox. What is certain, however, and what we have consistently seen, is that Cocteau's life and body are his work, and his work in turn is always mysteriously alive. This is Cocteau's final gift to his fellow human beings. Let us retain and celebrate the force of that gesture. He is resurrected before our eyes, ever-present, defiant and joyfully queer. Jean Cocteau is dead, long live Cocteau!

References

Introduction: The Living Artist and the Posthumous Work

1 Jean Cocteau, *The Art of Cinema* [1988], trans. and ed. Robin Buss (New York and London, 2001), p. 7.
2 See Jean Cocteau, *Le Cordon ombilical* [1962] (Paris, 2003), p. 19. All translations are my own unless otherwise stated.
3 Cited in Anthony Levi, *Guide to French Literature, 1789 to the present* (Chicago and London, 1992), p. 170.
4 See *Jean Cocteau: romans, poésies, œuvres diverses*, ed. Bernard Benech (Paris, 1995), p. 895.

1 Paradise Lived and Lost

1 On his military dossier he is named as 'Clément, Eugène, Jean, Maurice Cocteau'.
2 See 'Venise vue par un enfant', *La Revue hebdomadaire* (May 1913).
3 See Francis Steegmuller, *Cocteau: A Biography* (Boston, MA, and Toronto, 1970), pp. 11–12.

2 Natural-born Legend

1 Cited in Frederick Brown, *An Impersonation of Angels: A Biography of Jean Cocteau* (London, 1969), p. 13.

4 Russian Lessons

1 Jean Cocteau, *Le Potomak, 1913–1914, précédé d'un Prospectus (1916) et suivi de La Fin du Potomak (1939)*, vol. II of *Oeuvres complètes de Jean Cocteau* (Geneva, 1947), p. 39.
2 Ibid., p.123.

5 Cocteau's First War

1 See *Jean Cocteau: photographies et dessins de guerre,* ed. Pierre Caizergues (Arles, 2000).
2 Jean Cocteau, *Thomas l'imposteur* [1923] (Paris, 1973), p. 150.
3 See *Jean Cocteau: photographies et dessins de guerre*, pp. 107–23.
4 See Billy Kluver, *A Day with Picasso* (Cambridge, MA, 1997).

6 The Greatest Battle

1 See *Jean Cocteau: romans, poésies, œuvres diverses*, ed. Bernard Benech (Paris, 1995), p. 868.

7 Happy Families

1 See Jean Cocteau, *Diary of an Unknown*, trans. and ed. Jesse Browner (New York, 1988), pp. 194–5.

8 Genius of France

1 See Preface to Jean Cocteau, *Les Mariés de la Tour Eiffel* (Paris, 1924), pp. 9–23 (p. 18).

9 A Child Carrying a Cane

1 *Jean Cocteau: romans, poésies, œuvres diverses*, ed. Bernard Benech (Paris, 1995), p. 298.

10 *Annus Mirabilis / Annus Miserabilis*

1 See Jean Cocteau, *Diary of an Unknown*, trans. and ed. Jesse Browner (New York, 1988), p. 202.
2 Letter dated 3 November 1922, cited in Francis Steegmuller, *Cocteau: A Biography* (Boston, MA, and Toronto, 1970), pp. 294–5.
3 *Jean Cocteau: romans, poésies, œuvres diverses*, ed. Bernard Benech (Paris, 1995), p. 98.

11 Lost in the Wilderness

1 From Drawing 14 in Jean Cocteau, *Le Mystère de Jean l'Oiseleur: monologues*, ed. Milorad (Paris, 1983).
2 Cocteau's diary, 26 July 1958, cited in Francis Ramirez and Christian Rolot, 'L'acte graphique', *Le Magazine littéraire* 423 (2003), pp. 56–9 (p. 59).
3 See 'Le numéro Barbette', *Nouvelle Revue française* (July 1926).

12 An Ass Bearing the Lord

1 Cited in Francis Steegmuller, *Cocteau: A Biography* (Boston, MA, and Toronto, 1970), pp. 337–8.
2 In a letter written in 1963 to Mme Jeanette Kandaouroff, cited in full in Steegmuller, *Cocteau*, pp. 496–9.

13 Miracle or Simulacrum?

1 See *Jean Cocteau: romans, poésies, œuvres diverses*, ed. Bernard Benech (Paris, 1995), p. 219.

2 Ibid., p. 223.

14 Body and Blood of a Poet

1 See *Jean Cocteau: romans, poésies, œuvres diverses*, ed. Bernard Benech (Paris, 1995), p. 51.
2 See James S. Williams, *Jean Cocteau* (Manchester, 2006), chapter 2: 'All Is Possible: *Le Sang d'un poète*'.

15 Tripping Across the World

1 Cited in Peter France, ed., *The New Oxford Companion to Literature in French* (Oxford, 1995), p. 841.
2 Jean Cocteau, *Round the World Again in 80 Days*, trans. Stuart Gilbert (London, 1937), p. 249.

16 Enter Apollo

1 Cited in René Gilson, *An Investigation into his Films and Philosophy* [1964] (New York, 1969), pp. 172–3.

17 World War Redux

1 A. Laubreaux, 'Le Scandale des Ambassadeurs', *Je Suis partout* (13 January 1939).
2 See Gregory Sims, '*Tristan en chandail*: Poetics as Politics in Jean Cocteau's *L'Eternel Retour*', *French Cultural Studies*, 9 (1998), pp. 19–50.

18 No Man's Land

1 Jean Cocteau, *La Belle et la bête: journal d'un film* [1946] (Monaco, 1958), p. 61.
2 In *Empreintes*, 7–8 (1950).

19 Club Santo-Sospir

1 See James S. Williams, *Jean Cocteau* (Manchester, 2006), chapter 4: 'In the Zone: *Orphée*'.
2 See Jean Cocteau, *Diary of an Unknown*, trans. and ed. Jesse Browner (New York, 1988), p. 87.
3 Ibid., p. 89.

21 Jean Cocteau is Dead, Long Live Cocteau!

1 See Gilbert Adair, Programme Notes for the 'Jean Cocteau: The Naked Dandy' film season (March 2004, French Institute, London), p. 13.
2 See James S. Williams, *Jean Cocteau* (Manchester, 2006), chapter 6: 'For Our Eyes Only: Body and Sexuality in Reverse Motion', especially pp. 159–76.
3 For a full transcription, see 'Mon testament pour l'an 2000', in Jean Cocteau, *Jean Cocteau: 28 autoportraits*, ed. Pierre Caizergues (Paris, 2003).

Select Bibliography

Works by Cocteau

Cocteau's literary and dramatic works are all now available in the authoritatively annotated three-part Gallimard 'Pléaide' edition: *Oeuvres poétiques complètes*, ed. Michel Décaudin and David Gullentops (Paris, 1999); *Théâtre Complet*, ed. Michel Décaudin (Paris, 2003); and *Oeuvres romanesques complètes*, ed. Serge Linares and Henri Godard (Paris, 2006). Many of Cocteau's works were also republished in 2003 by Grasset (Collection 'Les Cahiers rouges') and Editions du Rocher with new or previously unavailable prefaces.

Poetry

Le Cap de Bonne-espérance (Paris: La Sirène, 1919)
Escales (Paris: La Sirène, 1920) [illustrations by André Lhote]
Poésies, 1917–1920 (Paris: La Sirène, 1920)
Vocabulaire (Paris: La Sirène, 1922)
Plain-chant (Paris: Stock, 1923)
'Discours du grand sommeil', *Nouvelle Revue française* (1924)
Le Mystère de Jean l'Oiseleur: monologues (Paris: Champion, 1925); ed. Milorad
    (Paris: Persona, 1983)
Opéra (Paris: Stock, 1927)
Allégories (Paris: Gallimard, 1941)
Léone (Paris: Gallimard, 1945)
La Crucifixion (Paris: Morihien, 1946)
Le Chiffre sept (Paris: Seghers, 1952)
Appogiatures (Monaco: Rocher, 1953)

Clair-obscur (Monaco: Rocher, 1954)

Poèmes, 1916–1955 (Paris: Gallimard, 1956)

Paraprosodies précédées de 7 dialogues (Monaco: Rocher, 1958)

Le Requiem (Paris: Gallimard, 1962)

Novels

Le Potomak [1919] (Paris: Stock, 1924); reprinted in *Le Potomak,* 1913–1914,
    *précédé d'un Prospectus (*1916*) et suivi de La Fin du Potomak (*1939*),* vol. II of
    Oeuvres complètes de Jean Cocteau (Geneva: Marguerat, 1947)

Le Grand Ecart (Paris: Stock, 1923); as *The Miscreant*, trans. Dorothy Williams
    (London, 2003)

Thomas l'imposteur (Paris: Gallimard, 1923); as *Thomas the Impostor*, trans.
    Dorothy Williams, ed. Gilbert Adair (London, 2005)

Le Livre blanc (Paris, 1928) [without name of publisher or author]; reprinted
    Paris: Editions du Signe, 1930; as *Le Livre blanc*, trans. and ed. Margaret
    Crosland (London, 1969) [with woodcuts by Jean Cocteau]; as *The White
    Book / Le Livre blanc* (San Francisco, 1989)

Les Enfants terribles (Paris: Grasset, 1929); as *The Holy Terrors*, trans. Rosamond
    Lehmann (New York, 1966)

Theatre

Les Mariés de la Tour Eiffel (Paris: *Nouvelle Revue française*, 1924); as 'The Eiffel
    Tower Wedding Party', in *The Infernal Machine and Other Plays*, trans.
    W. H. Auden et al. (New York, 1963)

Orphée (Paris: Stock, 1927); as 'Orpheus', trans. John Savacool, in *The Infernal
    Machine and Other Plays*

La Voix humaine (Paris: Stock, 1930); as *The Human Voice*, trans. Carl Wildman
    (London, 1951)

La Machine infernale (Paris: Grasset, 1934); as 'The Infernal Machine', trans.
    Albert Bermel, in *The Infernal Machine and Other Plays*

Les Parents terribles (Paris: Gallimard, 1938); as *Les Parents terribles*, trans. Jeremy
    Sams (London, 1994)

L'Aigle à deux têtes (Paris: Gallimard, 1946); as *The Eagle Has Two Heads*, trans.

and adapted Ronald Duncan (London, 1962)

Théâtre I: Antigone, Les Mariés de la tour Eiffel, Les Chevaliers de la Table Ronde,
    Les Parents terribles (Paris: Gallimard, 1948); *Antigone*, trans. Carl Wildman
    (New York, 1961); as *The Knights of the Round Table*, trans. W. H. Auden, in
    The Infernal Machine and Other Plays

Théâtre II: Les Monstres sacrés, La Machine à écrire, Renaud et Armide (Paris:
    Gallimard, 1948); *The Typewriter*, trans. Robert Duncan (London, 1947);
    The Holy Terrors, trans. Rosamond Lehman (New York, 1957)

Théâtre de poche (Paris: Morihien, 1949) [includes *Parade, Le Boeuf sur le toit,*
    Le Bel Indifférent, Le Fantôme de Marseilles, Chansons et monologues]

Bacchus (Paris: Gallimard, 1952); as 'Bacchus', trans. Mary C. Hoeck, in
    The Infernal Machine and Other Plays

L'Impromptu du Palais-Royal (Paris: Gallimard, 1962)

Criticism

Le rappel à l'ordre: Le Coq et l'Arlequin, Carte blanche, Visites à Barrès, Le Secret
    professionnel, D'un ordre considéré comme une anarchie, Autour de Thomas
    l'imposteur, Picasso (Paris: Stock, 1926); as *A Call to Order . . . Including 'Cock*
    and Harlequin', 'Professional Secrets', and Other Critical Essays, trans. Rollo
    H. Myers (London, 1926)

Lettre à Jacques Maritain / Réponse à Jean Cocteau [1926] (Paris: Stock, 1964); as
    Art and Faith: Letters between J. Maritain and J. Cocteau (New York, 1948)

Opium (Paris: Stock, 1930); as *Opium: The Illustrated Diary of His Cure*, trans.
    Margaret Crosland and S. Road (London, 1996)

Essai de critique indirecte: Le Mystère laïc, Des Beaux-arts considérés comme un
    assassinat (Paris: Grasset, 1932)

Portraits-Souvenir, 1900–1914 (Paris: Grasset, 1935); as *Paris-Album, 1900–1914,*
    trans. Margaret Crosland (London, 1987) [contains illustrations by
    Cocteau]

Mon premier voyage: Tour du monde en quatre-vingts jours (Paris: Gallimard, 1937);
    as *Round the World Again in 80 Days*, trans. Stuart Gilbert (London, 1937;
    reprinted 2000, with an introduction by Simon Callow)

La Mort et les statues (Paris: Editions du Compas, 1946; reprinted 1977) [con-
    tains photographs by Pierre Jahan]

La Difficulté d'être (Paris: Morihien, 1947); as *The Difficulty of Being*, trans.

Elizabeth Sprigge (New York, 1995)

Lettre aux Américains (Paris: Grasset, 1949)

Maalesh: journal d'une tournée de théâtre (Paris: Gallimard, 1949); as *Maalesh: A Theatrical Tour in the Middle-East,* trans. Mary C. Hoeck (London, 1956)

Jean Marais (Paris: Calmann-Lévy, 1951)

Le Journal d'un inconnu (Paris: Grasset, 1952); as *Diary of an Unknown*, trans. and ed. Jesse Browner (New York, 1988)

Jean Cocteau par lui-même, ed. André Fraigneau (Paris: Seuil, 1957)

Poésie critique, 2 vols (Paris: Gallimard, 1959–60)

Le Cordon ombilical (Paris: Plon, 1962, reprinted Paris: Allia, 2003)

Du Cinématographe, ed. André Bernard and Claude Gauteur (Paris: Belfond, 1973: reprinted 1988); as *The Art of Cinema*, trans. and ed. Robin Buss (New York and London, 2001)

Entretiens autour du Cinématographe (Paris: Bonne, 1951; as *Cocteau on the Film: Conversations with Jean Cocteau recorded by André Fraigneau*, trans. V. Traill, ed. George Amberg (New York, 1972)

Other works by Cocteau available in English

The Journals of Jean Cocteau, ed. and trans. Wallace Fowlie (New York, 1956; reprinted Bloomington, IN, 1964)

My Contemporaries, trans. Margaret Crosland (London, 1967; reprinted 2007)

Professional Secrets: An Autobiography of Jean Cocteau, ed. Robert Phelps, trans. Richard Howard (New York, 1970)

Past Tense: The Cocteau Diaries [1983–1985], 2 vols, ed. Pierre Chanel and Ned Rorem, trans. Richard Howard (London, 1987–90)

Tempest of Stars: Selected Poems, trans. Jeremy Reed (London, 1992) [with drawings by David Austen]

The Passionate Penis: Erotic Drawings (London, 1993)

Jean Cocteau: Erotic Drawings, ed. Annie Guédras (Cologne, 1999)

Films written and directed by Cocteau

Jean Cocteau fait du cinéma (1925), 16 mm, black and white [short, now lost]

Le Sang d'un poète (*The Blood of a Poet*), 1930 (released 1932), 53 minutes, black and white

La Belle et la bête (*Beauty and the Beast*), 1946, 90 minutes, black and white

L'Aigle à deux têtes (*The Eagle with Two Heads*), 1947 (released 1948), 94 minutes,
    black and white

Les Parents terribles (*The Storm Within* aka *Intimate Relations*), 1948, 98 minutes,
    black and white

Orphée (*Orpheus*), 1950, 91 minutes, black and white

Coriolan, 1950 (never released), 16 mm, black and white [short]

La Villa Santo-Sospir, 1951 (never released), 36 minutes, 16 mm, Kodachrome
    colour [short]

Le Testament d'Orphée; ou, ne me demandez pas pourquoi (*The Testament of
    Orpheus*), 1960, 79 minutes, black and white, with one brief scene in colour

Published screenplays and film diaries

Two Screenplays: The Blood of a Poet / The Testament of Orpheus, trans. Carol
    Martin-Sperry (London and New York, 1968)

Three Screenplays: L'Eternel retour, *Orphée* and *La Belle et la bête*, trans. Carol
    Martin-Sperry (New York, 1972)

La Belle et la bête: Journal d'un film [1946] (Monaco, 2003); as *Beauty and the
    Beast: Diary of a Film*, trans. Ronald Duncan, ed. George Amberg (New
    York, 1972)

Orphée [1950] (Paris, 1994); trans. Carol Martin-Sperry in *Three Screenplays*

Les Dames du Bois du Boulogne (dir. R. Bresson), *Cahiers du cinéma*, 75–7 (1957)

Le Testament d'Orphée [1961] (Monaco, 1983) [with photographs by Lucien
    Clergue]; trans. Carol Martin-Sperry in *Two Screenplays*

Discography

Cocteau: anthologie (Frémeaux, 2000) (four-CD set of recordings)

Poètes et chansons: Jean Cocteau (EPM, 2003)

Cocteau et la musique (Centre Pompidou, 2003)

Books on Cocteau

Arnaud, Claude, *Jean Cocteau* (Paris, 2003)

Azoury, Paul, and Jean-Marc Lalanne, *Cocteau et le cinéma: désordres* (Paris, 2003)

Clergue, Lucien, *Jean Cocteau and the Testament of Orpheus* (New York, 2001) [with introduction by David LeHardy Sweet]

Marais, Jean, *L'Inconcevable Jean Cocteau* (Monaco, 1993)

Moyen, Dominique, ed., *Jean Cocteau: sur le fil du siècle*, exh. cat., Centre Pompidou, Paris (2003); trans. Trista Selous (London, 2003)

Oxenhandler, Neal, *Scandal and Parade: The Theatre of Jean Cocteau* (Rutgers, NJ, 1957)

Peters, Arthur King, ed., *Jean Cocteau and the French Scene* (New York, 1984)

Rolot, Christian, and Francis Ramirez, eds, *Jean Cocteau: l'œil architecte* (Courbevoie, 2000)

Steegmuller, Francis, *Cocteau: A Biography* (Boston, MA, and Toronto, 1970)

Williams, James S., *Jean Cocteau* (Manchester, 2006)

Acknowledgements

I would like first to thank Michael Leaman for proposing the idea for this book in the first place, and for his excellent support and patience throughout. I would also like to thank Robert Williams for his excellent editorial assistance and reassuring calm, and Harry Gilonis for his superb help and expertise with the images. I am extremely grateful to M. Pierre Bergé of the Comité Jean Cocteau for granting me permission to publish the book, and to the School of Modern Languages, Literatures and Cultures at Royal Holloway, London, for its generous funding of the illustrations. Thanks are due also to the staff of the following: The British Library, the Bibliothèque Nationale de France, BIFI (Paris), the Fonds Cocteau in Montpellier (in particular Florence Chaudoreille) and the British Film Institute Stills Library. I am especially indebted to Dr Katie Grant for her unwavering support and inspiration during the long haul and for being such a wonderful friend. Finally, I would like to express my deepest gratitude to Dr Jason Gittens for his love and encouragement in every way possible.

Photo Acknowledgements

The author and publishers wish to express their thanks to the following sources of illustrative material and/or permission to reproduce it:

Photos © ADAGP, Paris and DACS, London 2007: pp. 119 (Autoportrait no. 16 – Editions Champion), 136; Art Institute of Chicago (given in memory of Charles Barnett Goodspeed by Mrs Charles B. Goodspeed, 1947.851): p. 138 (photo © The Art Institute of Chicago/© ADAGP, Paris and DACS, London 2007); photos Cecil Beaton (courtesy Sotheby's): pp. 127, 152; photos Bibliothèque Interuniversitaire Montpellier: pp. 26, 56 (ADAGP, Paris and DACS, London 2007), 59, 69, 74, 107, 170, 171 (photo Boris Lipnitzki), 177, 184 (Galerie MARCO Edition), 196, 206 (photo Pierre Vals), 221 (photo André Ostier), 223; photos courtesy British Film Institute: pp. 150, 182, 189, 198, 202, 203, 228, 231, 235; photo CNAC/MNAM Dist RMN/© RMN/Jean-François Tomasian: p. 35; photo Herbert List: p. 207 (courtesy Magnum); photo Magnum: p. 15; photos © Man Ray Trust/ ADAGP, Paris and DACS, London 2007: p. 144; photo Patrick Mesner (P. Mesner/Gamma/Eyedea): p. 173; Musée des Beaux-Arts, Rouen: p. 36; Musée de Grenoble (gift of the artist, 1929): p. 136; Musée National d'Art Moderne, Paris: p. 35; photo Rex Features/ Sipa Press: p. 157 (633019B); photo Rex Features/Everett Collection: p. 188 (AD); photos Roger-Viollet/Rex Features: pp. 19 (676347A), 36 (676344A), 80 (photo Boris Lipnitzki – 676188B), 93 (581467B), 95 (676346A), 99 (676193B), 134 (676193A), 156 (photo Boris Lipnitzki – 676188A), 158 (photo Boris Lipnitzki – 676188C), 160 (676192A), 163 (676191A), 167 (676188D), 226 (photo Raymond Voinquel – 162593F); photos Telimage/© Man Ray Trust/ ADAGP, Paris and DACS, London 2007: pp. 6, 77.